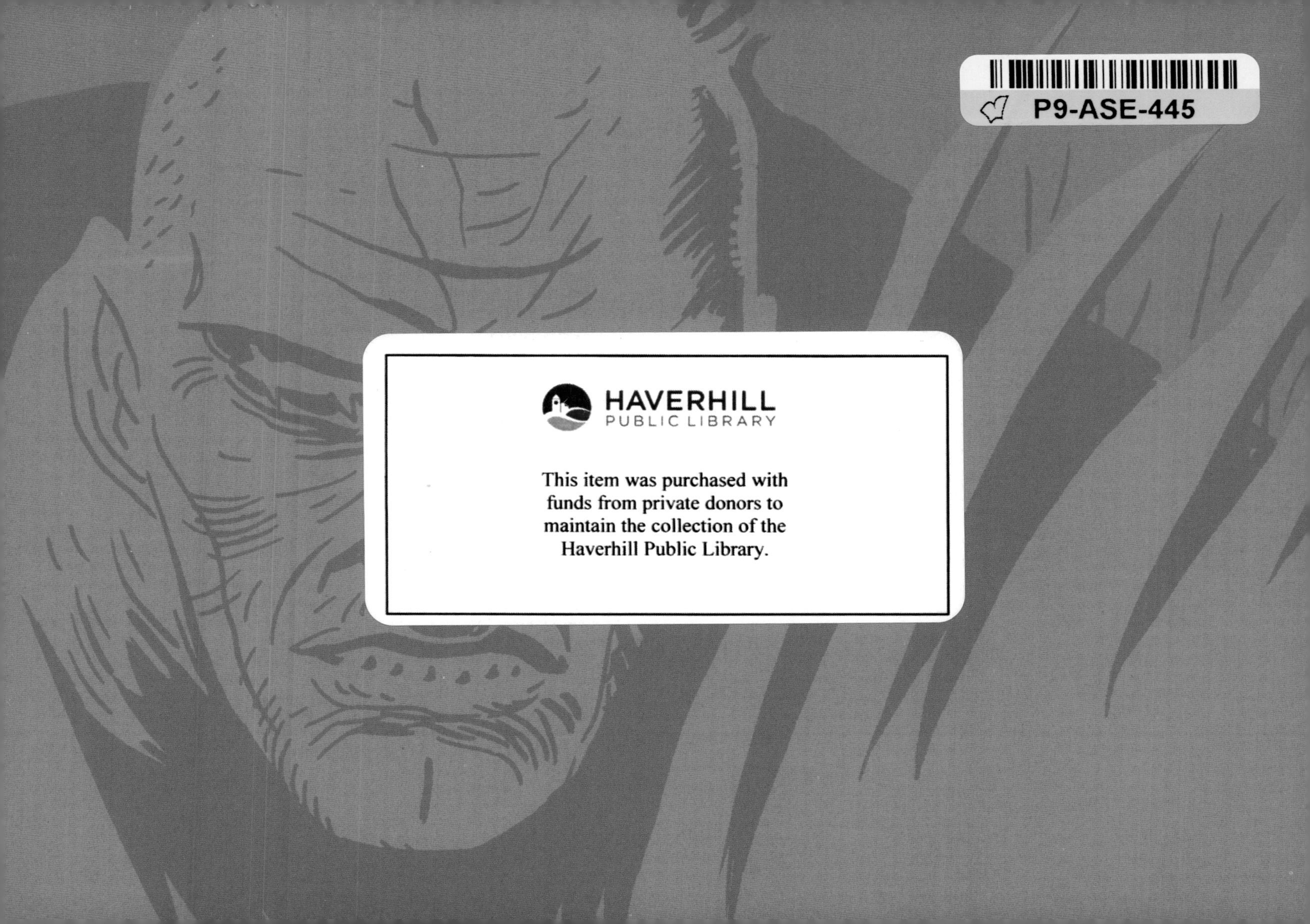

POLAR

THE KAISER FALLS

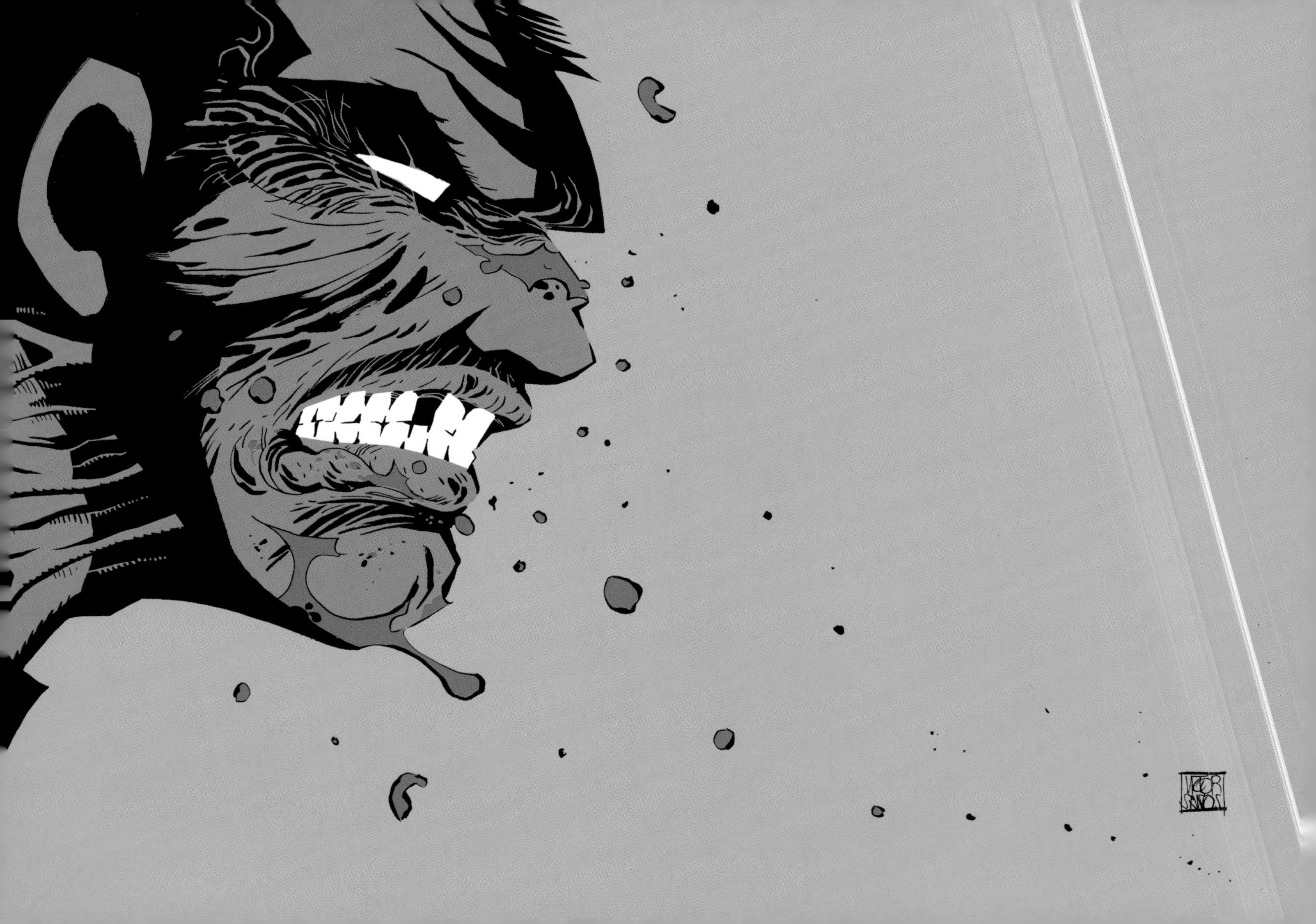

POLAR™
THE KAISER FALLS

VICTOR SANTOS

DARK HORSE BOOKS ®

PRESIDENT & PUBLISHER
MIKE RICHARDSON

EDITOR
SPENCER CUSHING

ASSISTANT EDITOR
KONNER KNUDSEN

DIGITAL PRODUCTION
SAMANTHA HUMMER

DESIGN
SARAH TERRY

NEIL HANKERSON Executive Vice President • TOM WEDDLE Chief Financial Officer • RANDY STRADLEY Vice President of Publishing • NICK McWHORTER Chief Business Development Officer • DALE LaFOUNTAIN Chief Information Officer • MATT PARKINSON Vice President of Marketing • CARA NIECE Vice President of Production and Scheduling • MARK BERNARDI Vice President of Book Trade and Digital Sales • KEN LIZZI General Counsel • DAVE MARSHALL Editor in Chief • DAVEY ESTRADA Editorial Director • CHRIS WARNER Senior Books Editor • CARY GRAZZINI Director of Specialty Projects • LIA RIBACCHI Art Director • VANESSA TODD-HOLMES Director of Print Purchasing • MATT DRYER Director of Digital Art and Prepress • MICHAEL GOMBOS Senior Director of Licensed Publishing • KARI YADRO Director of Custom Programs • KARI TORSON Director of International Licensing

Published by Dark Horse Books
A division of Dark Horse Comics LLC
10956 SE Main Street, Milwaukie, OR 97222

DarkHorse.com PolarComic.com
Comic Shop Locator Service: comicshoplocator.com

First Edition: March 2019 | ISBN 978-1-50671-117-1

10 9 8 7 6 5 4 3 2 1
Printed in China

POLAR VOLUME 4: THE KAISER FALLS

Library of Congress Cataloging-in-Publication Data

Names: Santos, Victor, 1977- author, artist.
Title: The kaiser falls / Victor Santos.
Description: Milwaukie, OR : Dark Horse Books, [2019] | Series: Polar ;
  Volume 4
Identifiers: LCCN 2018049851 | ISBN 9781506711171 (hardback)
Subjects: LCSH: Comic books, strips, etc. | BISAC: COMICS & GRAPHIC NOVELS /
  Media Tie-In. | COMICS & GRAPHIC NOVELS / Crime & Mystery.
Classification: LCC PN6777.S29 K35 2019 | DDC 741.5/946--dc23
LC record available at https://lccn.loc.gov/2018049851

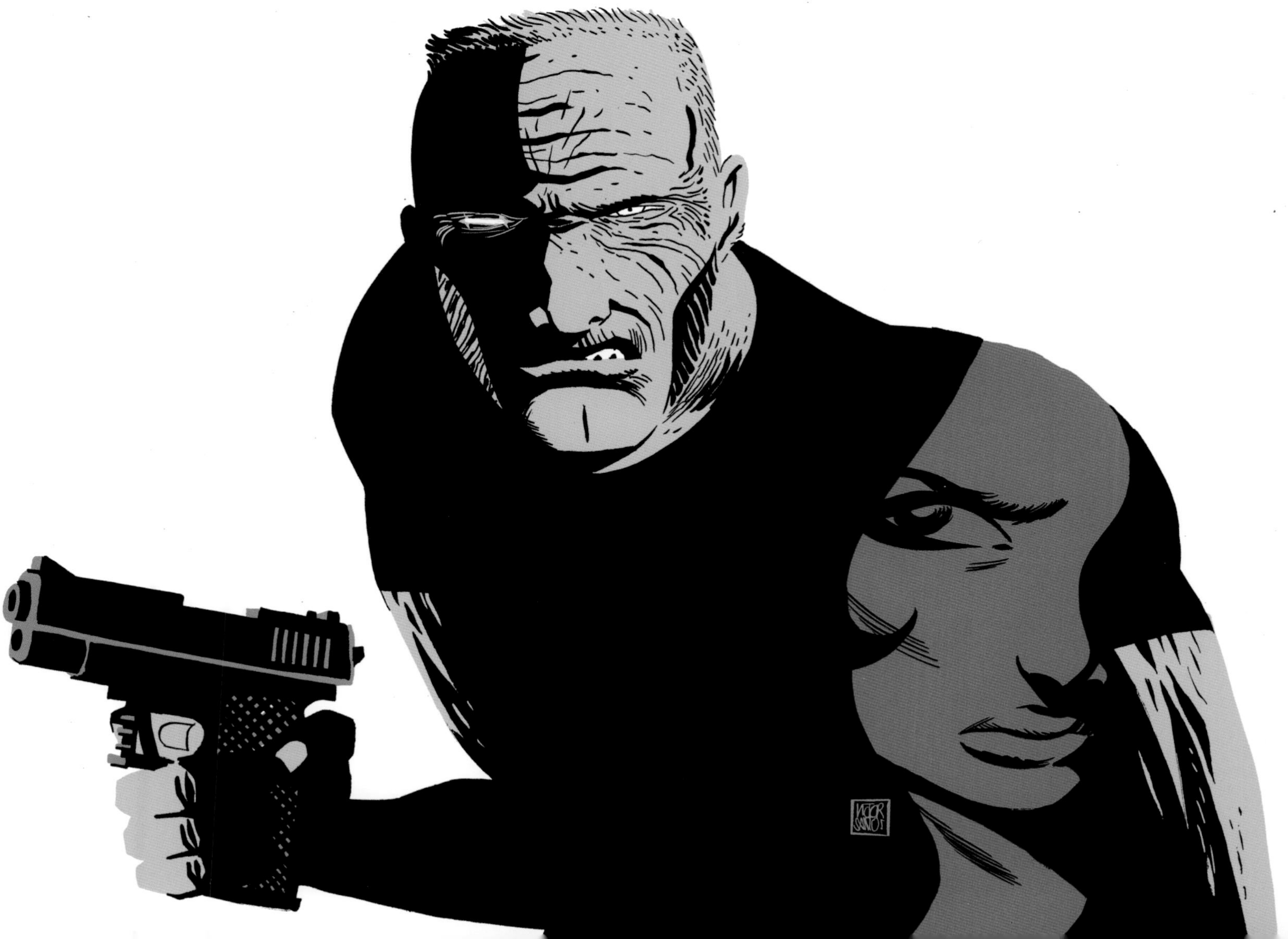

THE KAISER FALLS

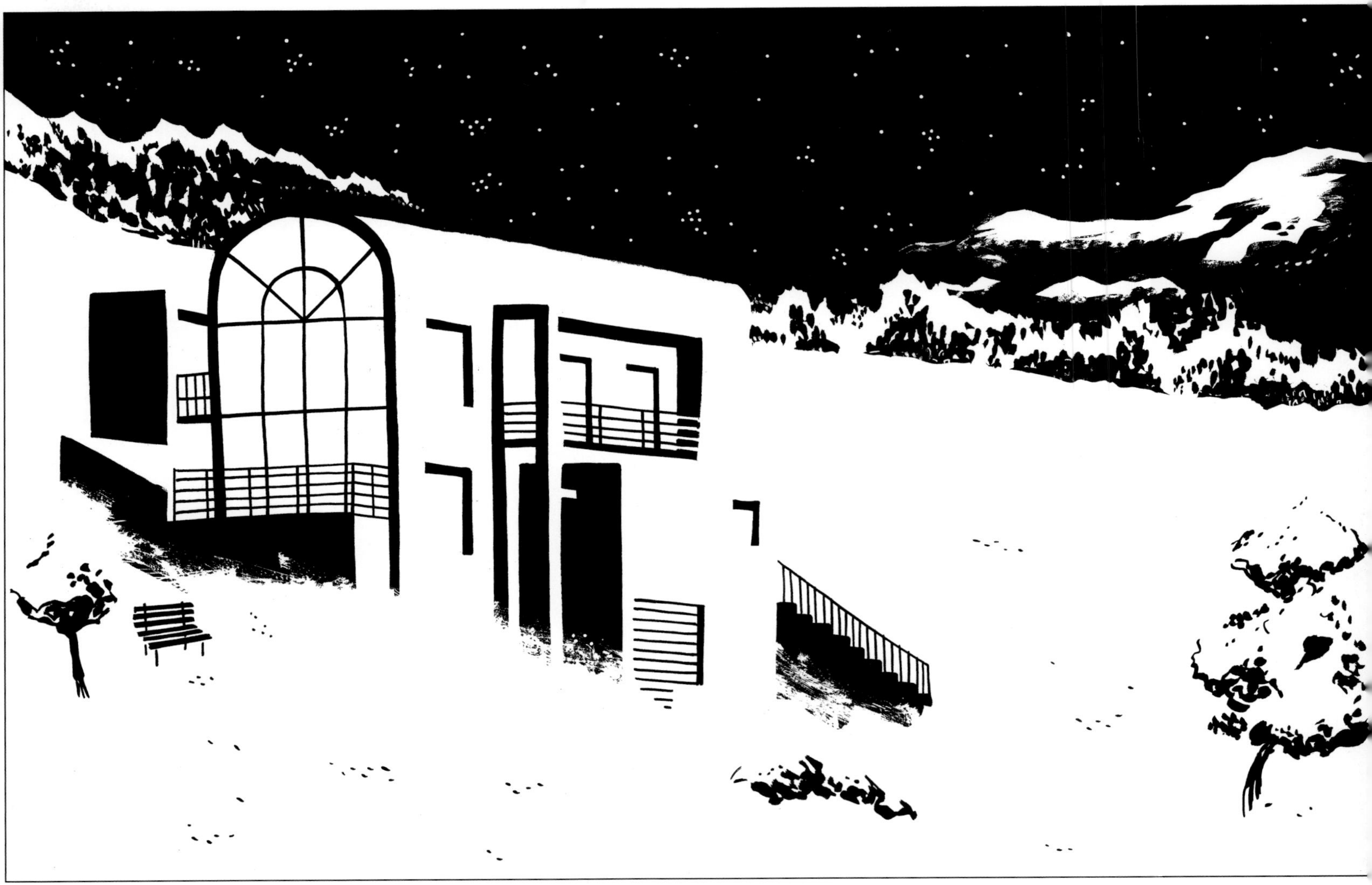

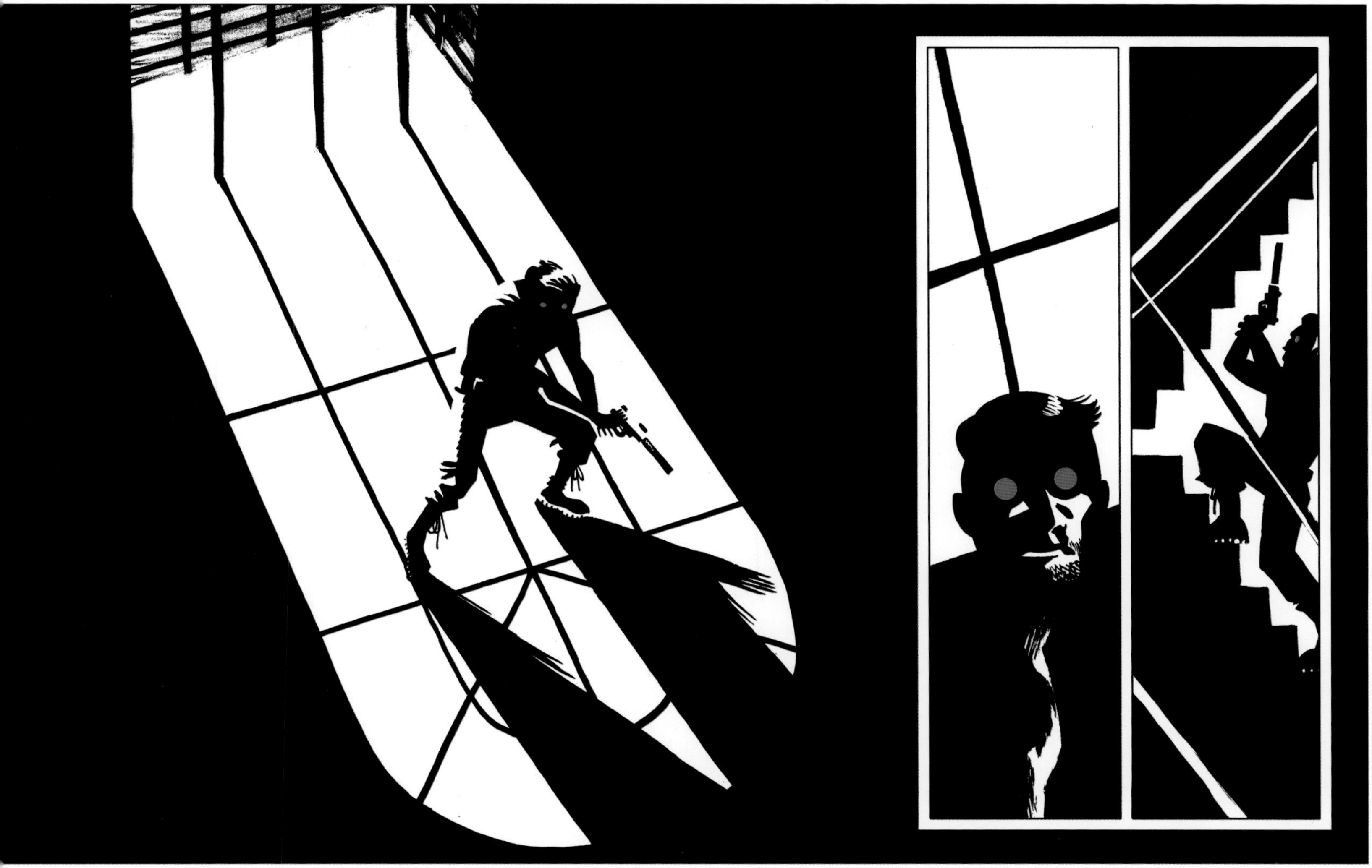

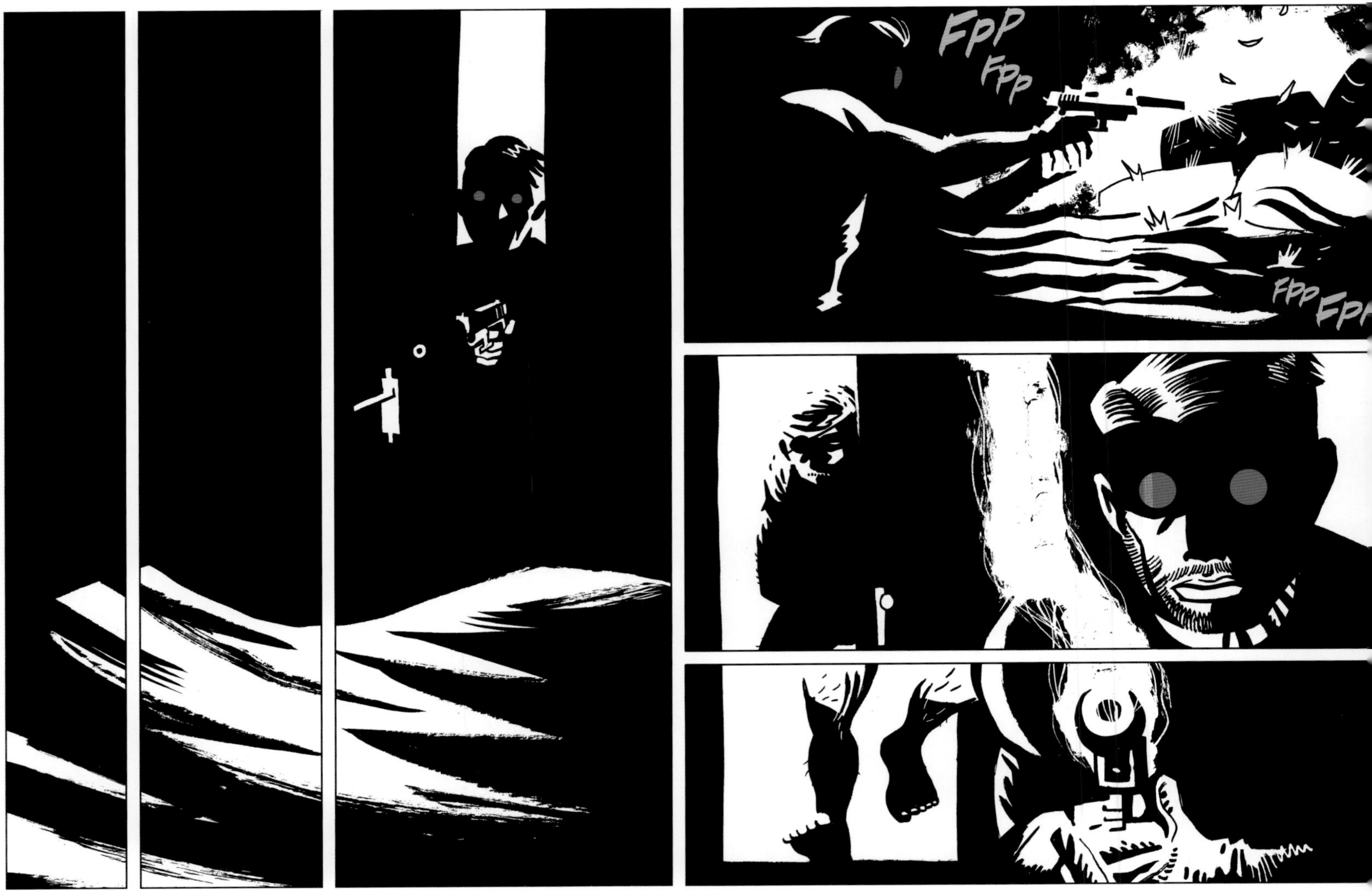
FPP
FPP
FPP

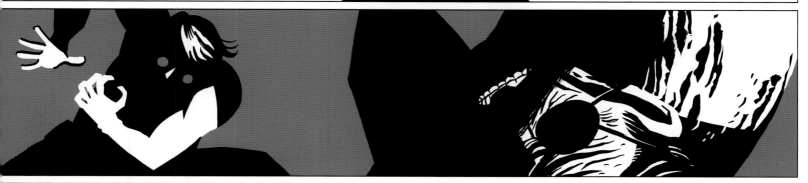

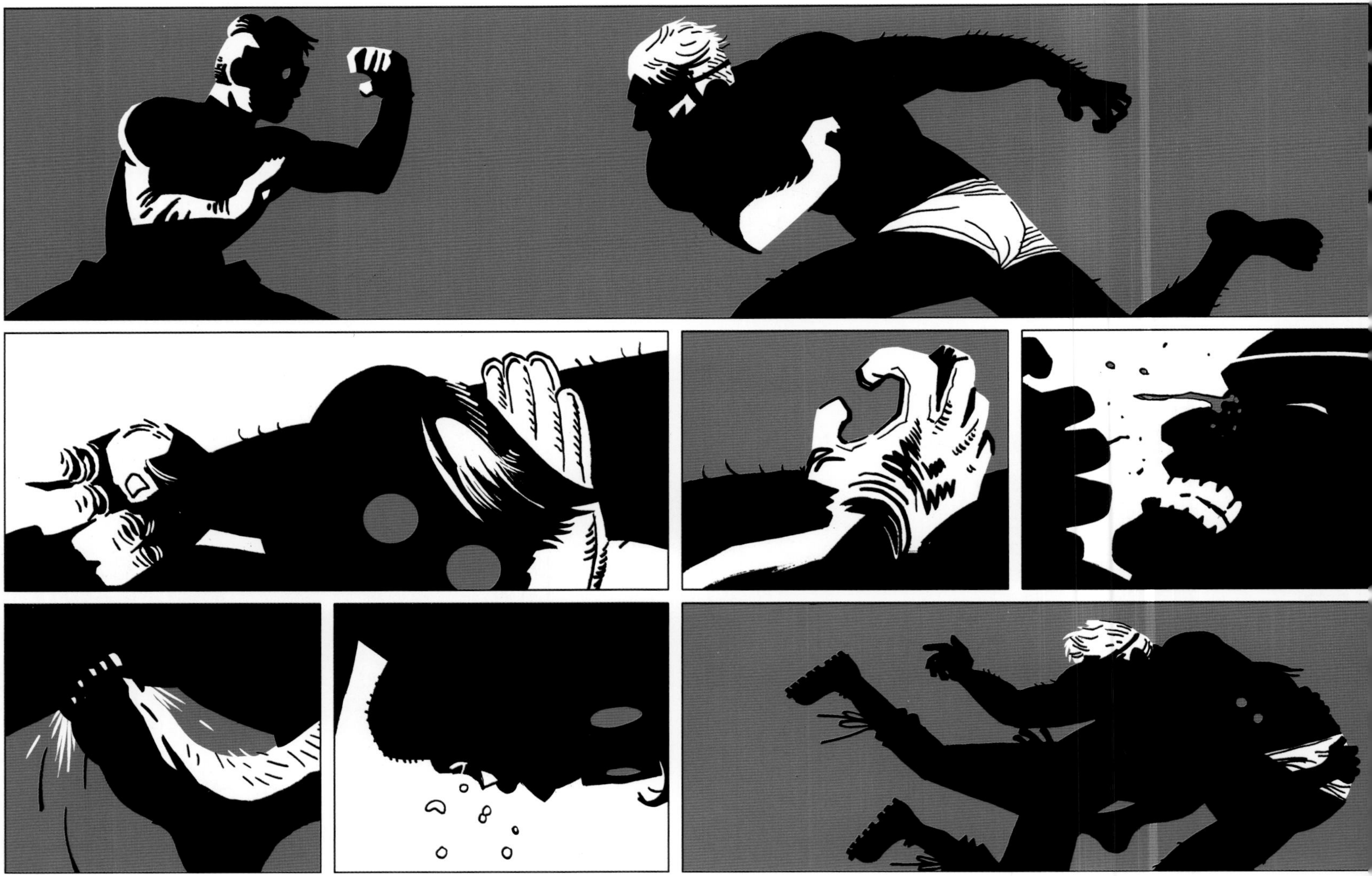

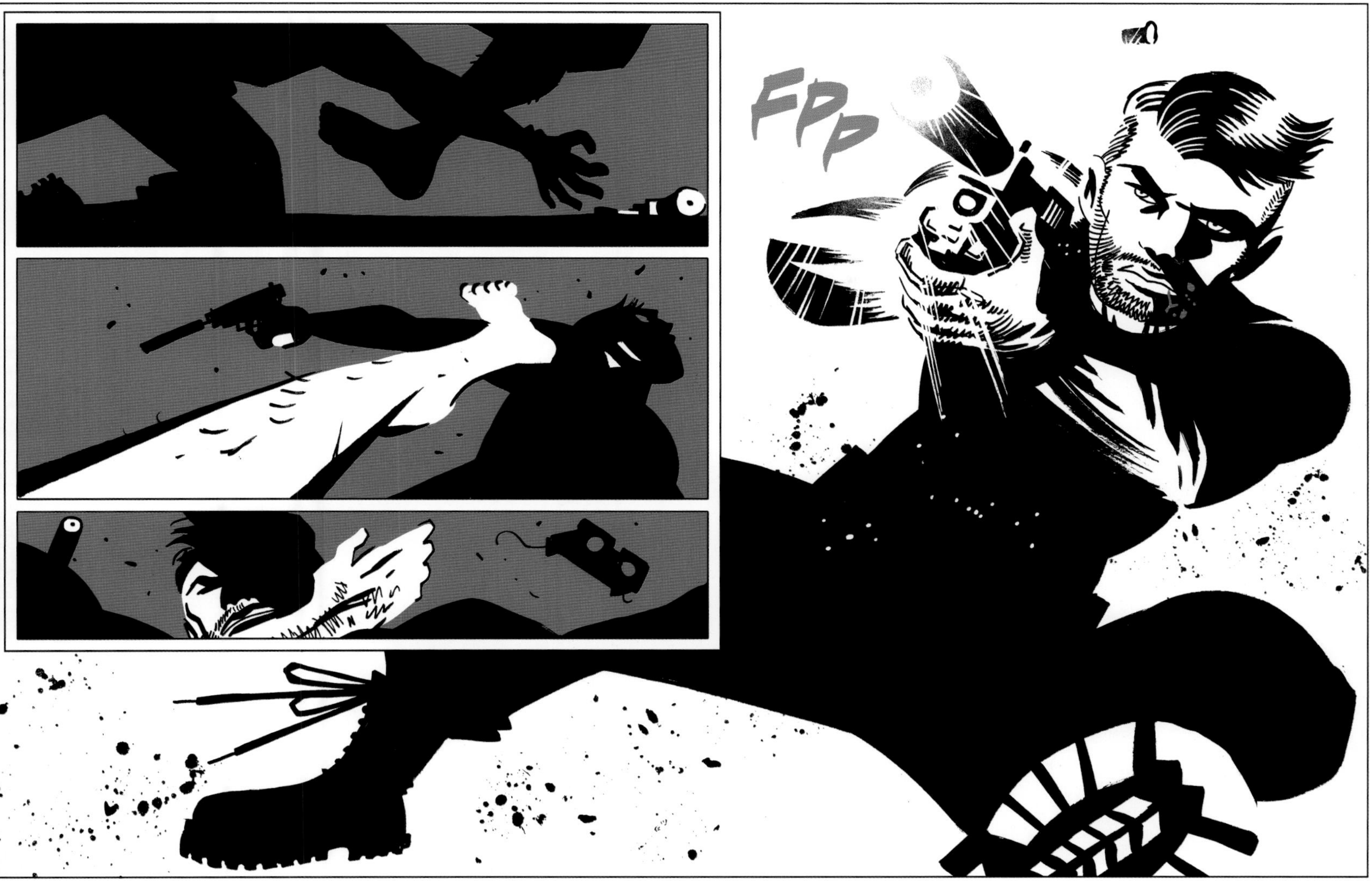
FPP

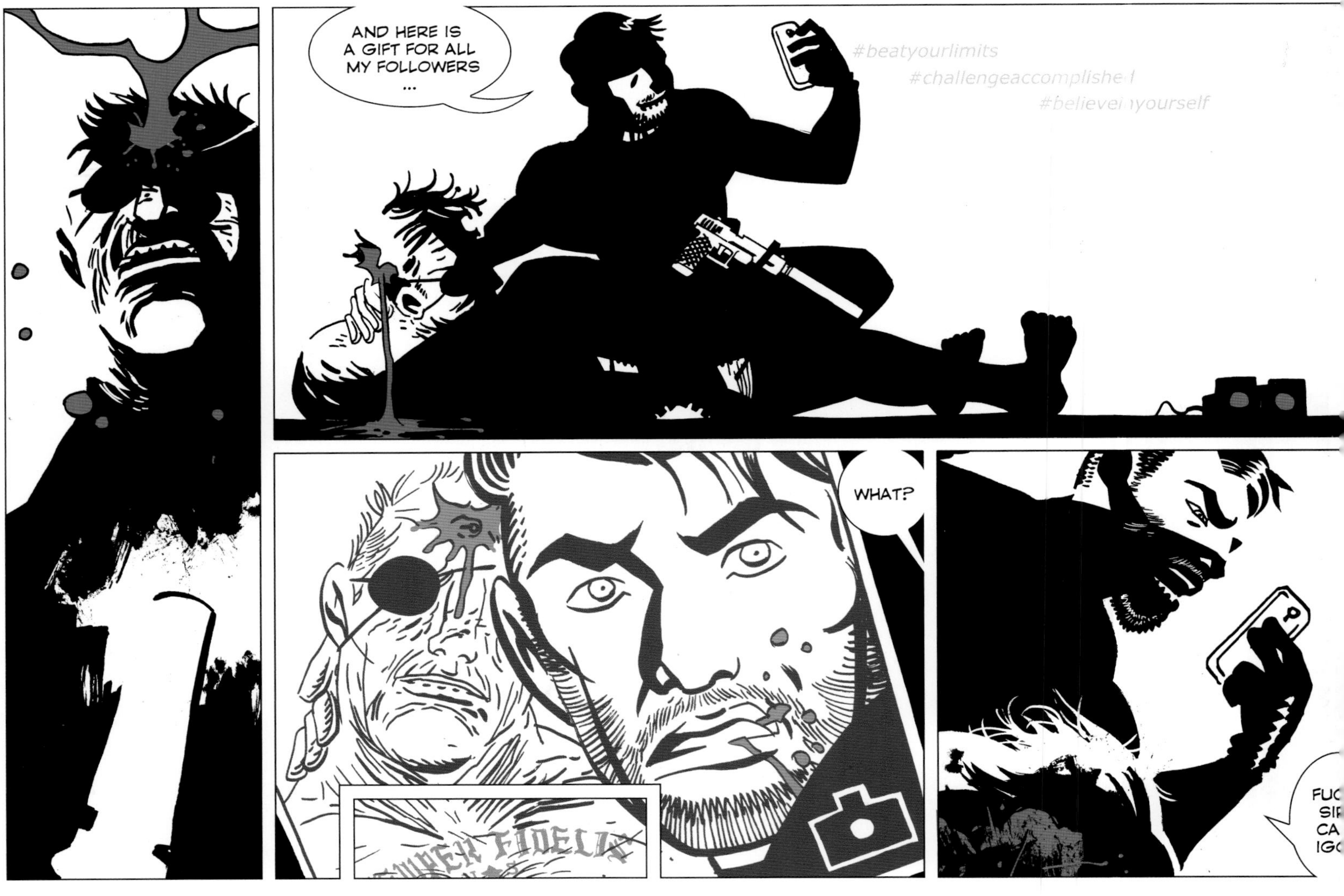
AND HERE IS A GIFT FOR ALL MY FOLLOWERS ...
#beatyourlimits
#challengeaccomplished
#believeinyourself
WHAT?

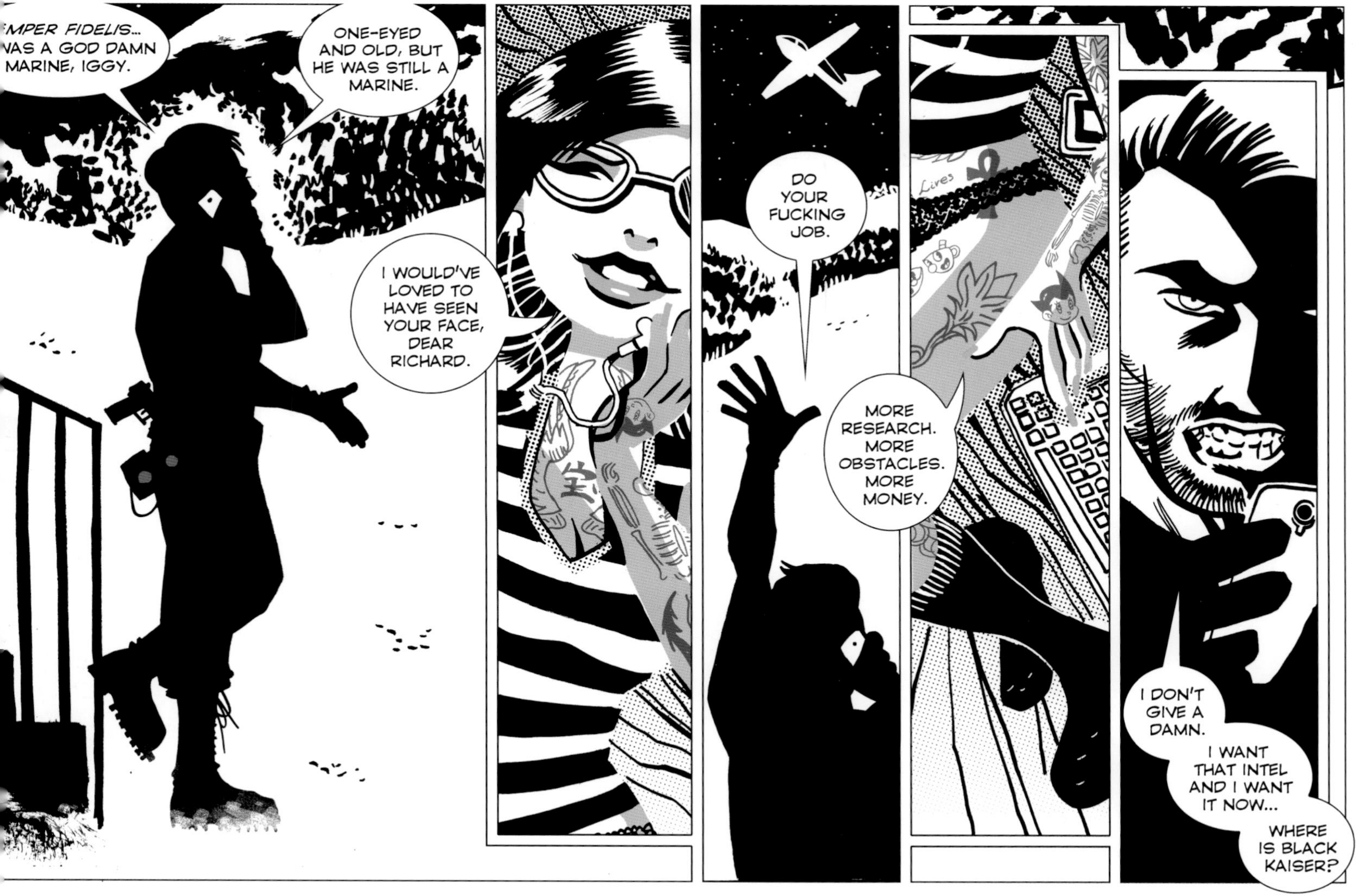

MPER FIDELIS... WAS A GOD DAMN MARINE, IGGY.
ONE-EYED AND OLD, BUT HE WAS STILL A MARINE.
I WOULD'VE LOVED TO HAVE SEEN YOUR FACE, DEAR RICHARD.
DO YOUR FUCKING JOB.
MORE RESEARCH. MORE OBSTACLES. MORE MONEY.
I DON'T GIVE A DAMN.
I WANT THAT INTEL AND I WANT IT NOW...
WHERE IS BLACK KAISER?

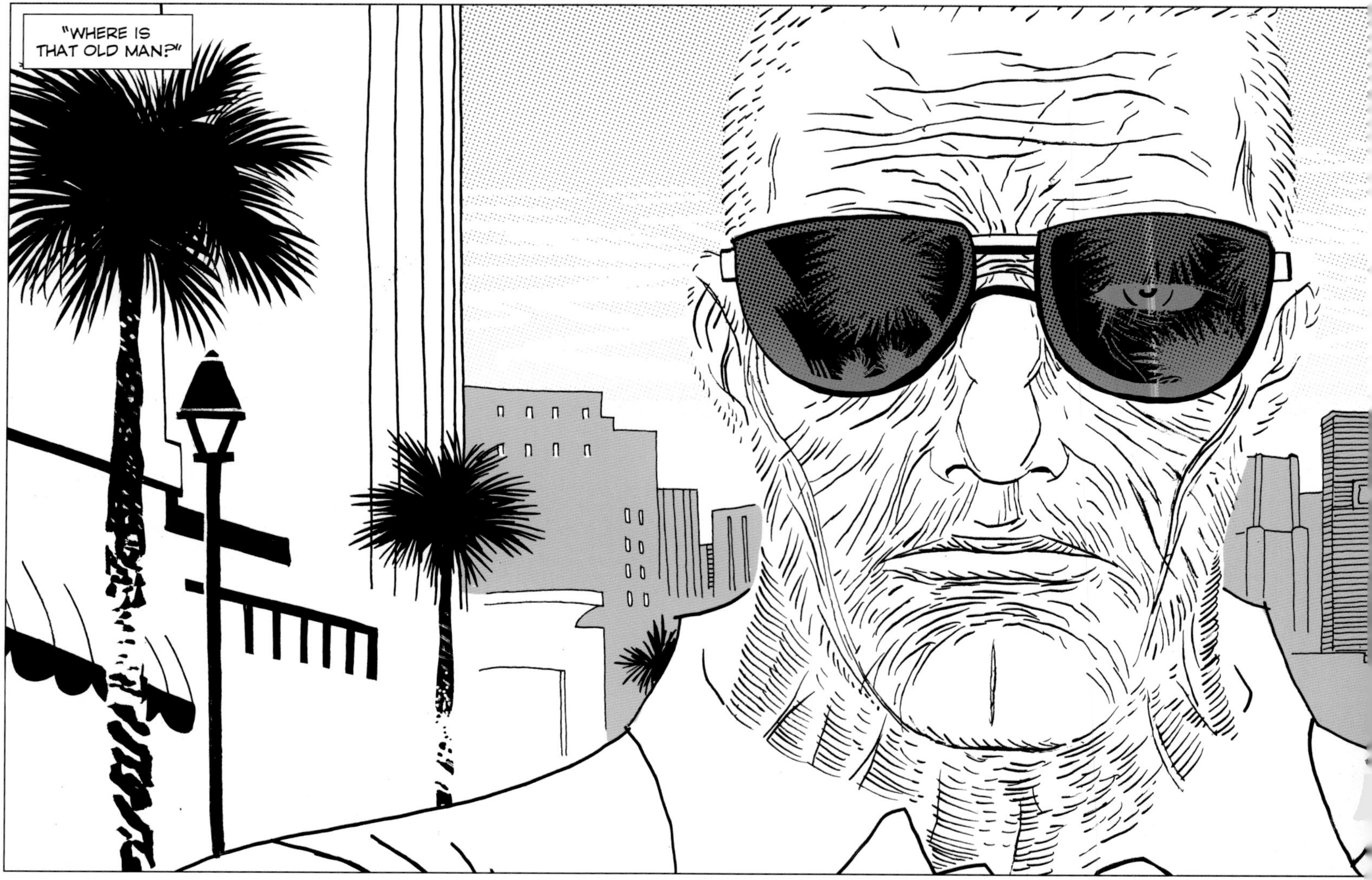
"WHERE IS
THAT OLD MAN?"

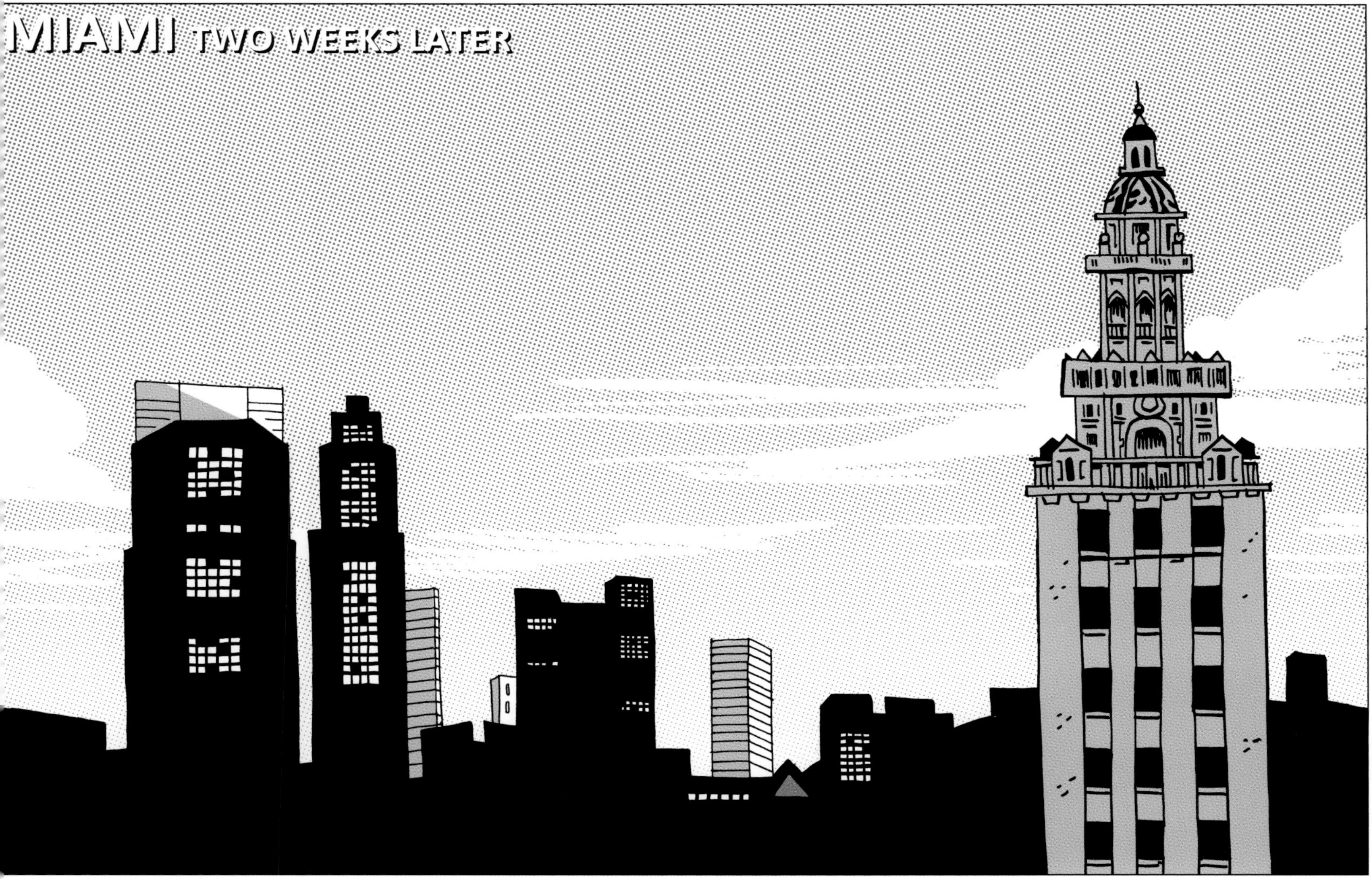
MIAMI TWO WEEKS LATER

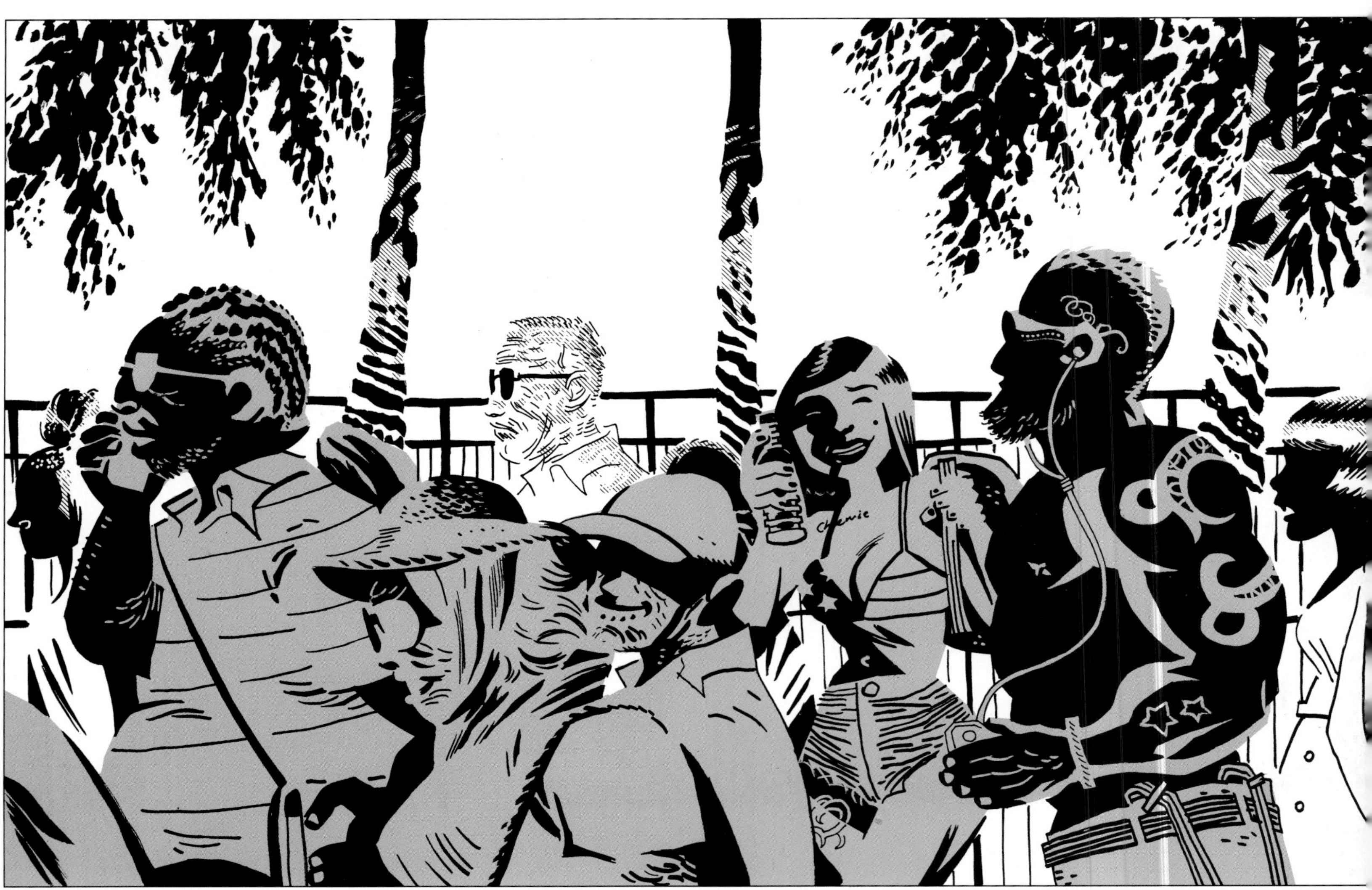

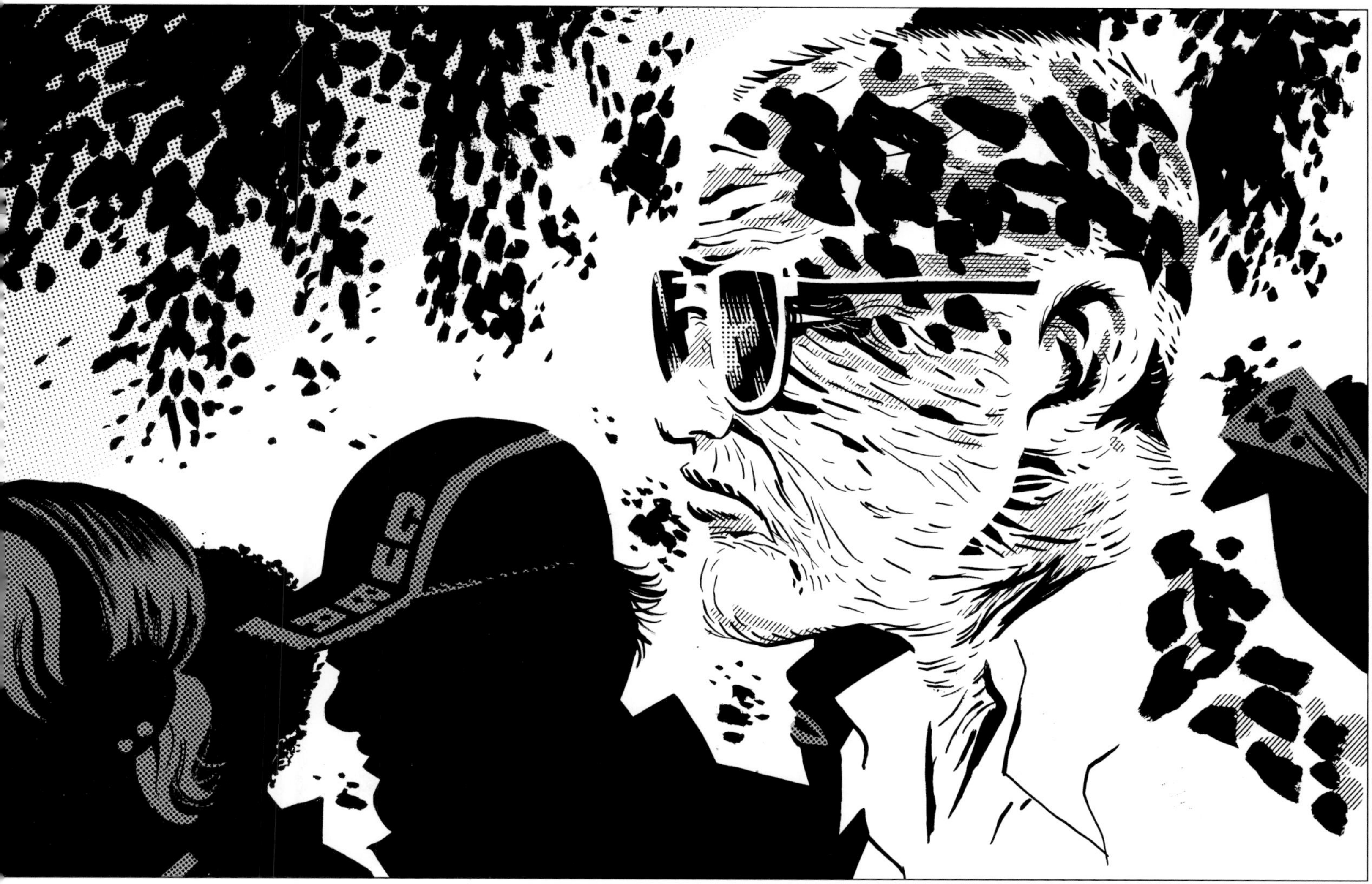

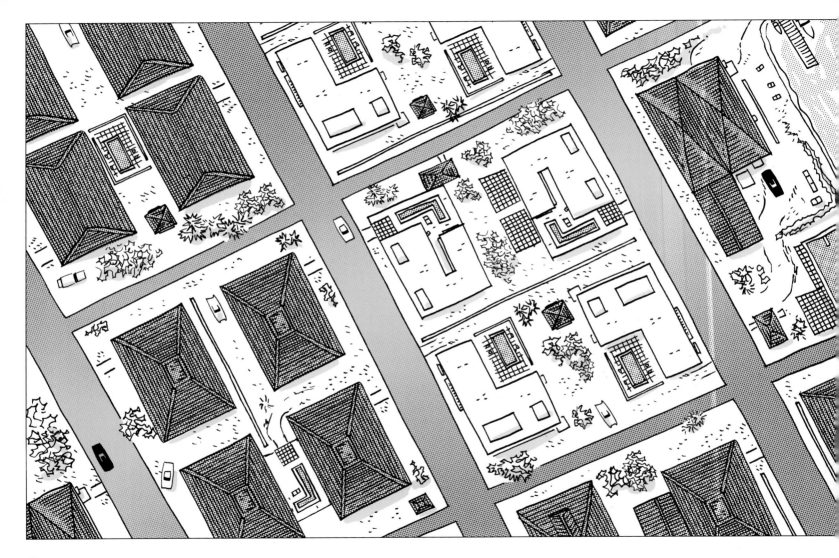

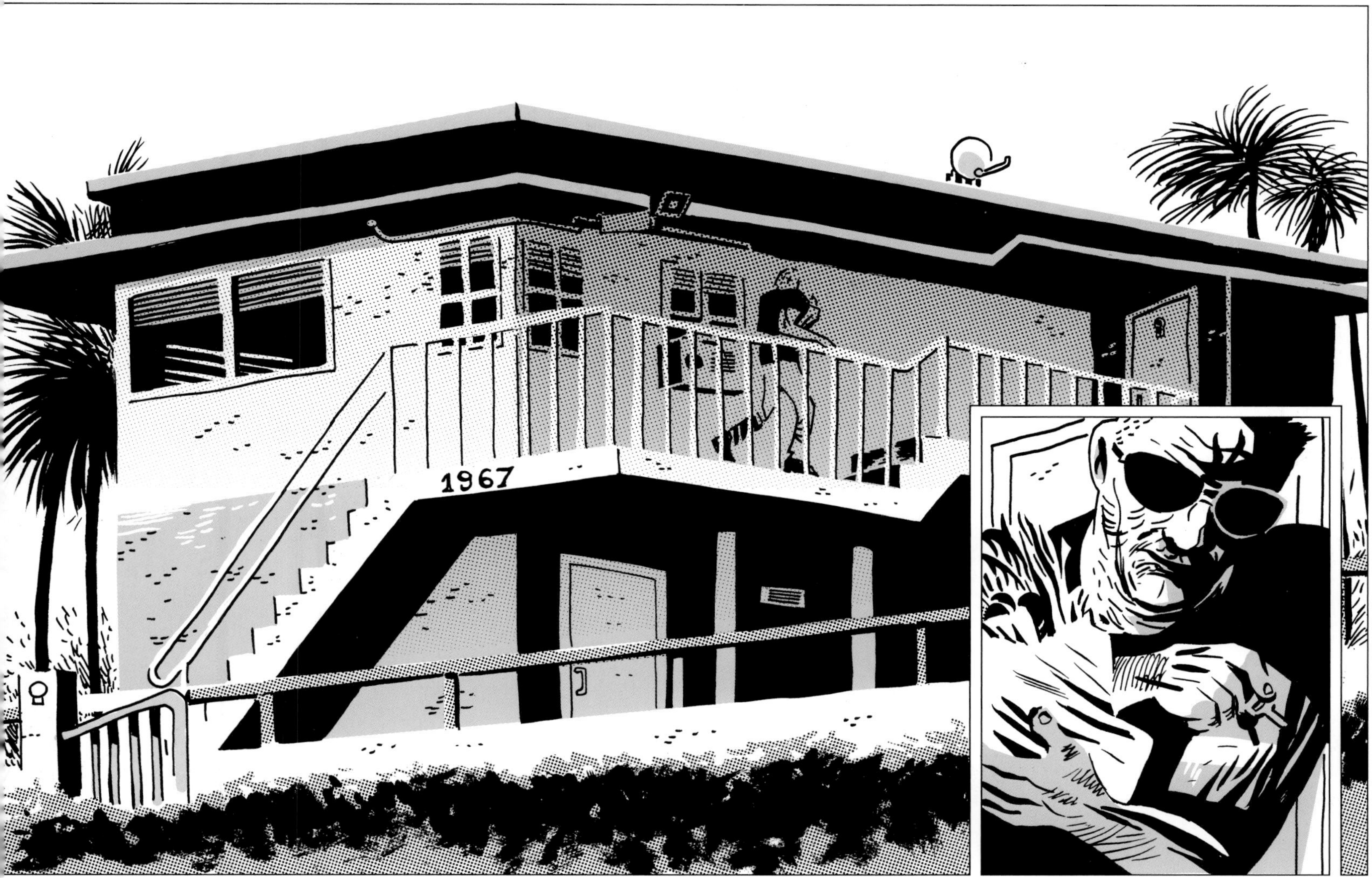
1967

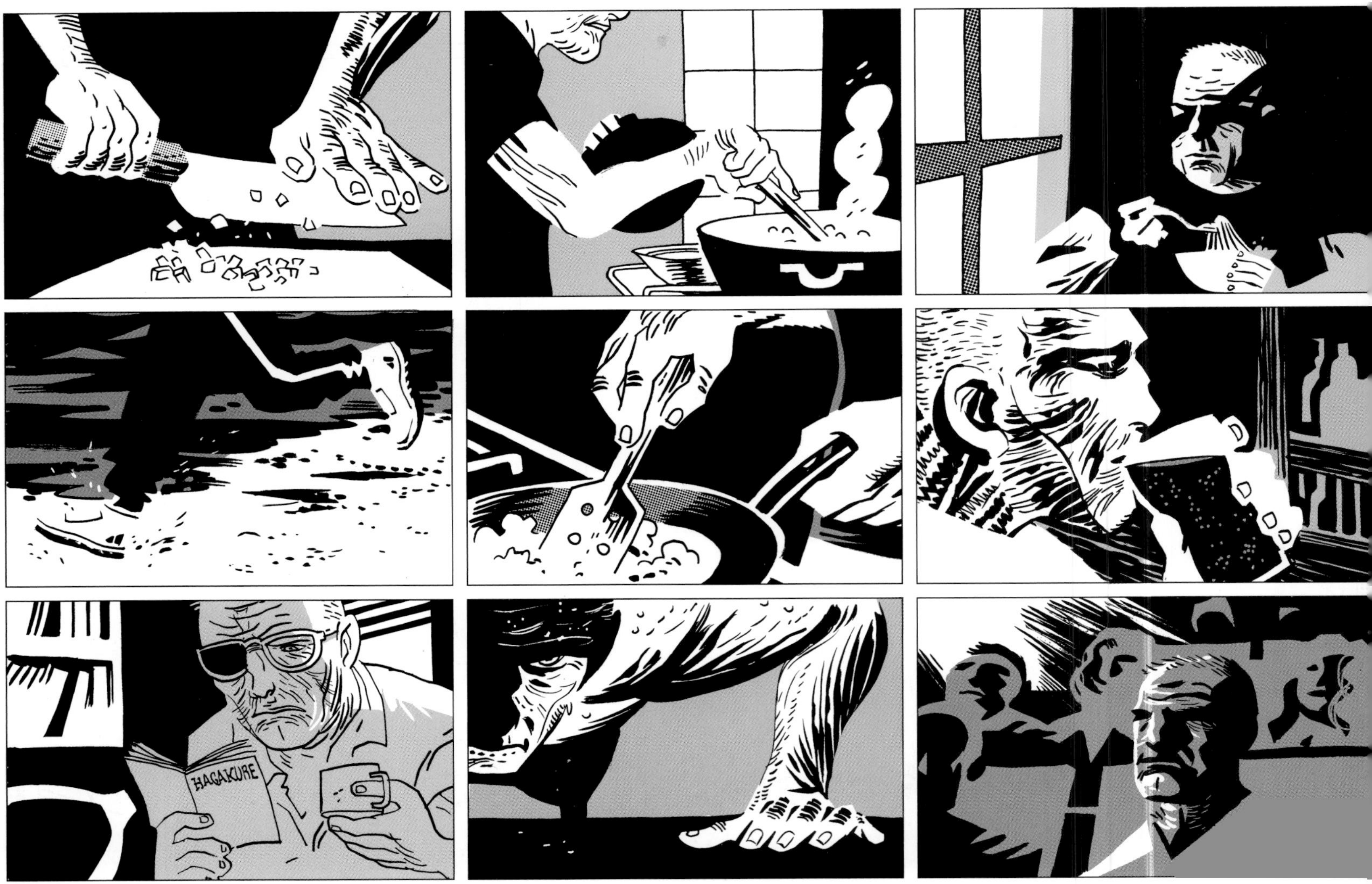
HAGAKURE

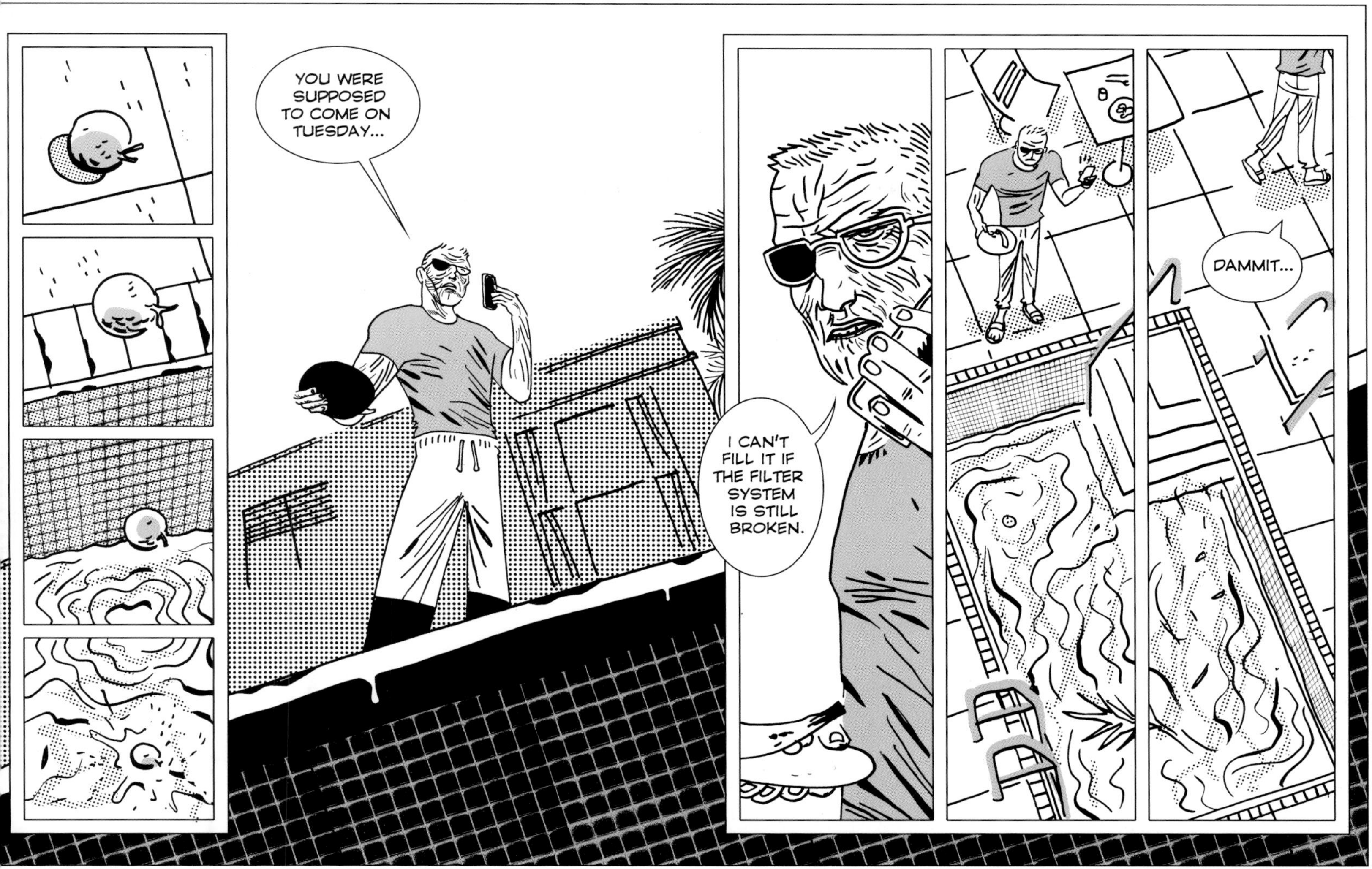
YOU WERE SUPPOSED TO COME ON TUESDAY...
I CAN'T FILL IT IF THE FILTER SYSTEM IS STILL BROKEN.
DAMMIT...

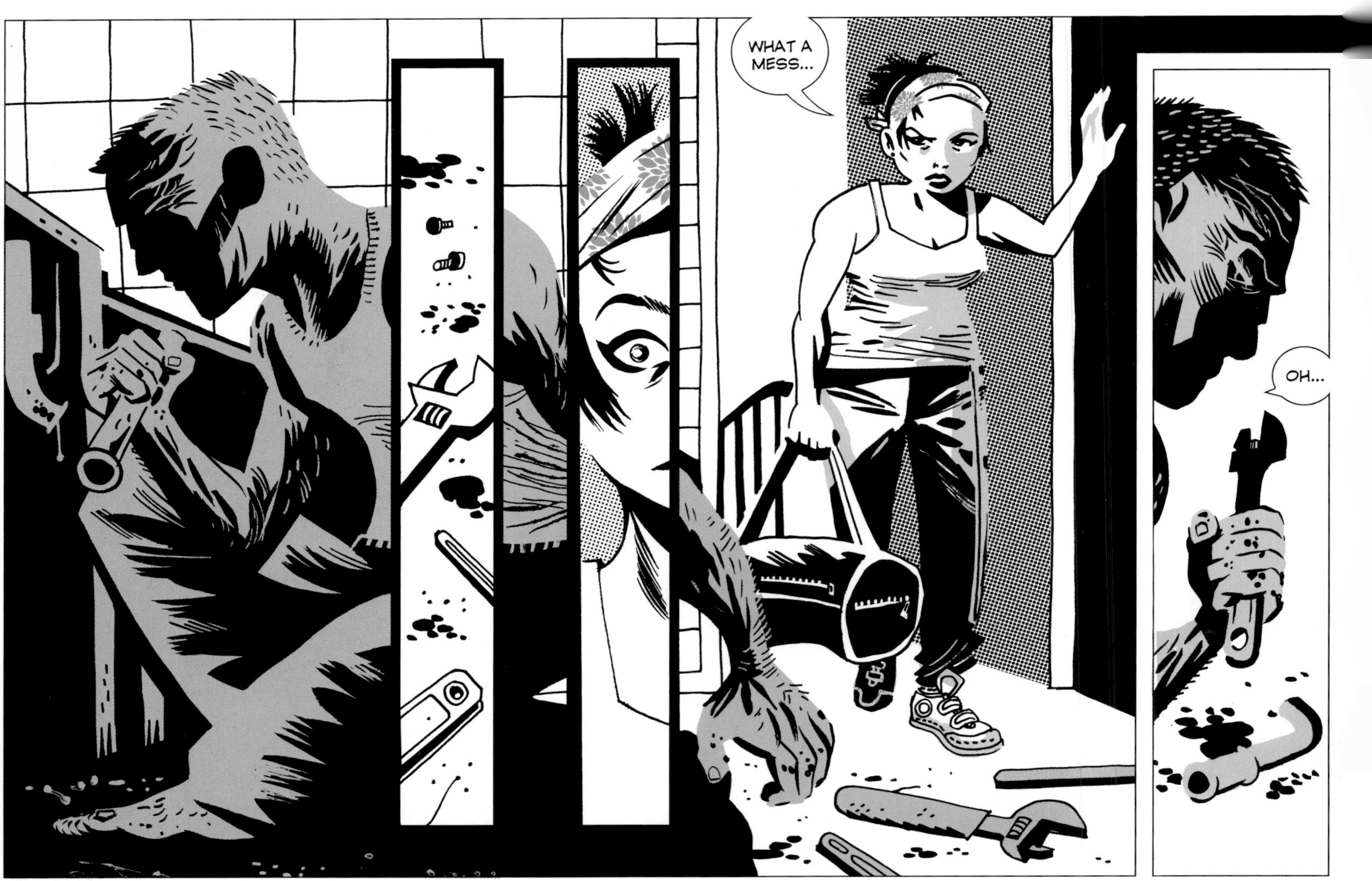
WHAT A MESS...
OH...

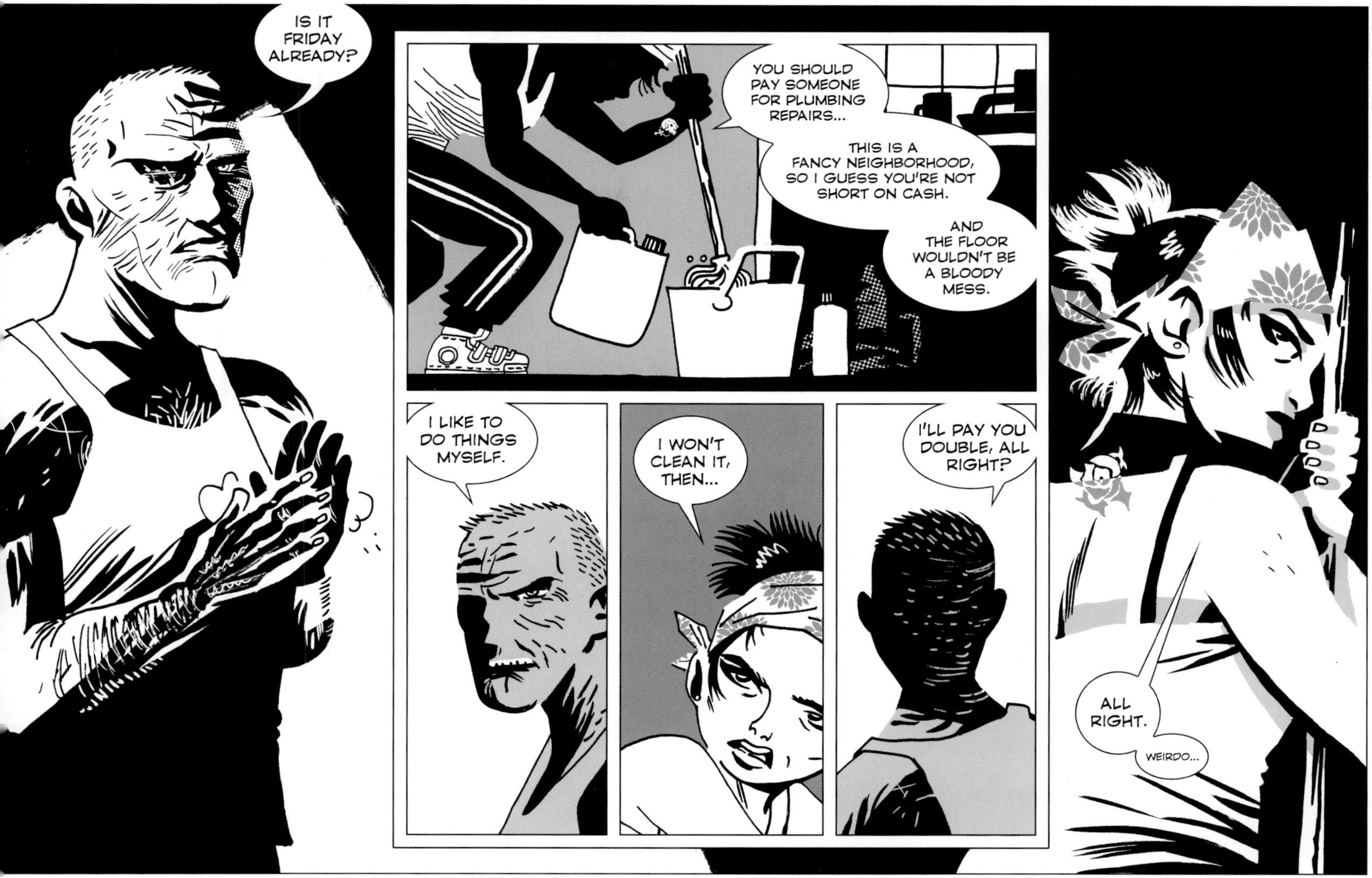

IS IT FRIDAY ALREADY?
YOU SHOULD PAY SOMEONE FOR PLUMBING REPAIRS...
THIS IS A FANCY NEIGHBORHOOD, SO I GUESS YOU'RE NOT SHORT ON CASH.
AND THE FLOOR WOULDN'T BE A BLOODY MESS.
I LIKE TO DO THINGS MYSELF.
I WON'T CLEAN IT, THEN...
I'LL PAY YOU DOUBLE, ALL RIGHT?
ALL RIGHT.
WEIRDO...

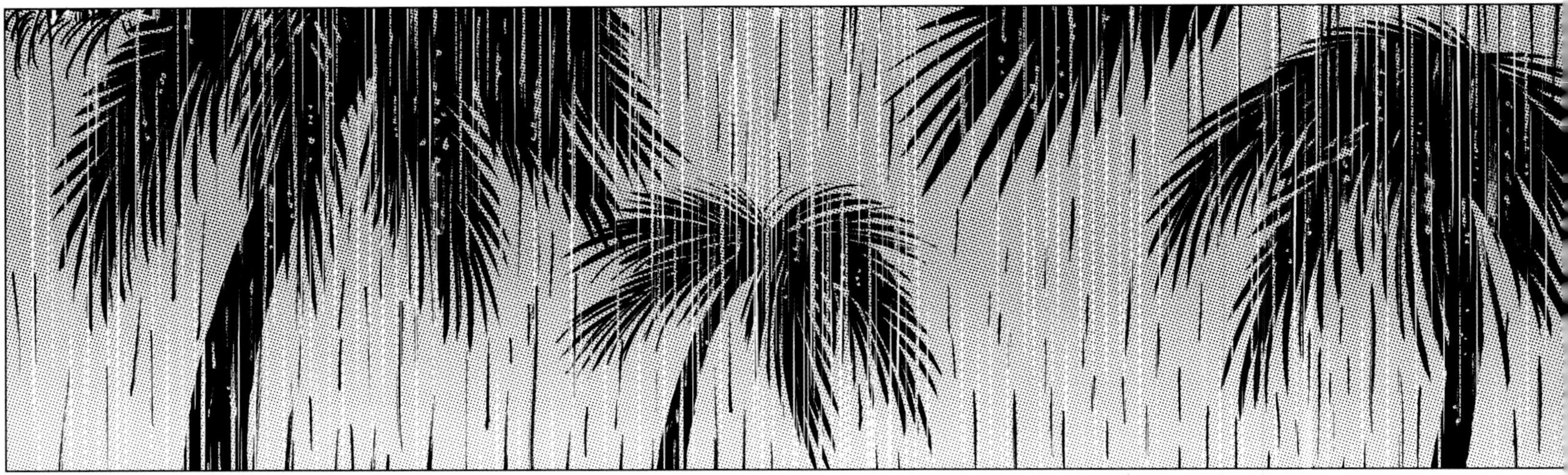

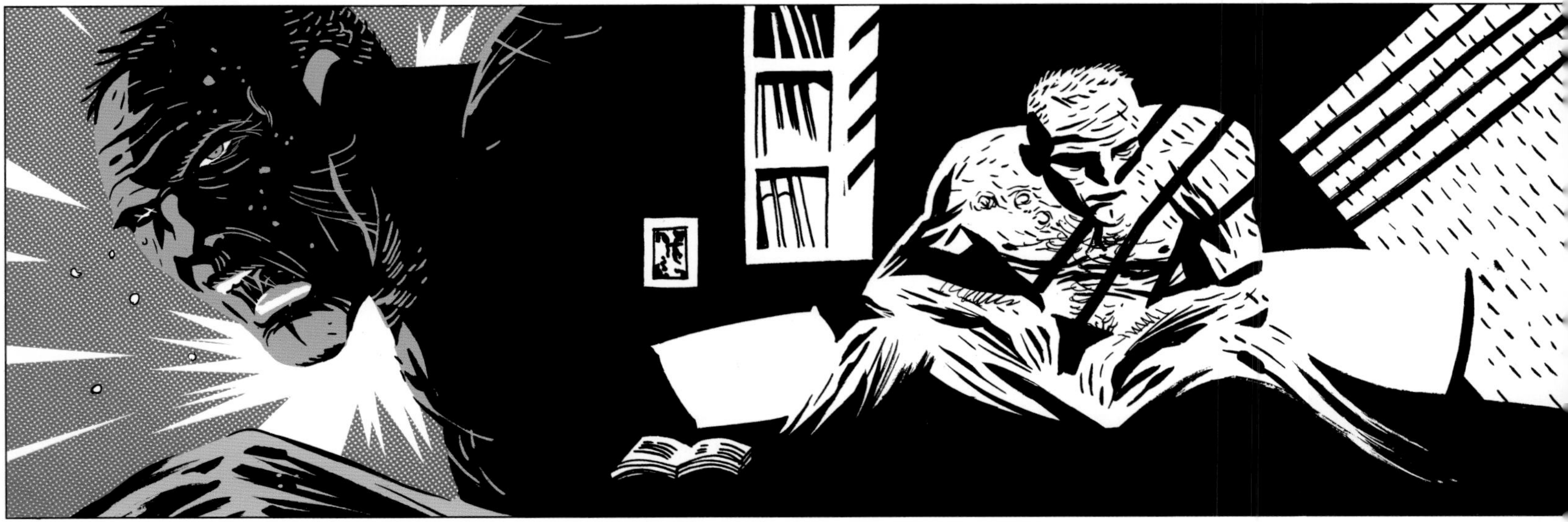

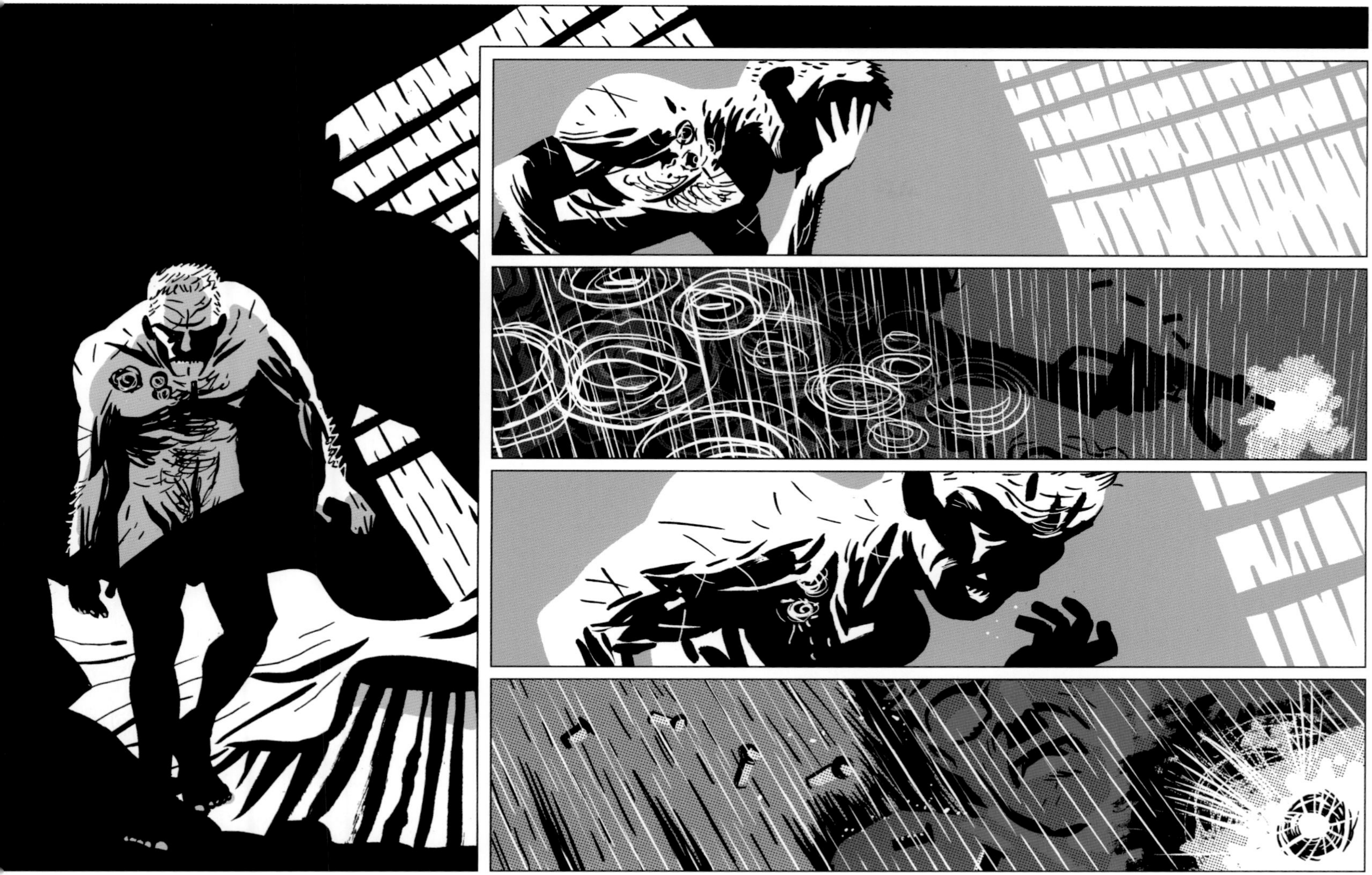

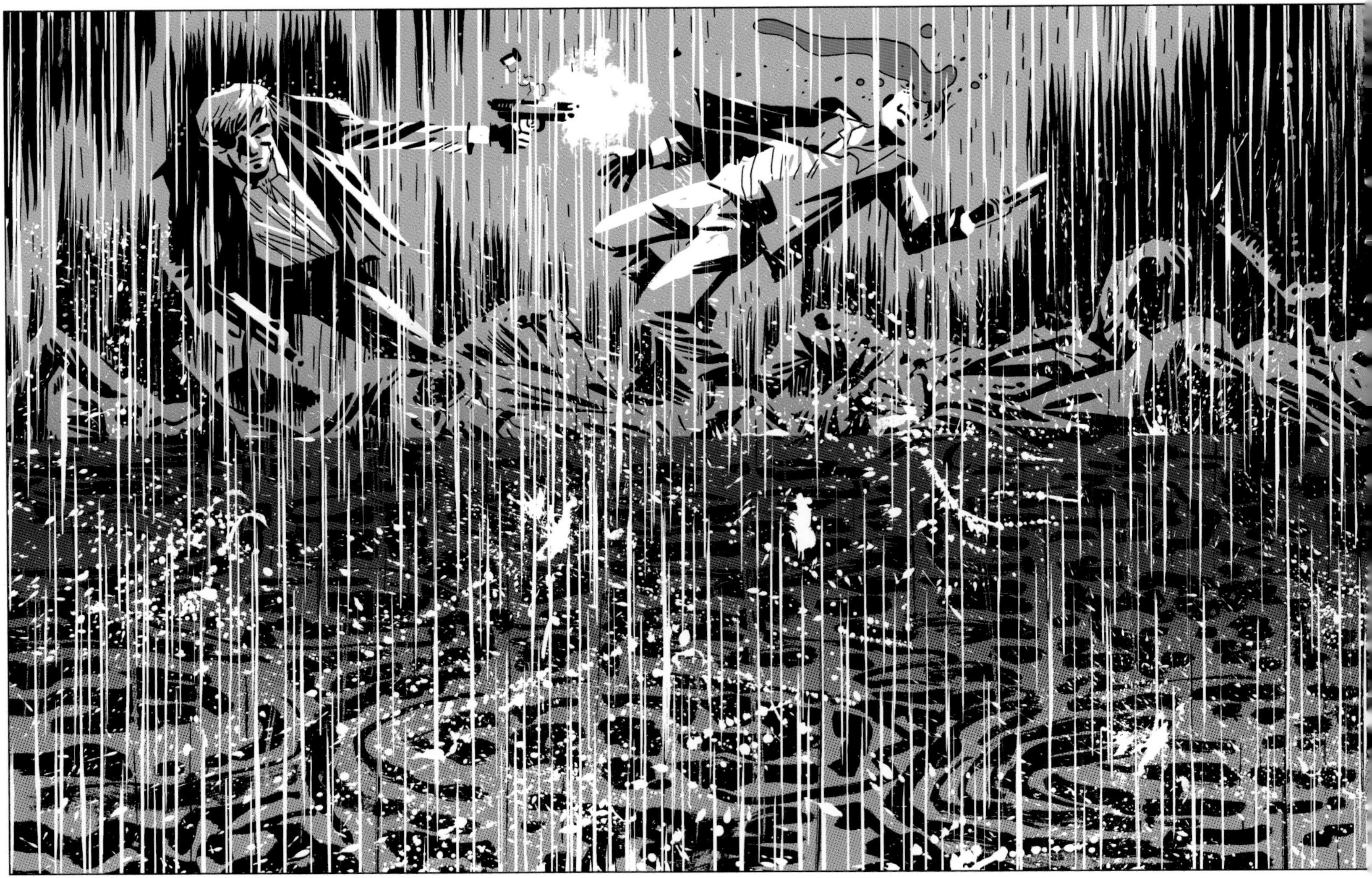

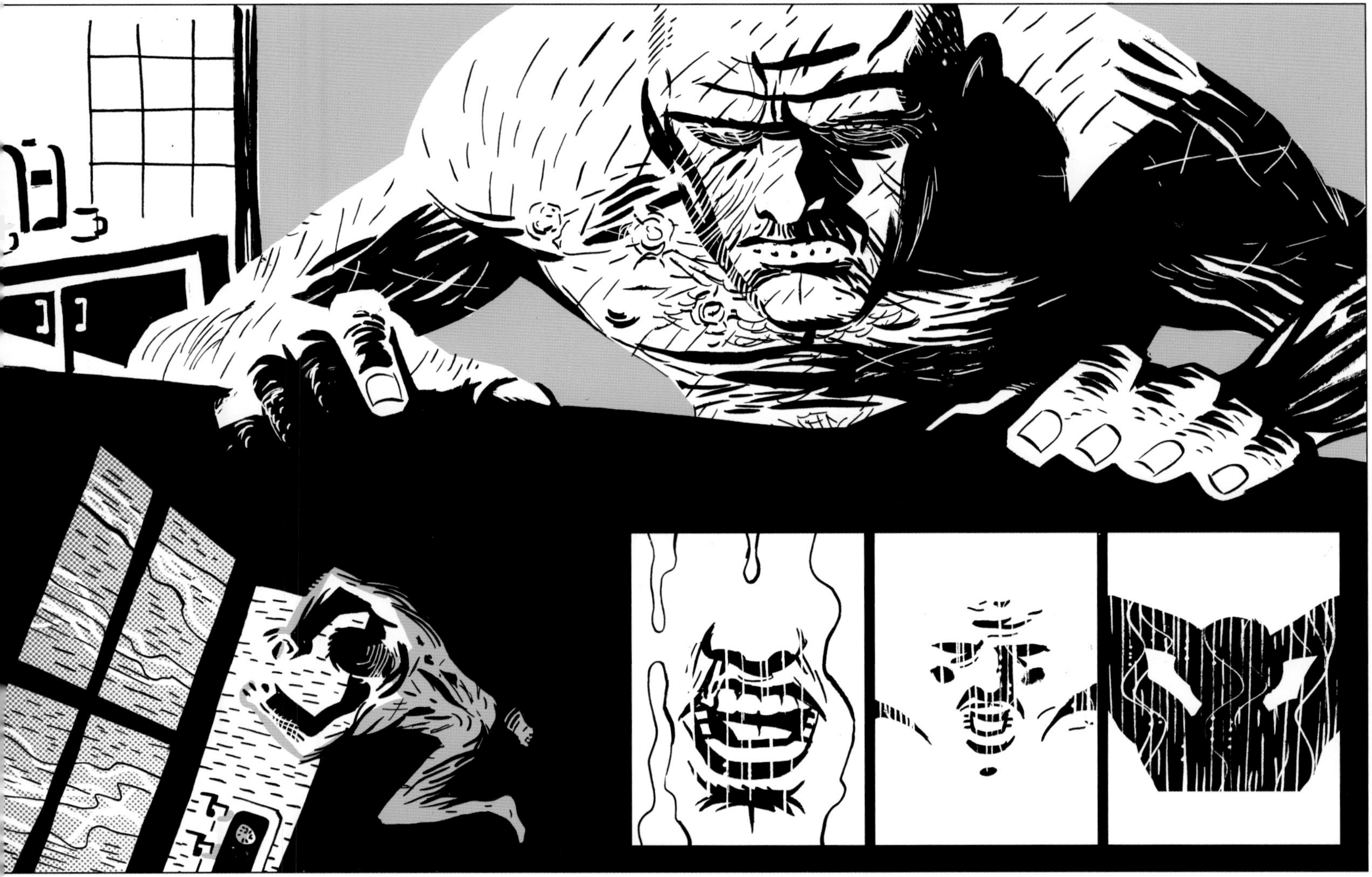

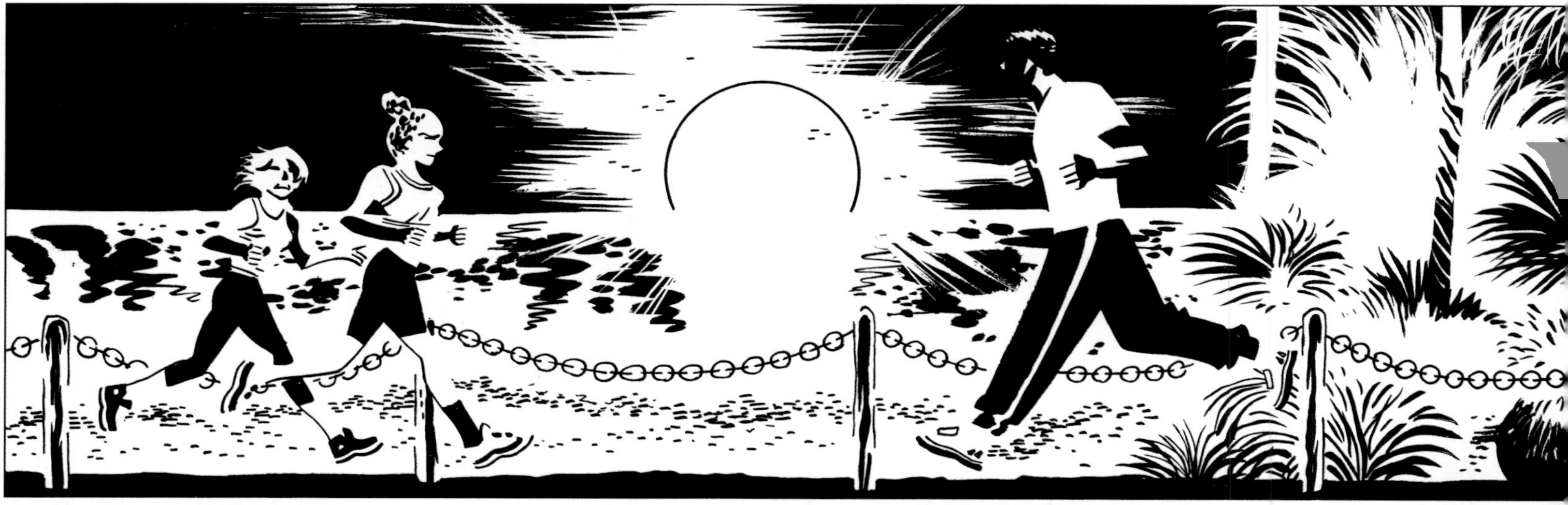

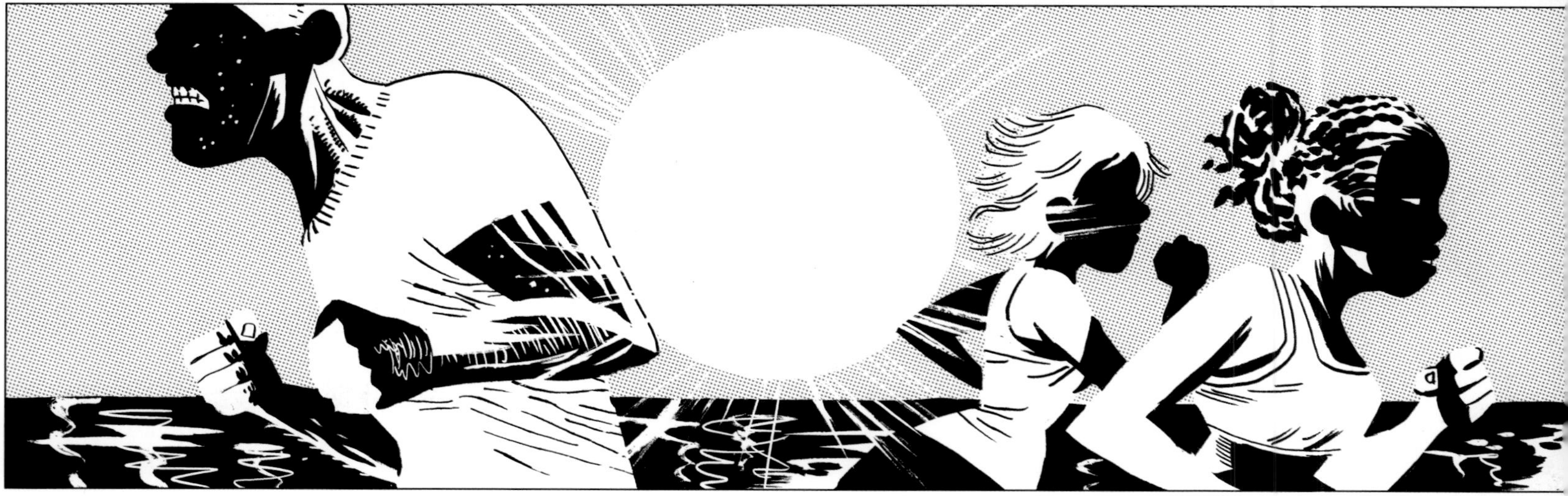

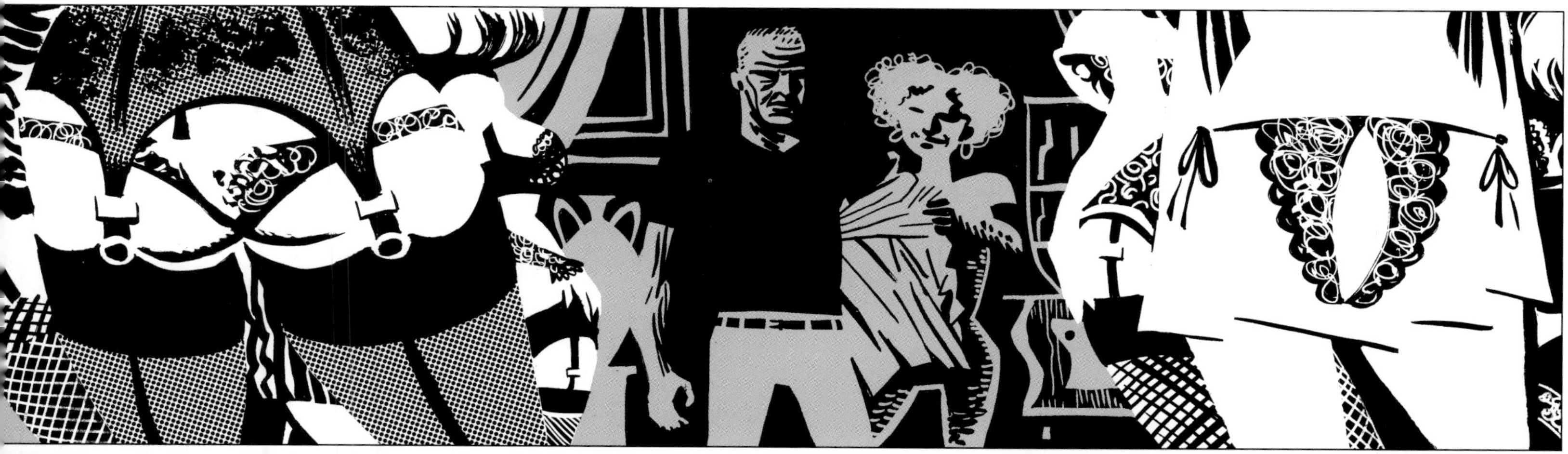

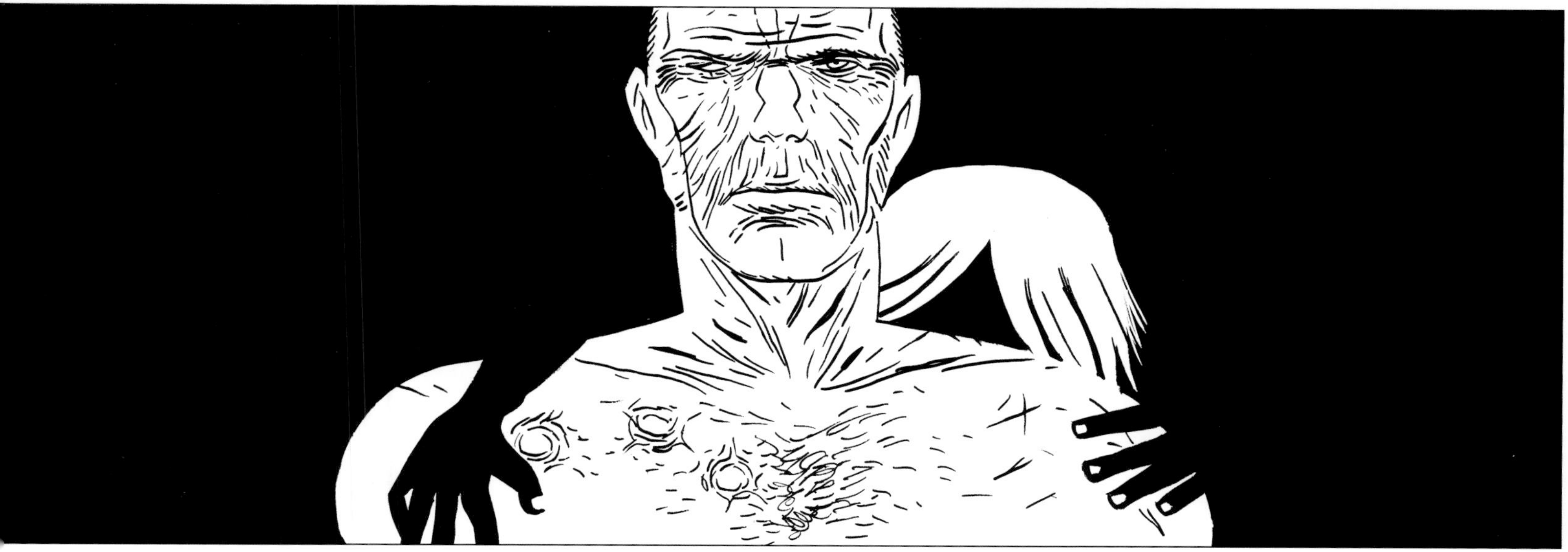

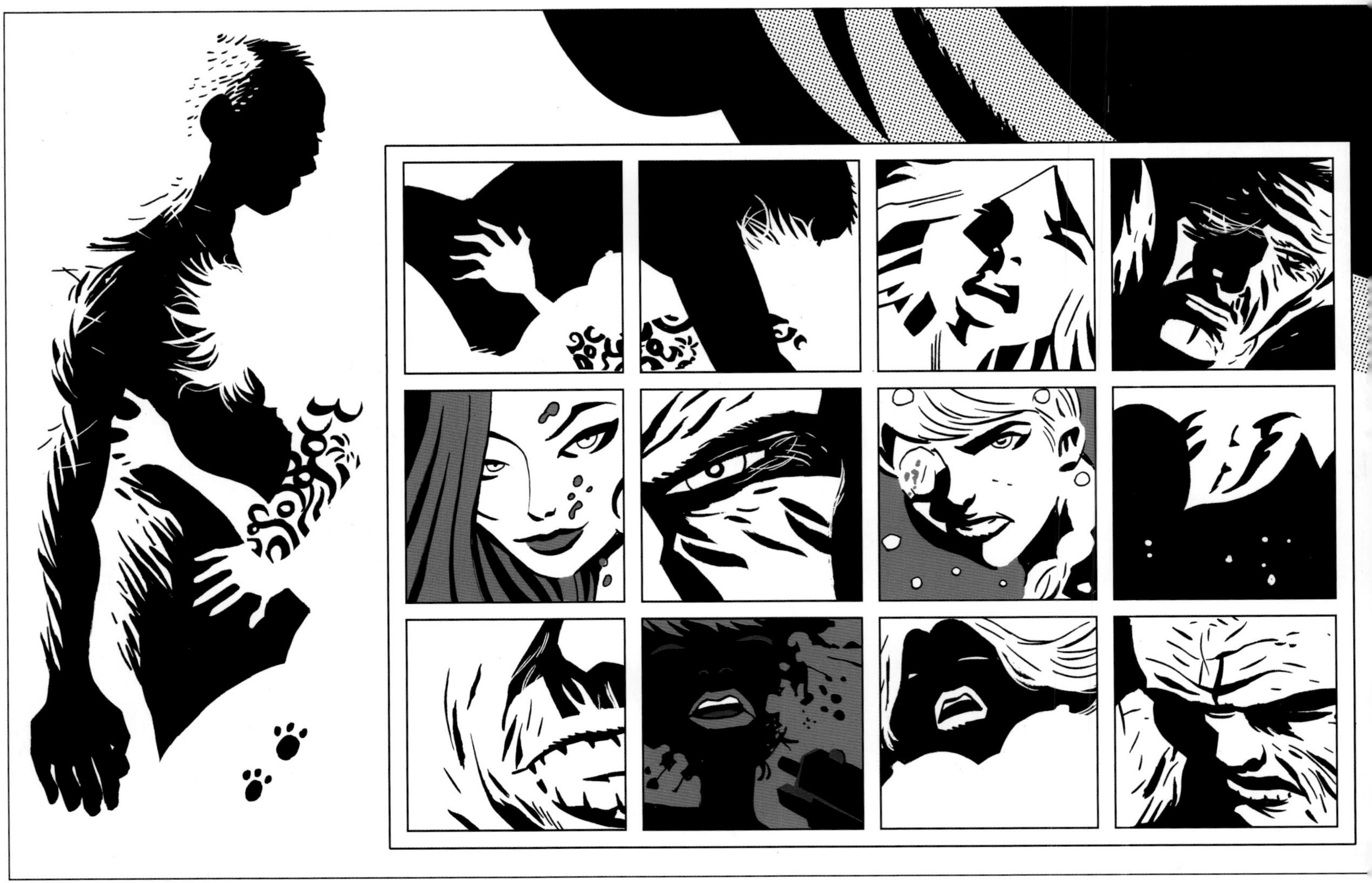

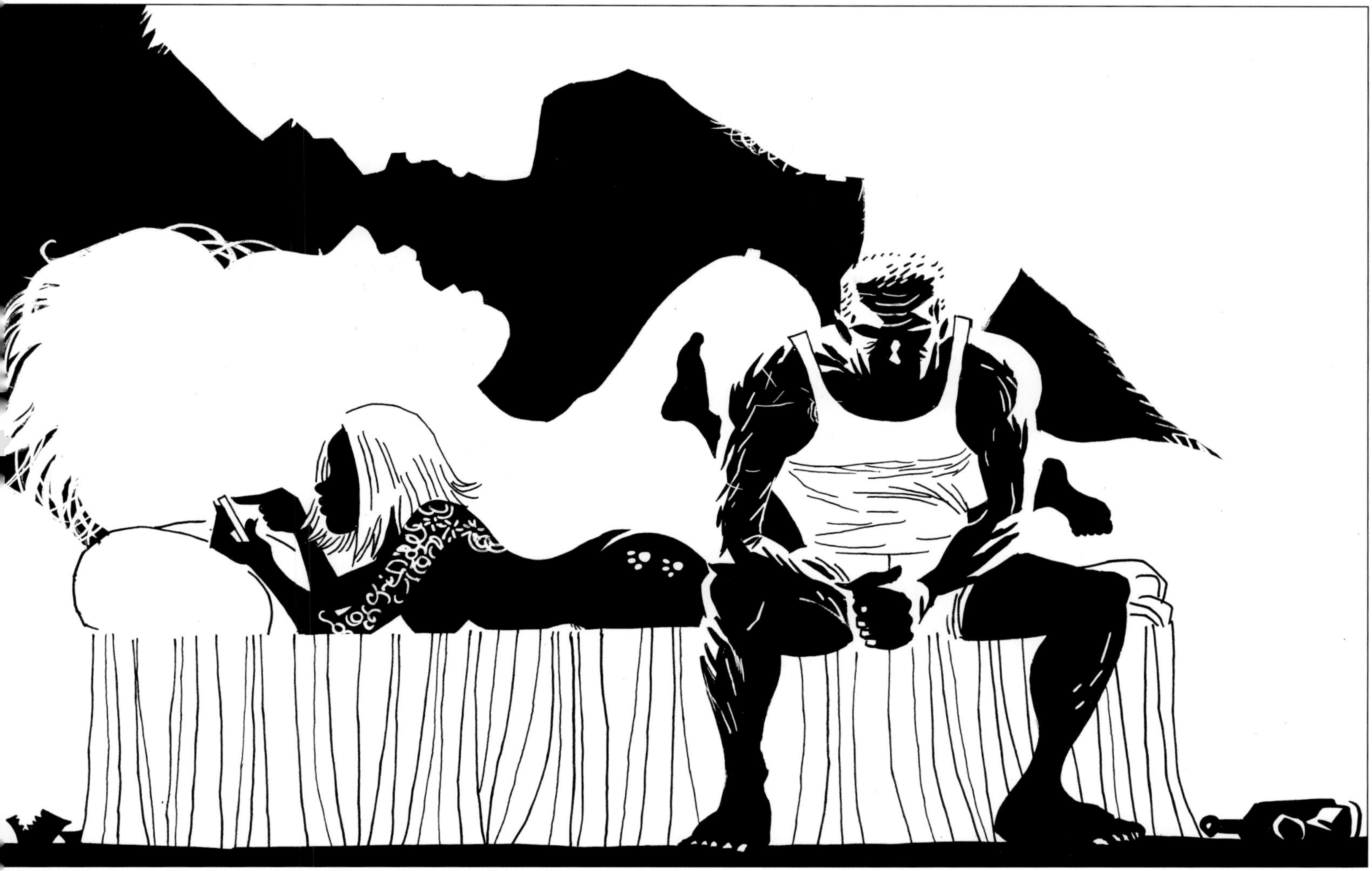

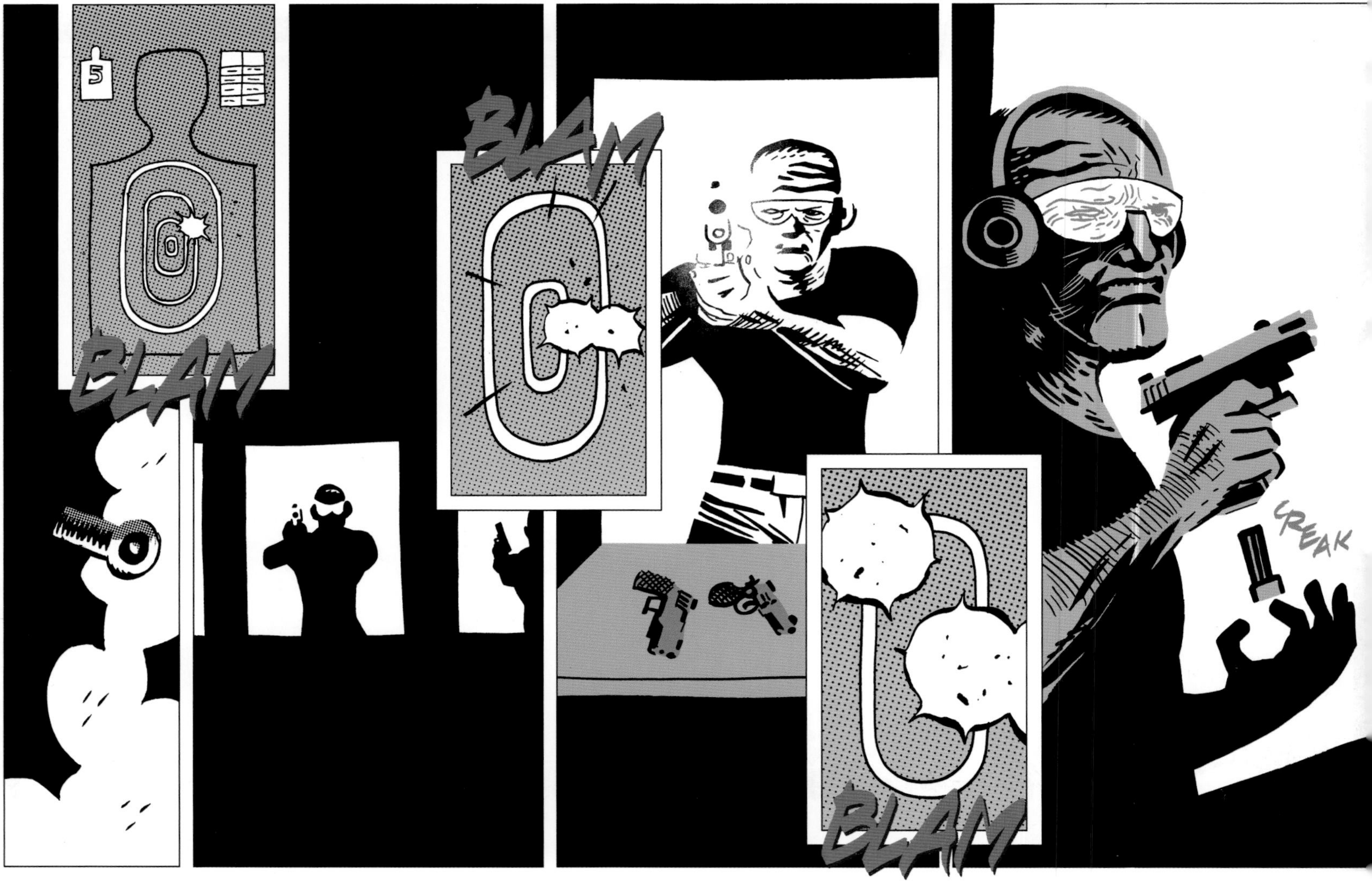
BLAM
BLAM
BLAM
CREAK

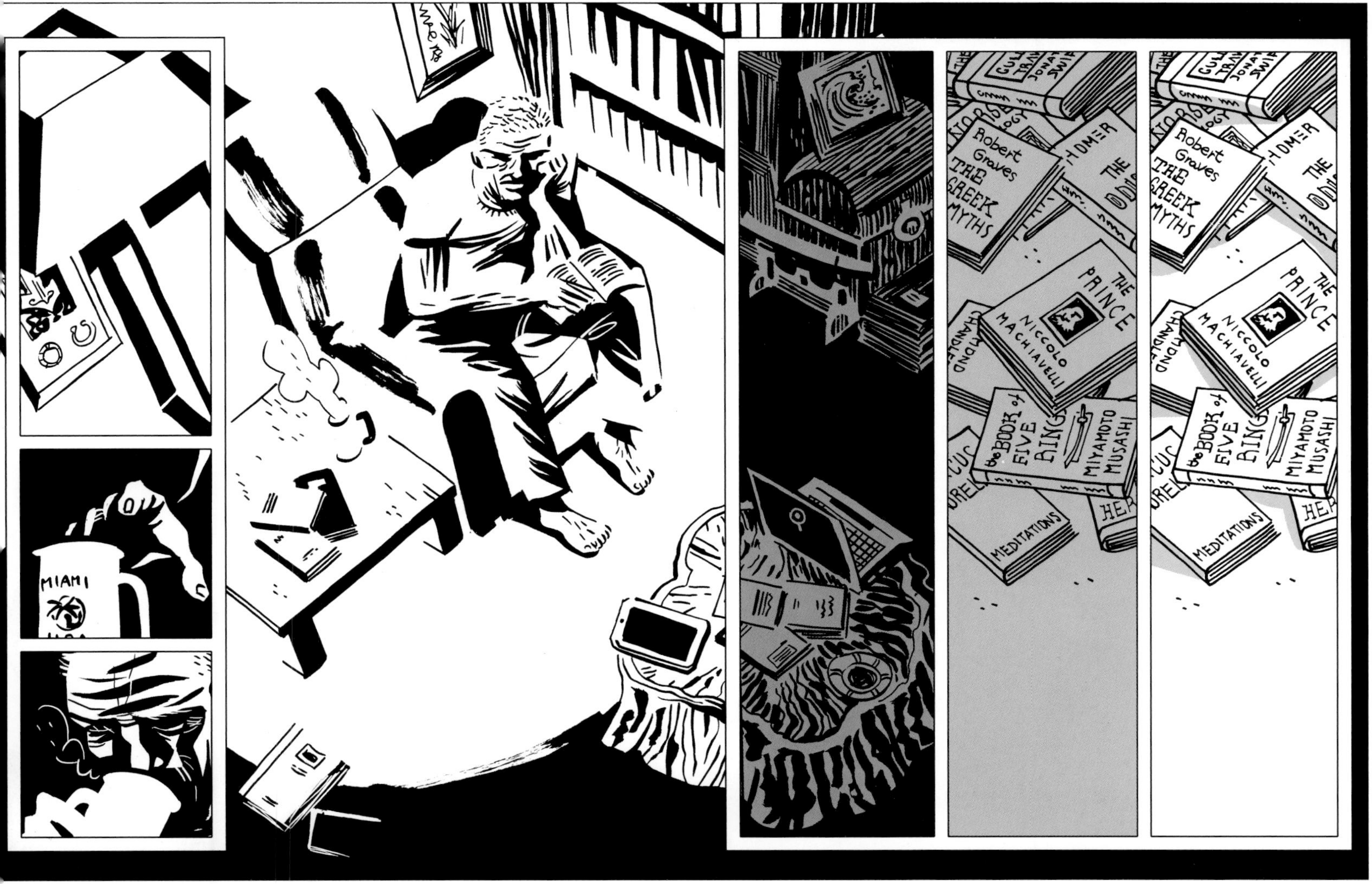
MIAMI
Robert Graves
THE GREEK MYTHS
HOMER
THE PRINCE
NICCOLO MACHIAVELLI
the BOOK of FIVE RINGS
MIYAMOTO MUSASHI
MEDITATIONS
Robert Graves
THE GREEK MYTHS
HOMER
THE PRINCE
NICCOLO MACHIAVELLI
the BOOK of FIVE RINGS
MIYAMOTO MUSASHI
MEDITATIONS

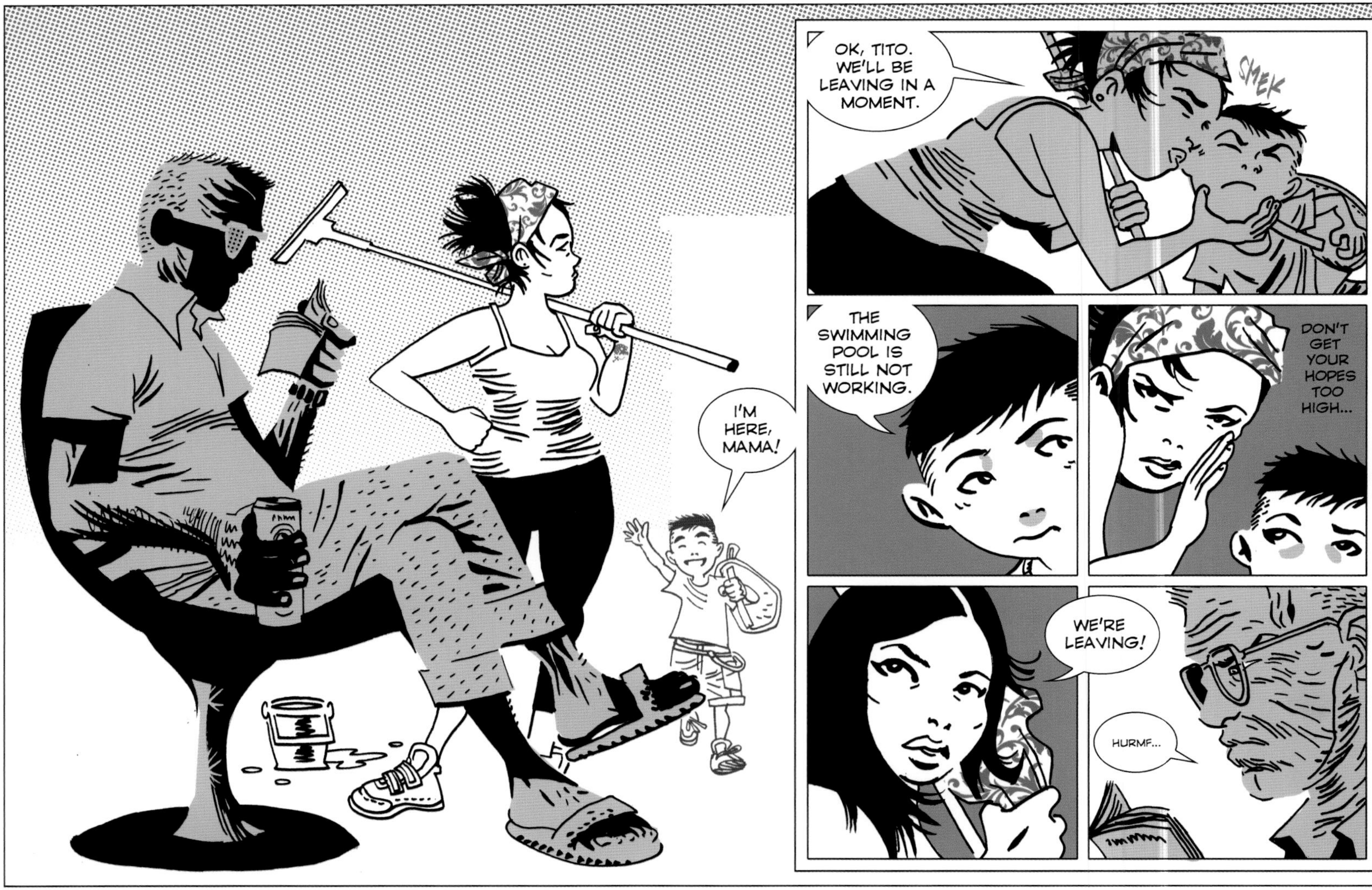
I'M HERE, MAMA!
OK, TITO. WE'LL BE LEAVING IN A MOMENT.
SMEK
THE SWIMMING POOL IS STILL NOT WORKING.
DON'T GET YOUR HOPES TOO HIGH...
WE'RE LEAVING!
HURMF...

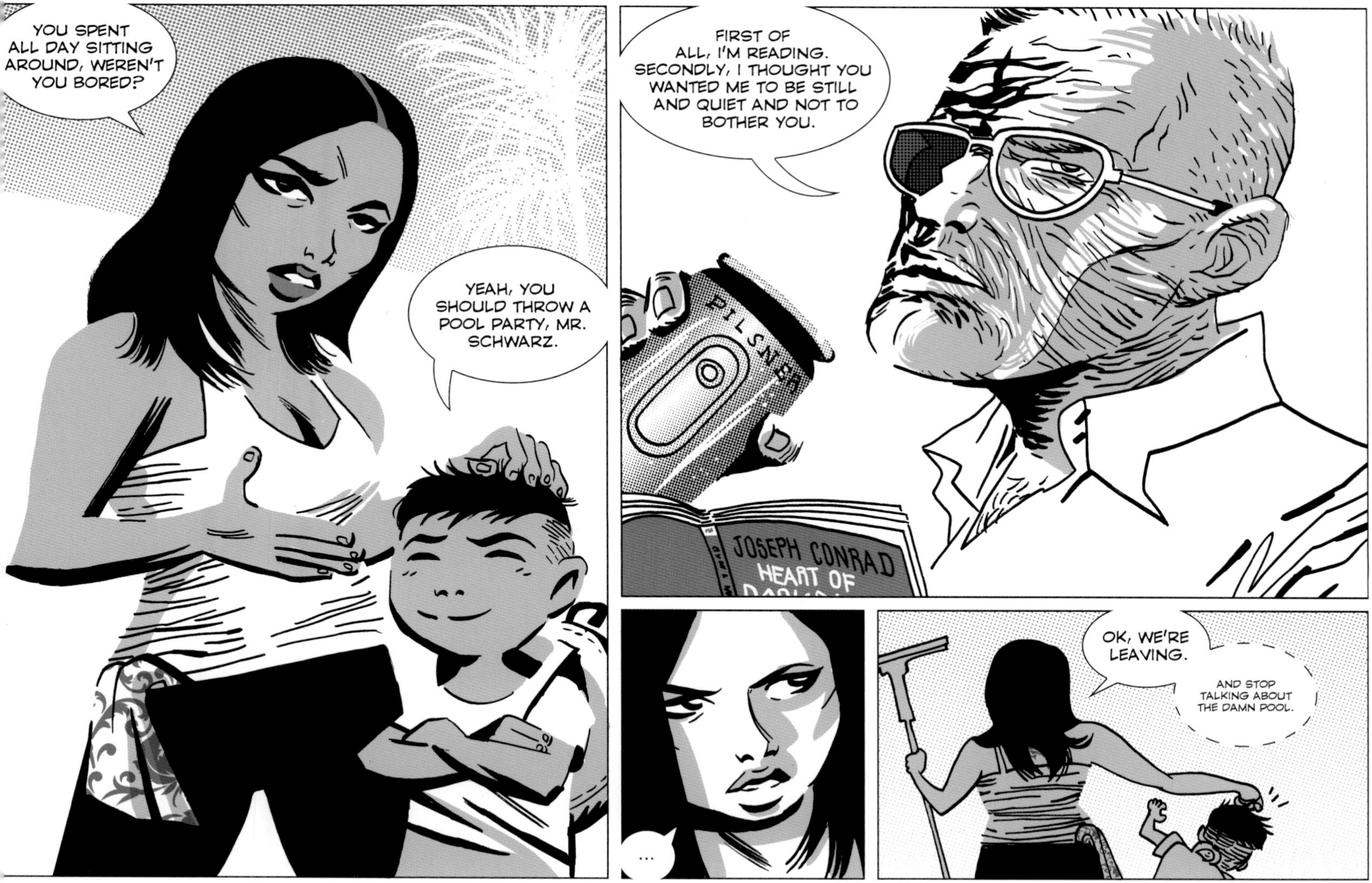
YOU SPENT ALL DAY SITTING AROUND, WEREN'T YOU BORED?
YEAH, YOU SHOULD THROW A POOL PARTY, MR. SCHWARZ.
FIRST OF ALL, I'M READING. SECONDLY, I THOUGHT YOU WANTED ME TO BE STILL AND QUIET AND NOT TO BOTHER YOU.
PILSNER
JOSEPH CONRAD
HEART OF
...
OK, WE'RE LEAVING.
AND STOP TALKING ABOUT THE DAMN POOL.

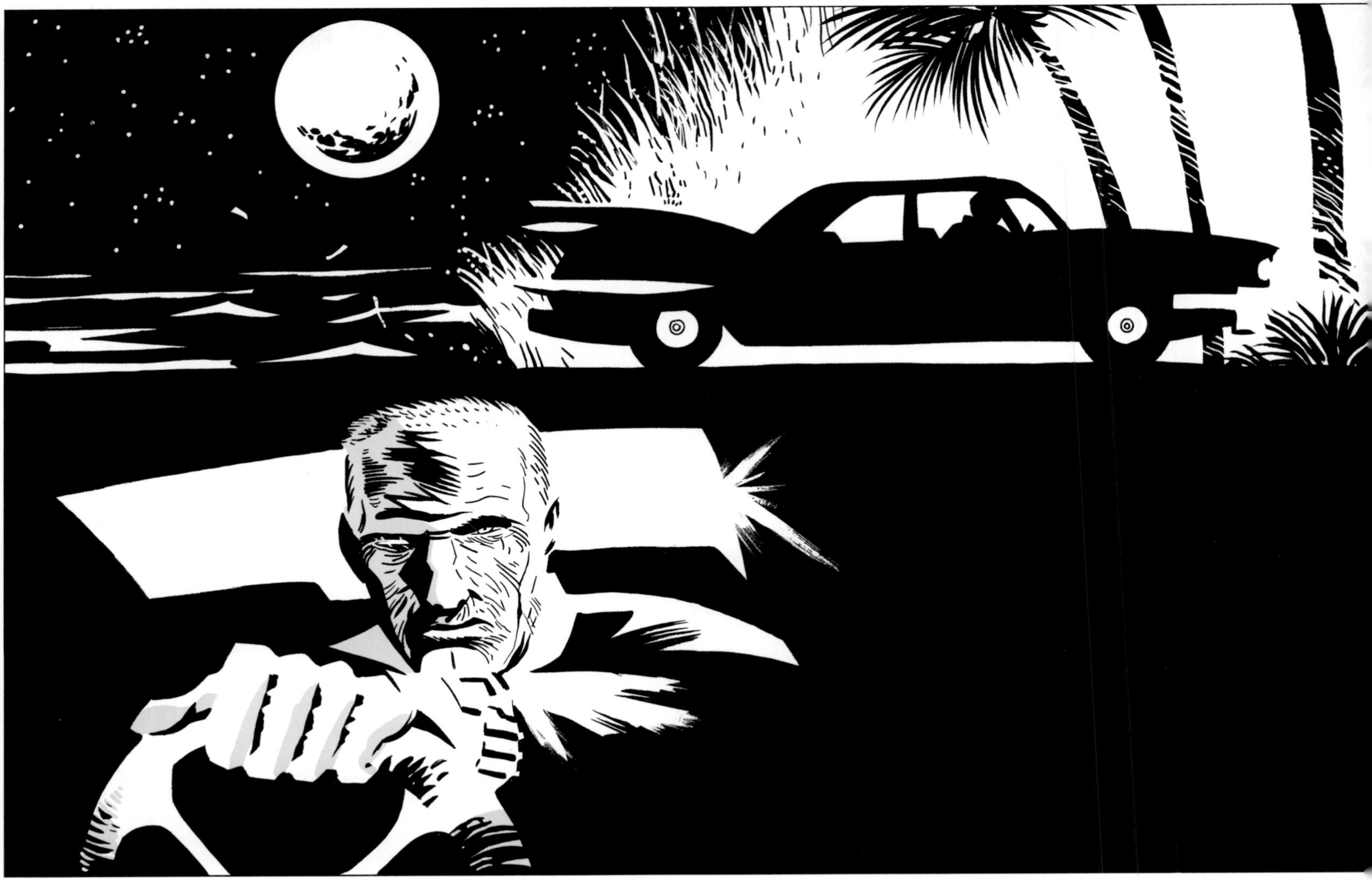

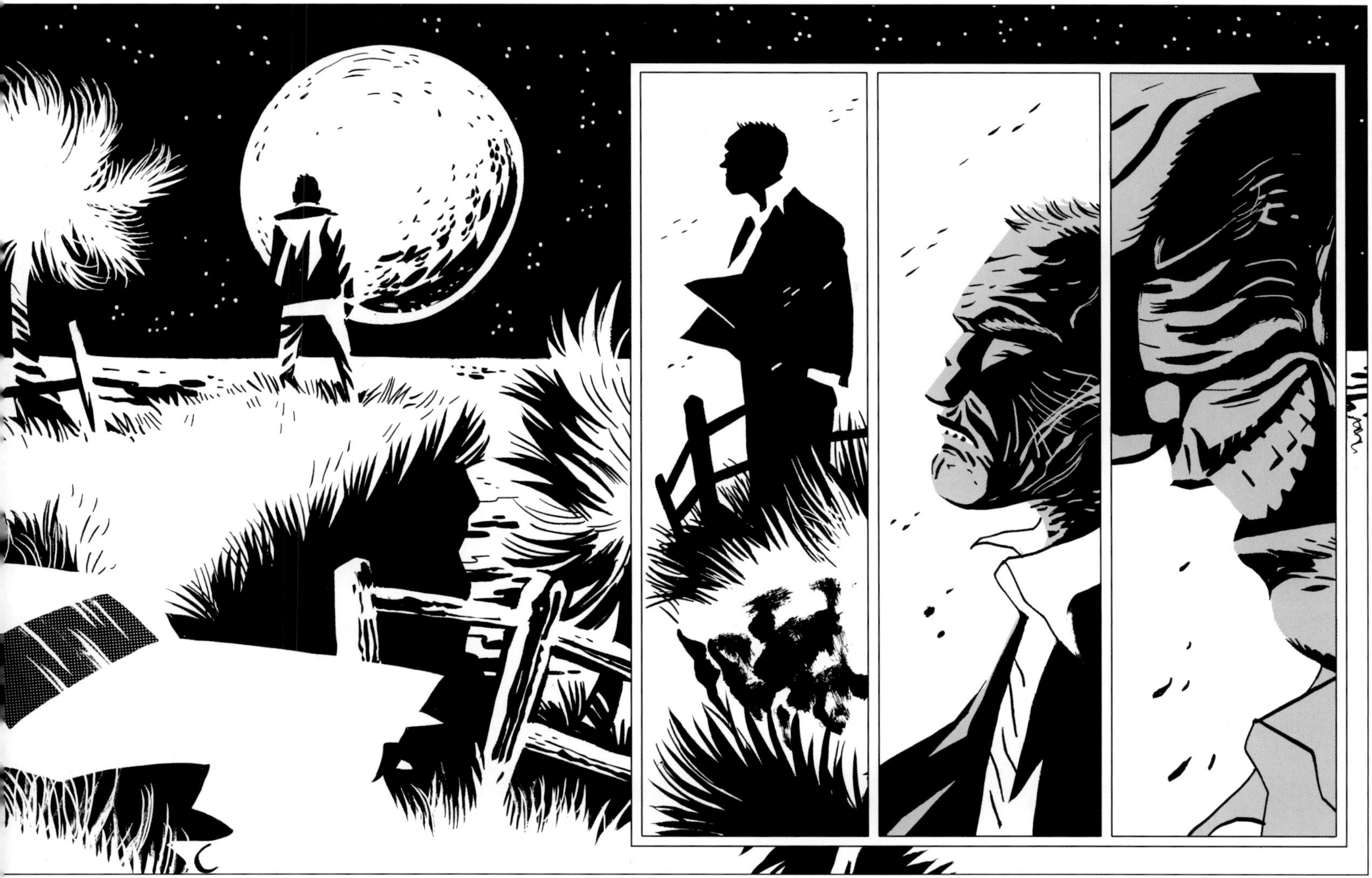

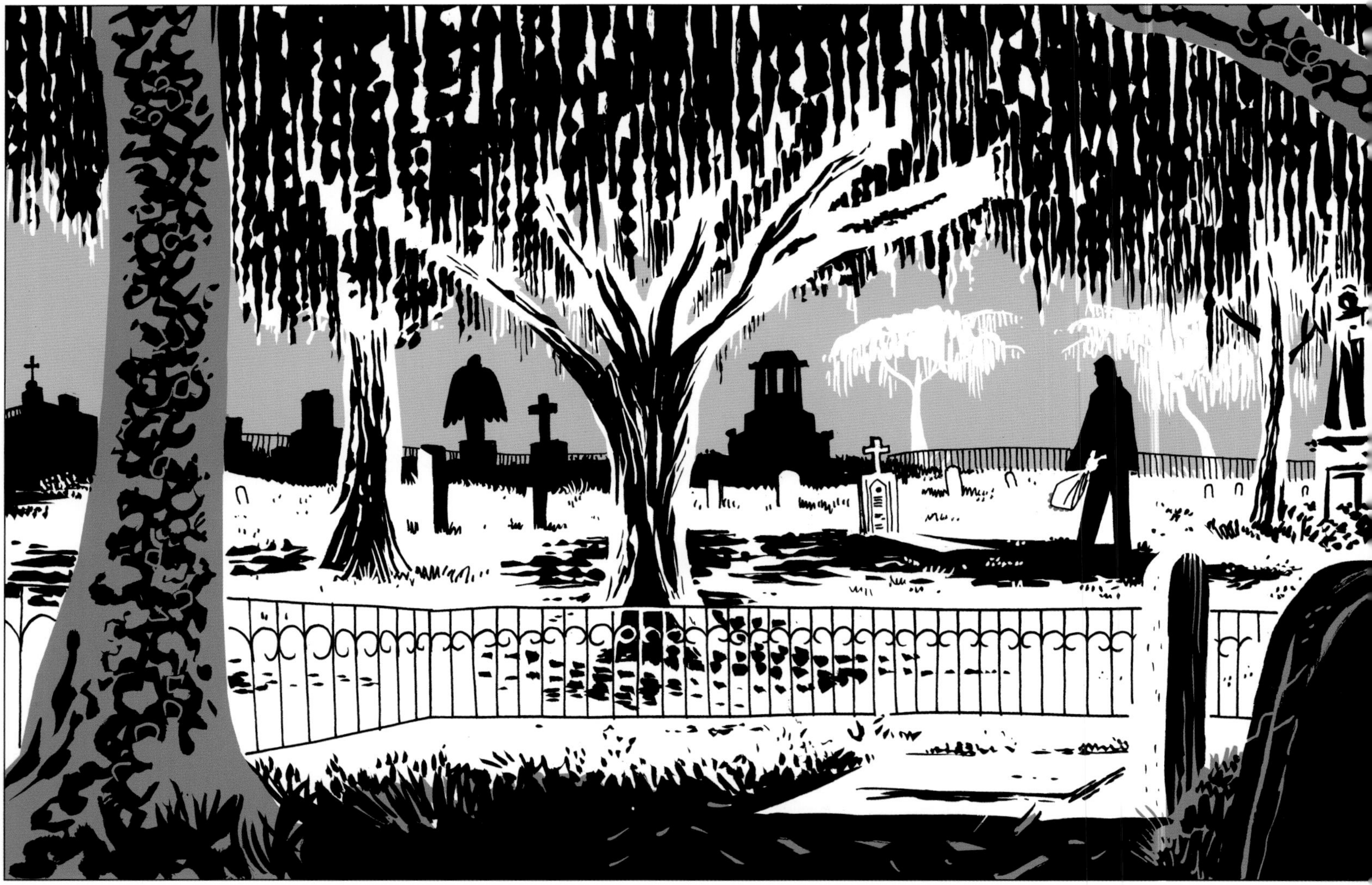

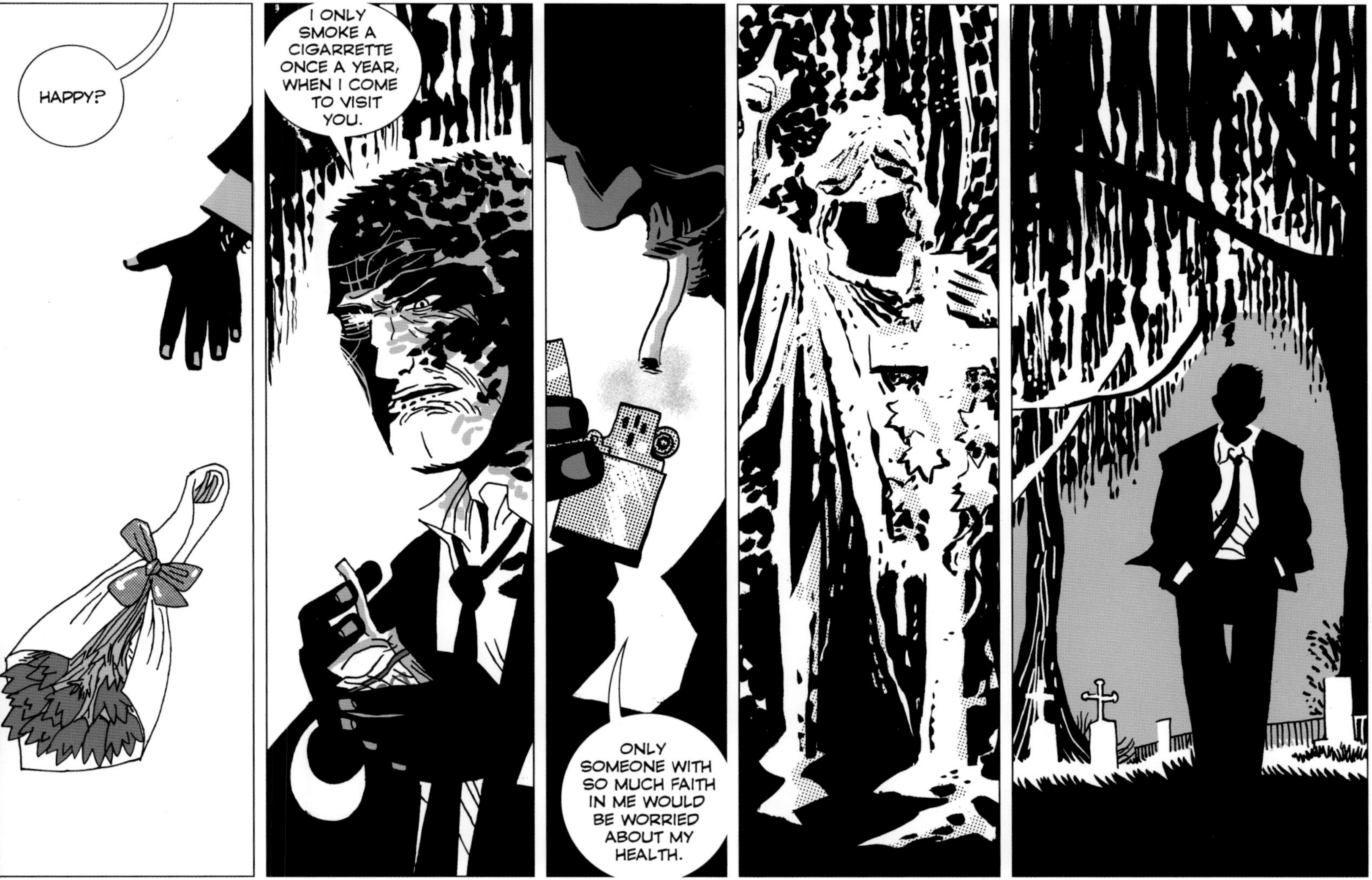
HAPPY?
I ONLY SMOKE A CIGARRETTE ONCE A YEAR, WHEN I COME TO VISIT YOU.
ONLY SOMEONE WITH SO MUCH FAITH IN ME WOULD BE WORRIED ABOUT MY HEALTH.

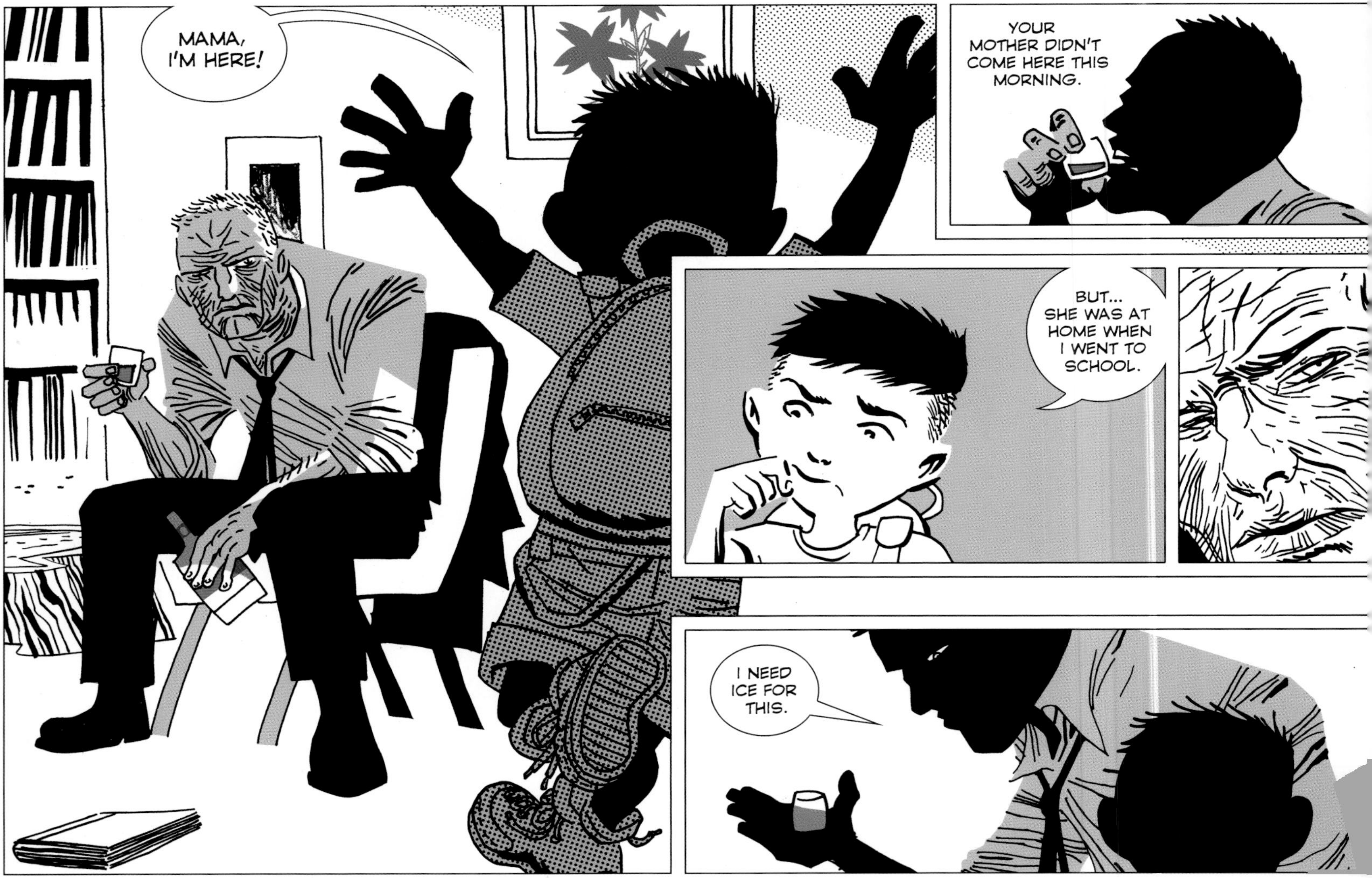
MAMA, I'M HERE!
YOUR MOTHER DIDN'T COME HERE THIS MORNING.
BUT... SHE WAS AT HOME WHEN I WENT TO SCHOOL.
I NEED ICE FOR THIS.

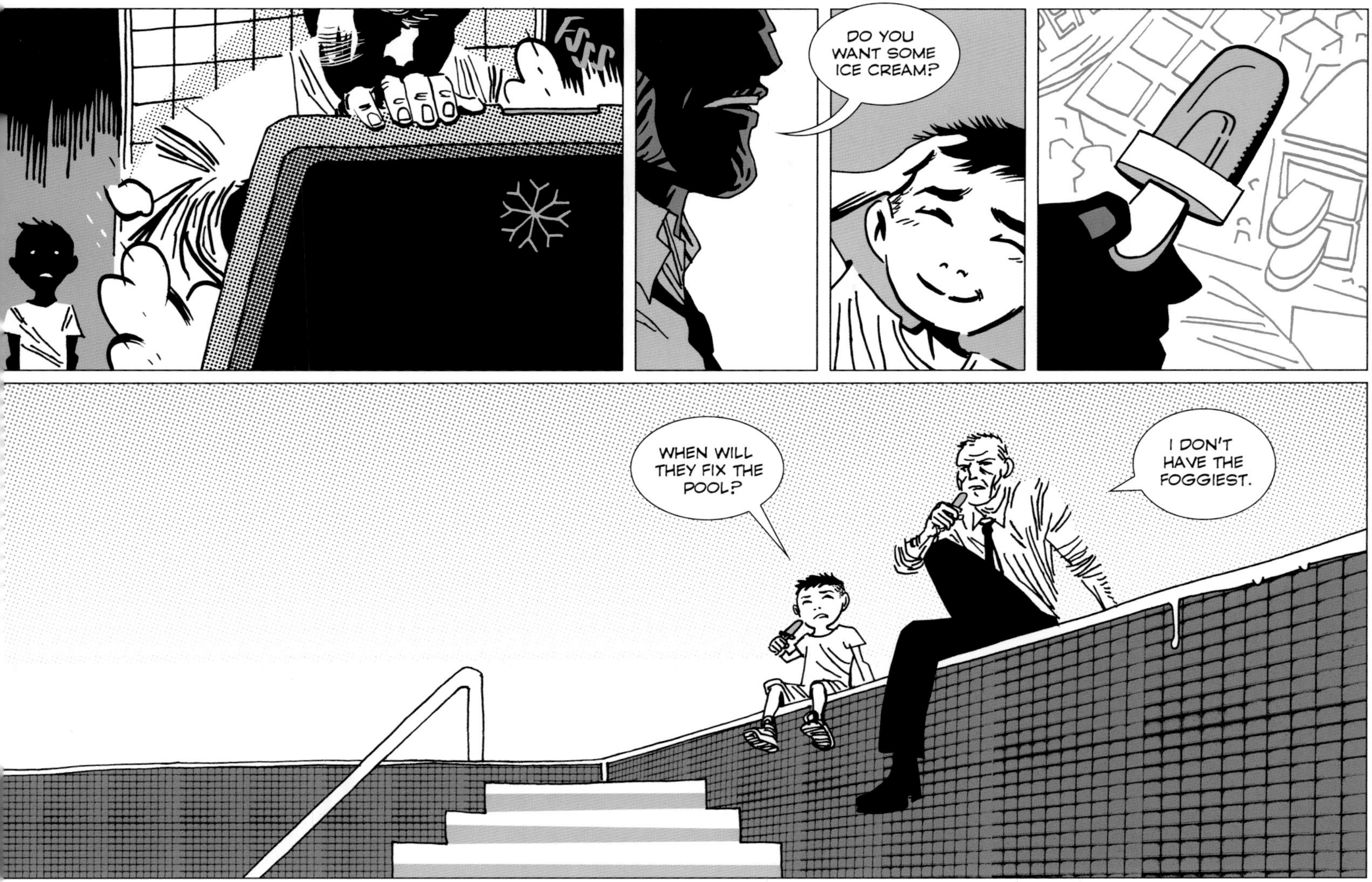
FSSS
DO YOU WANT SOME ICE CREAM?
WHEN WILL THEY FIX THE POOL?
I DON'T HAVE THE FOGGIEST.

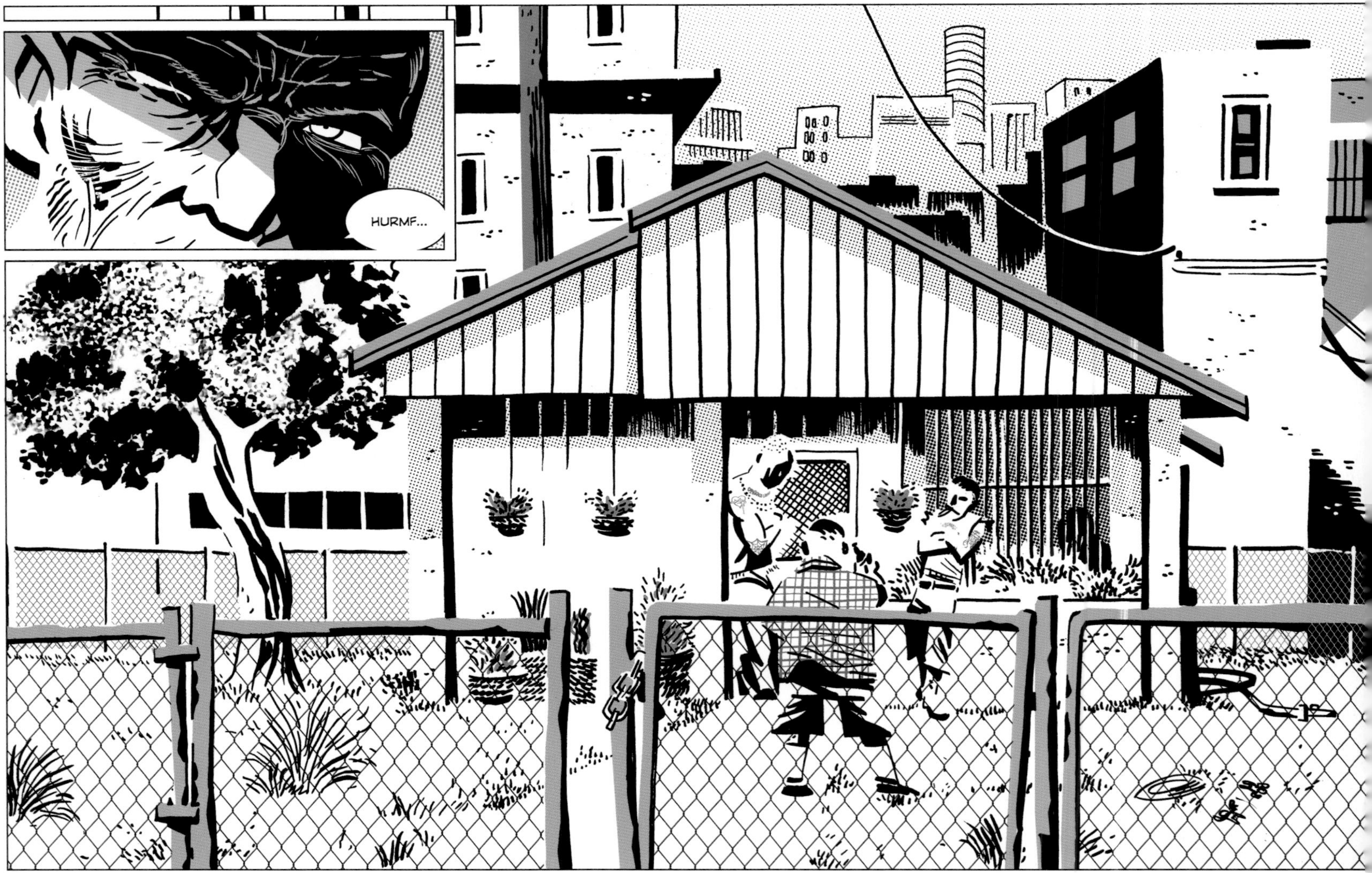
HURMF...

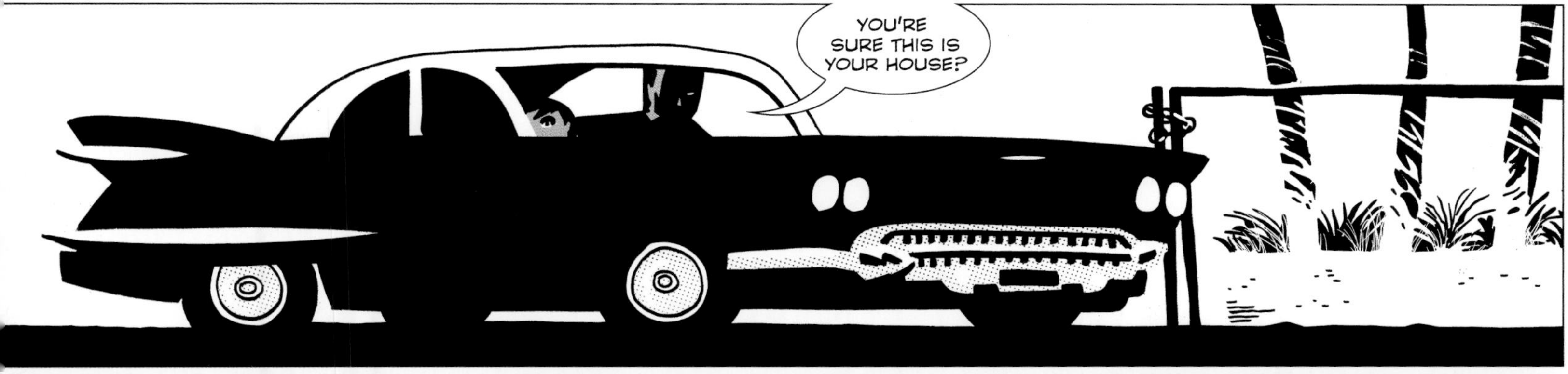
YOU'RE SURE THIS IS YOUR HOUSE?

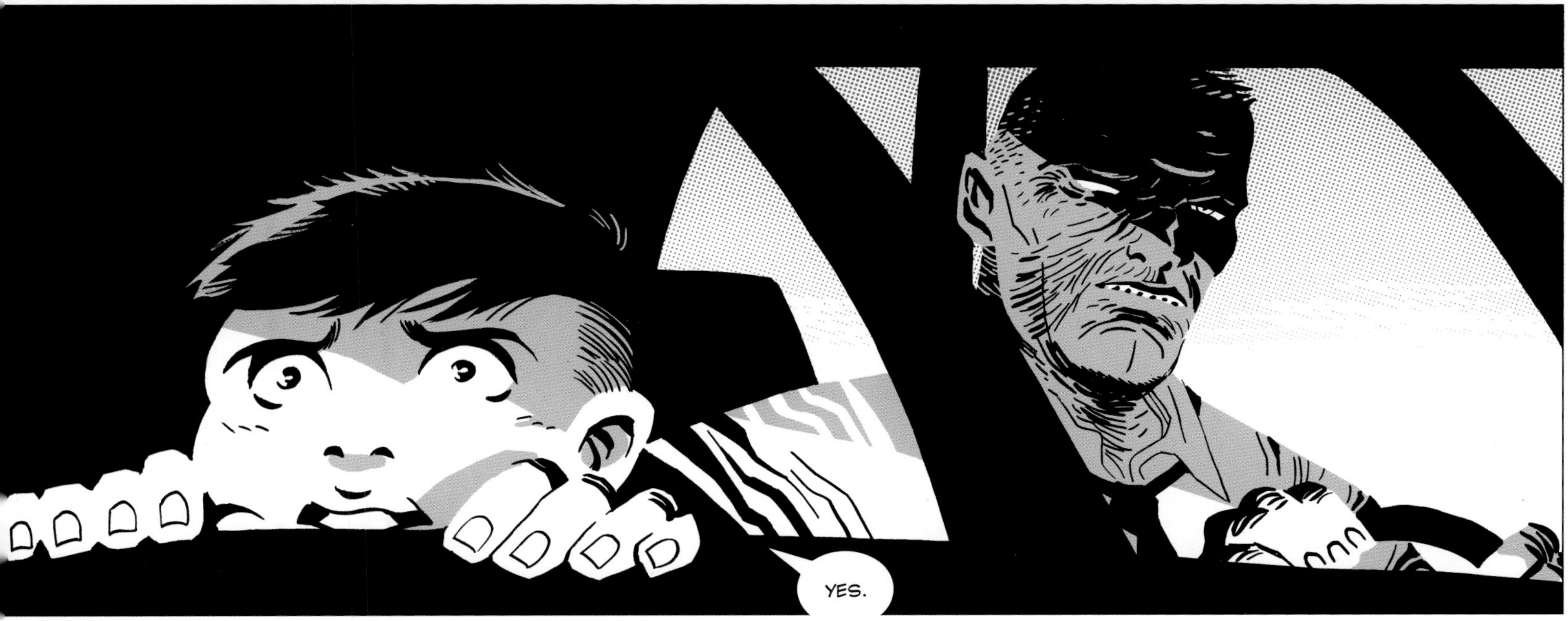
YES.

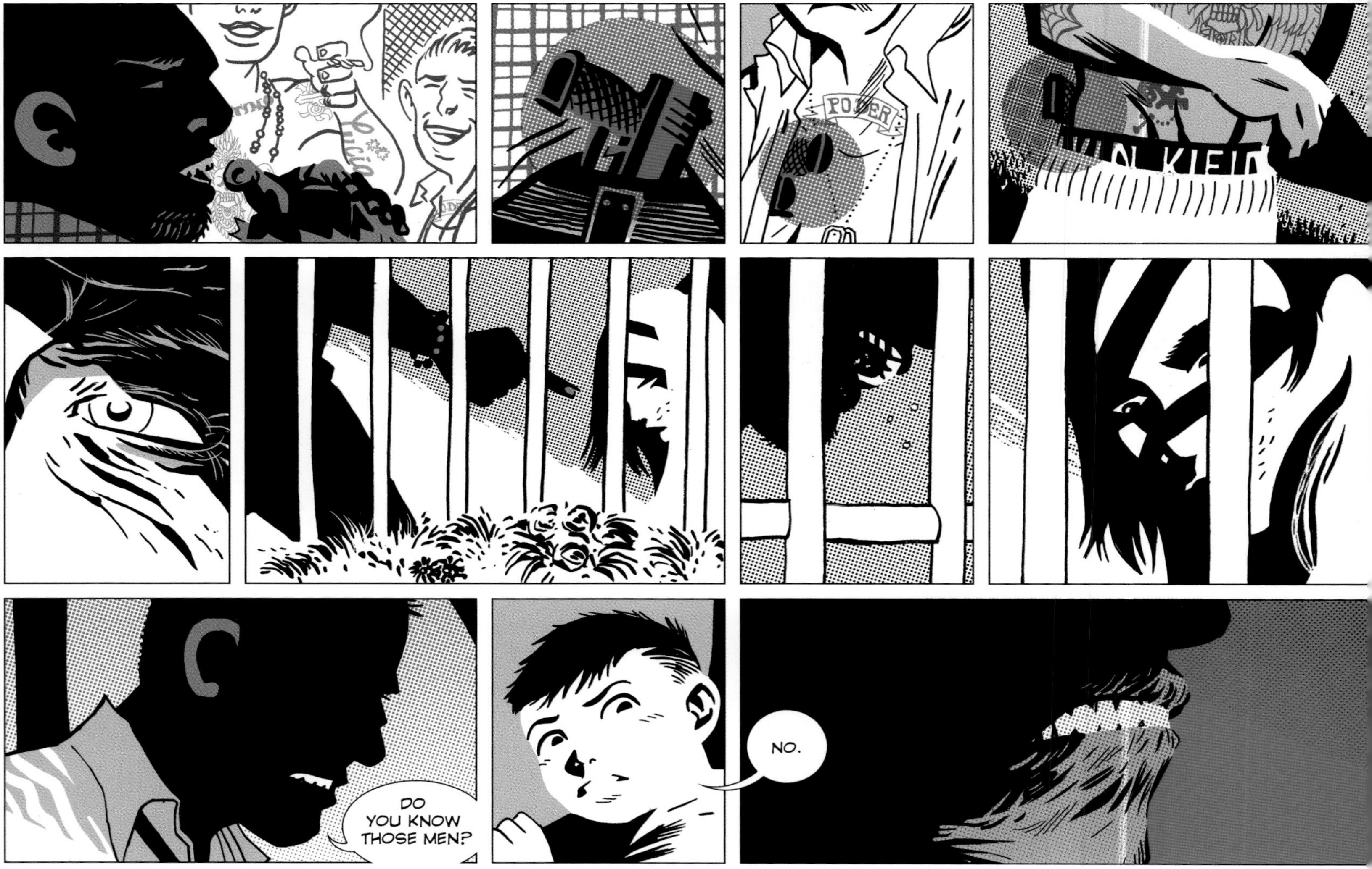
PODER
DO YOU KNOW THOSE MEN?
NO.

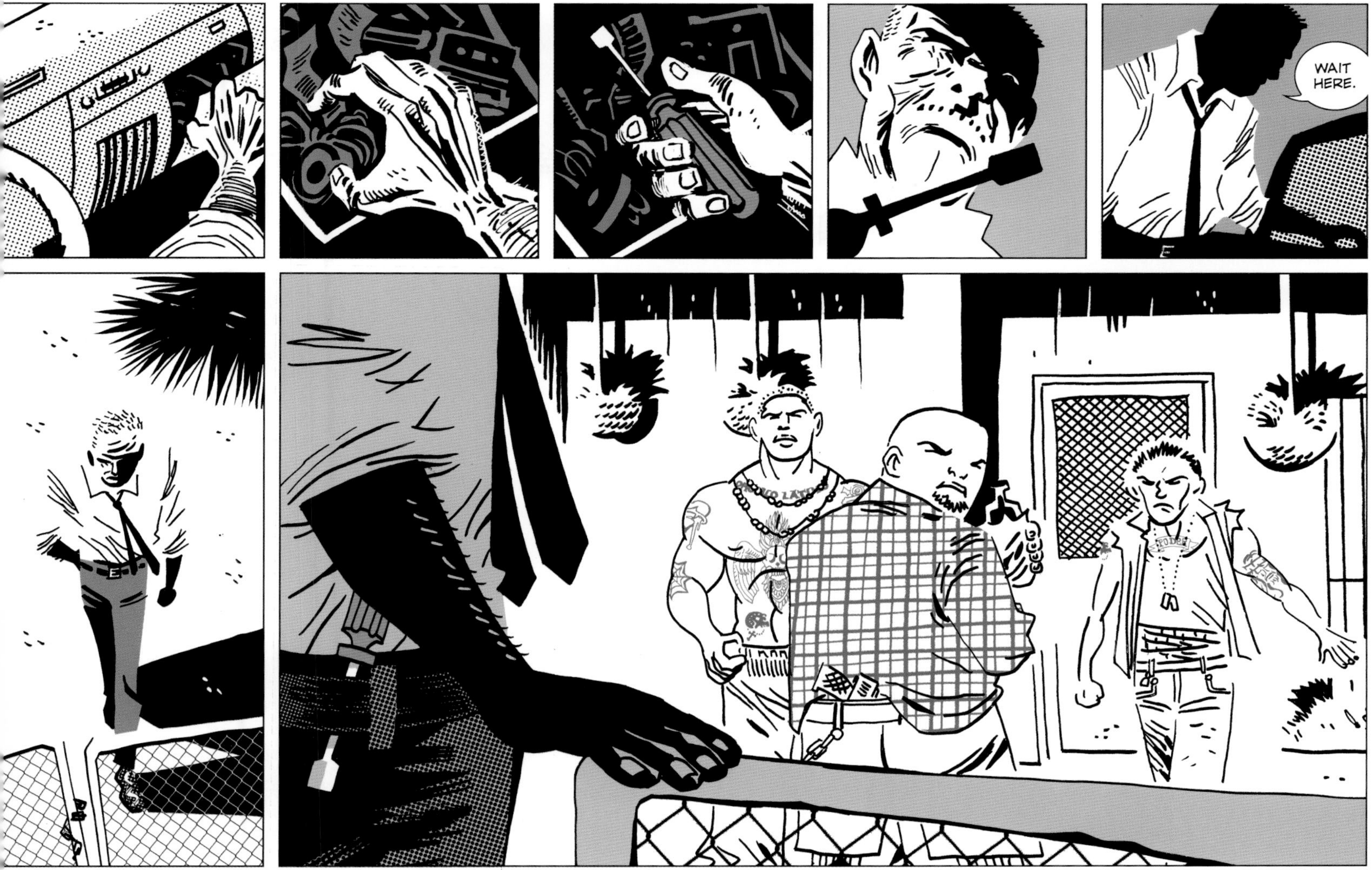
WAIT HERE.

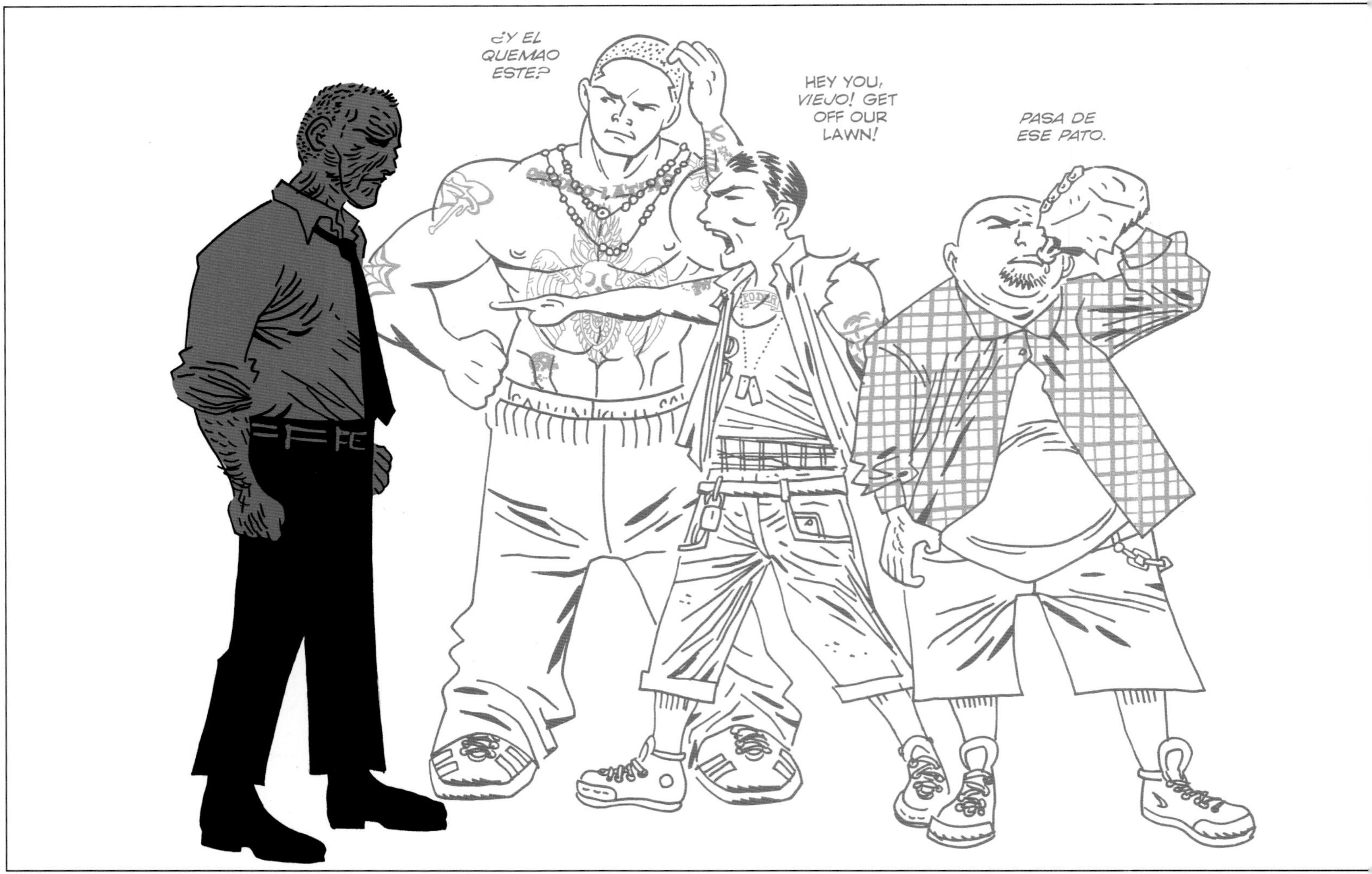
¿Y EL QUEMAO ESTE?
HEY YOU, VIEJO! GET OFF OUR LAWN!
PASA DE ESE PATO.

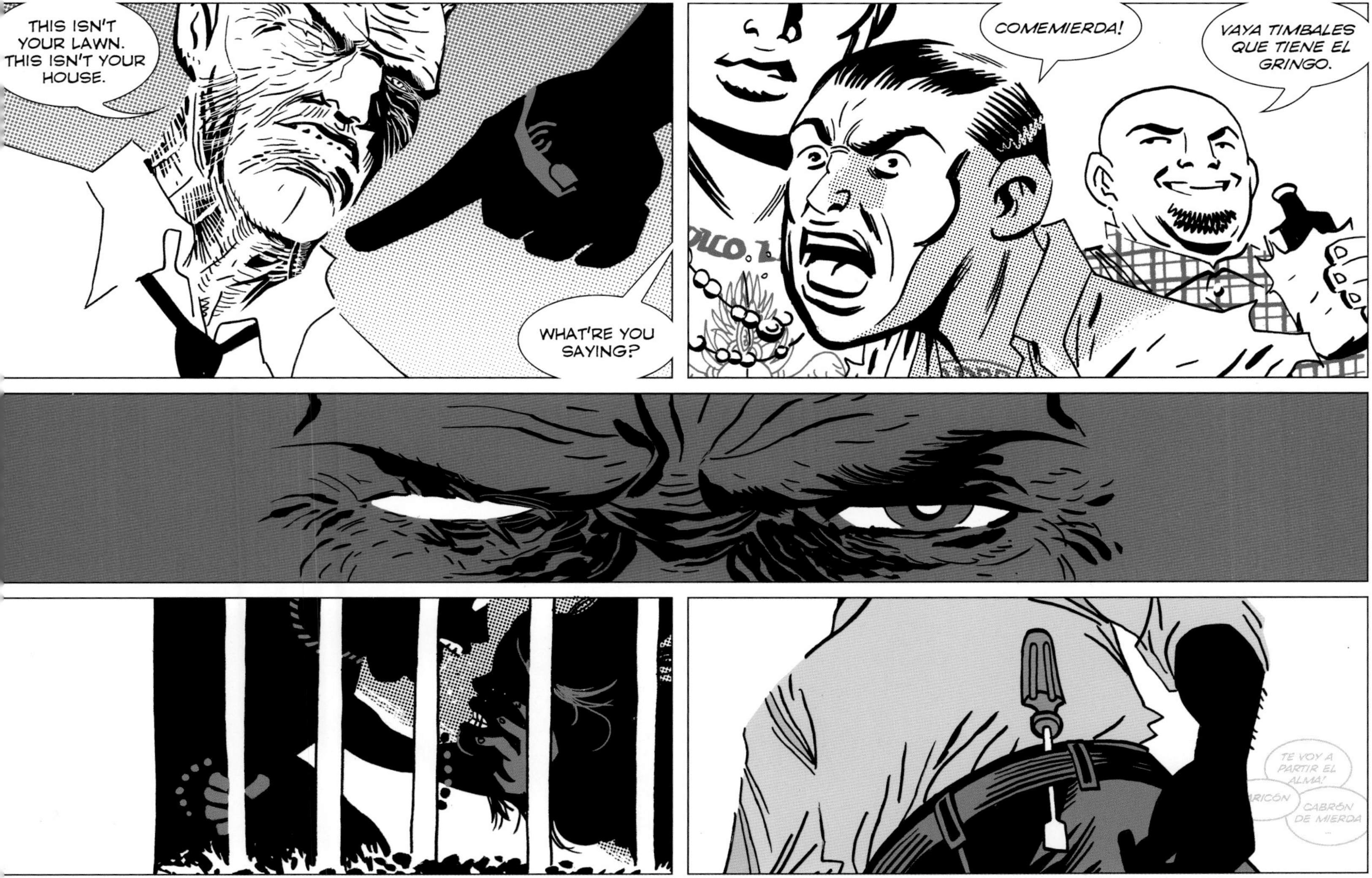
THIS ISN'T YOUR LAWN. THIS ISN'T YOUR HOUSE.
WHAT'RE YOU SAYING?
COMEMIERDA!
VAYA TIMBALES QUE TIENE EL GRINGO.
TE VOY A PARTIR EL ALMA!
CABRÓN DE MIERDA

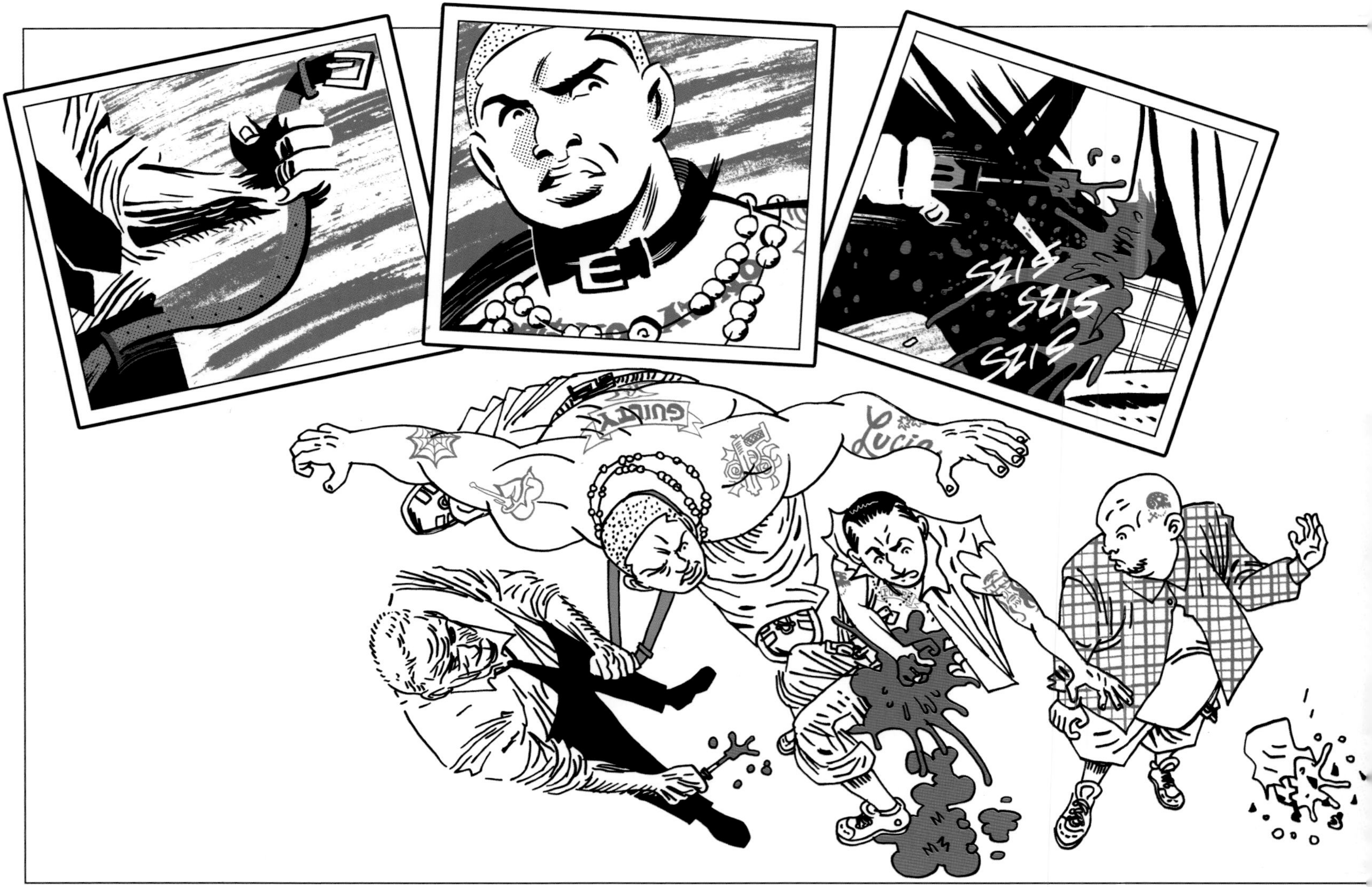
SZIS
SZIS
SZIS
GUILTY
Lucia

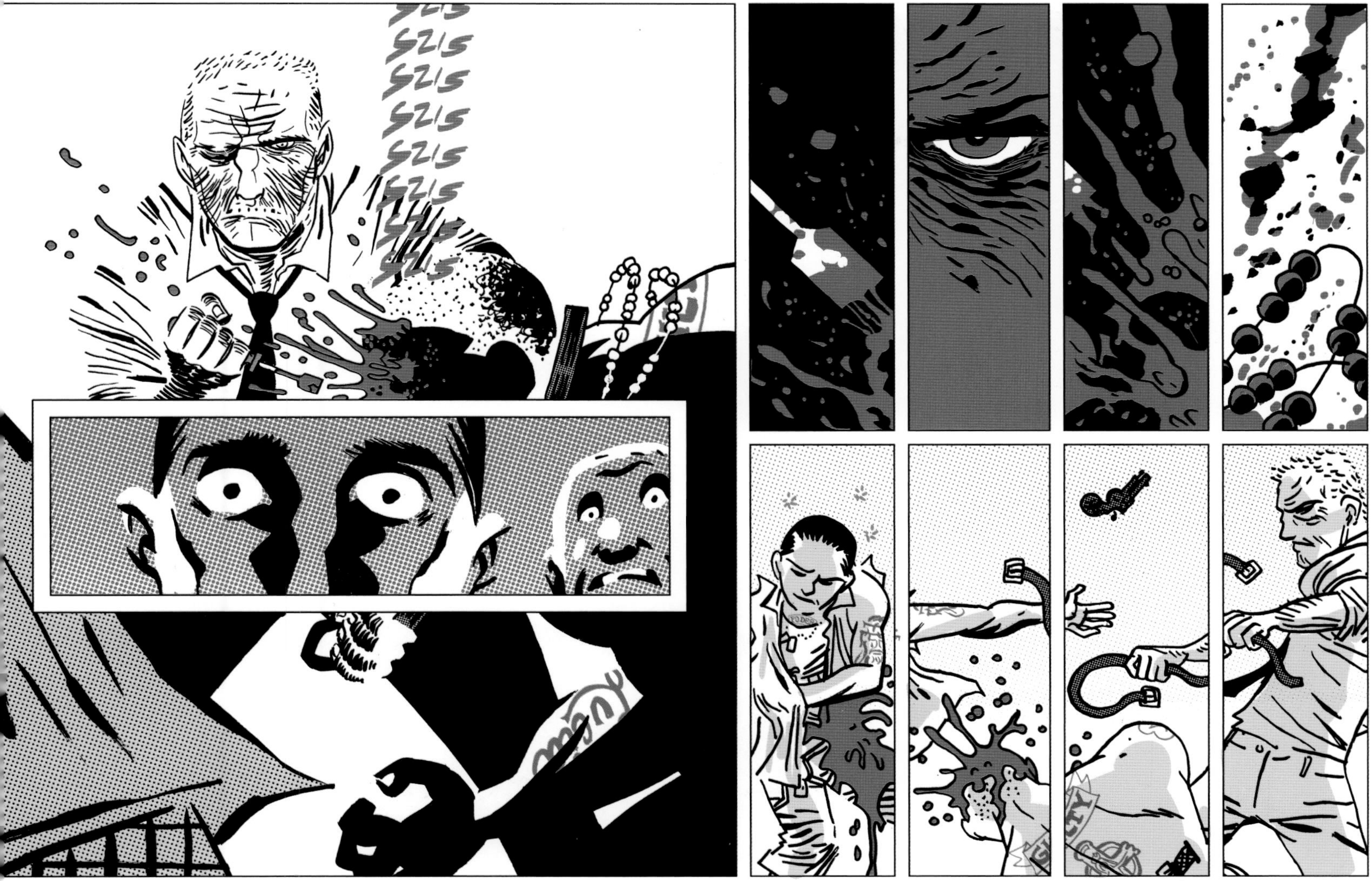
SZIS
SZIS
SZIS
SZIS
SZIS
SZIS
SZIS
SZIS

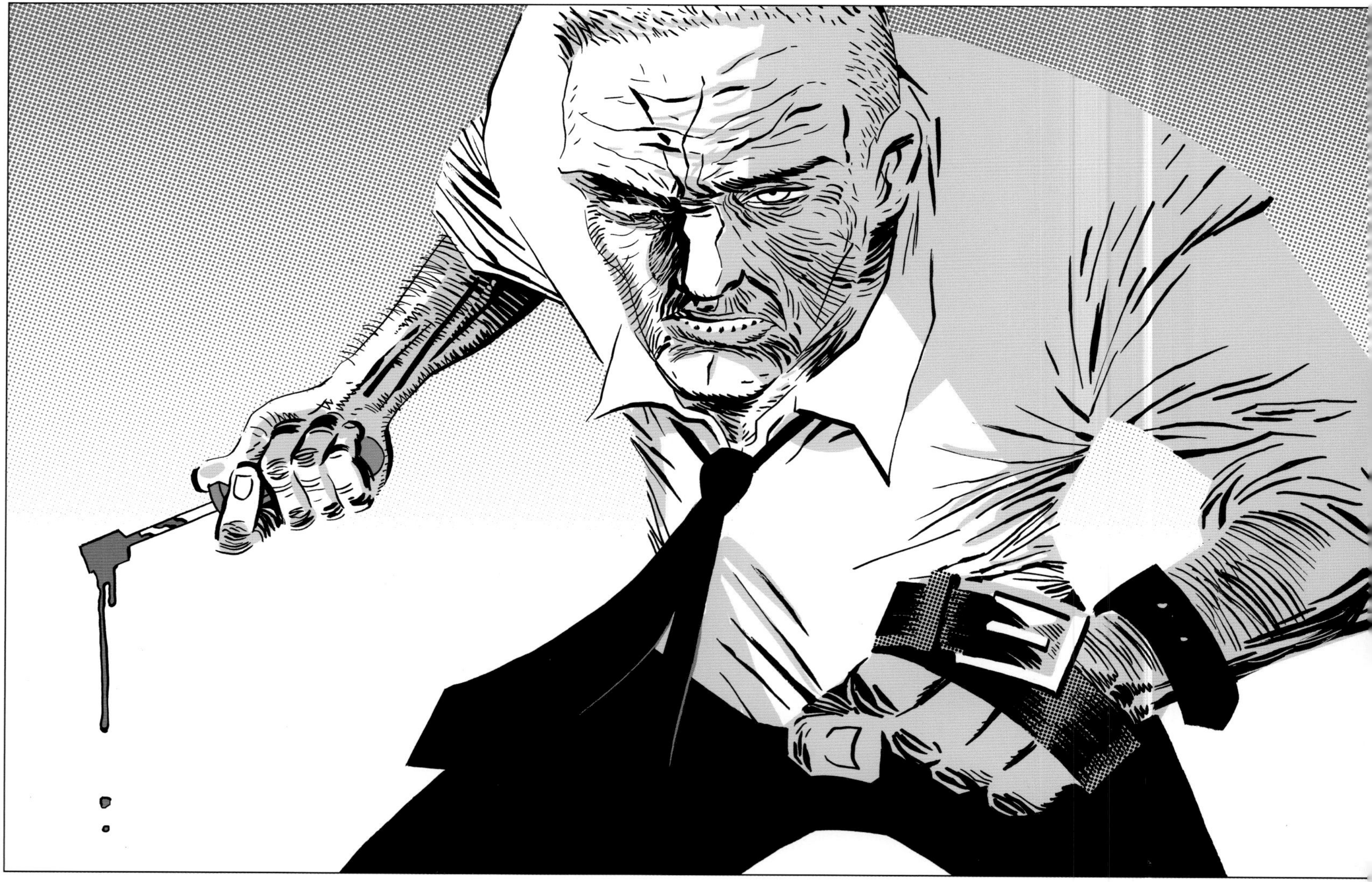

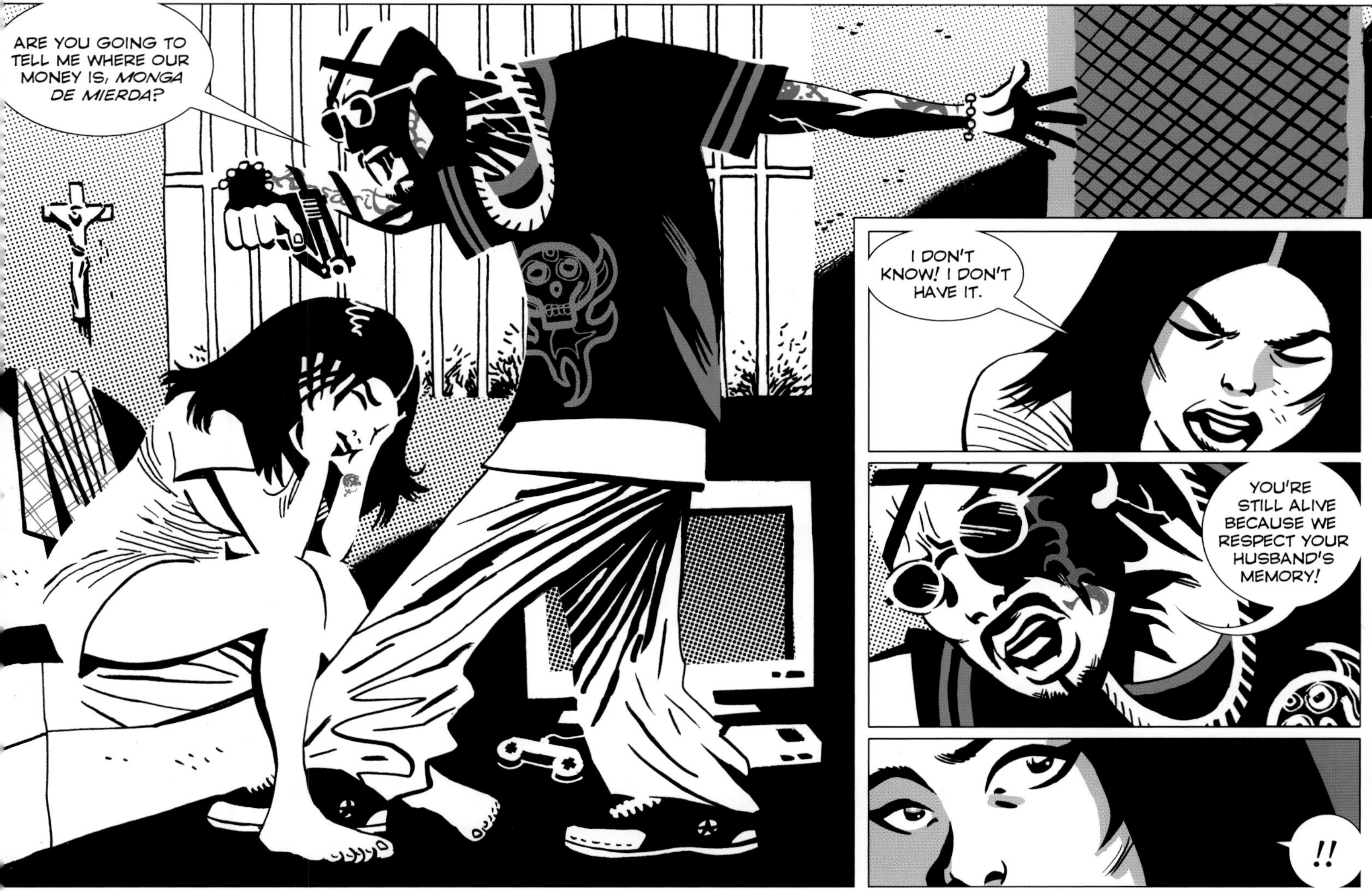
ARE YOU GOING TO TELL ME WHERE OUR MONEY IS, *MONGA DE MIERDA*?
I DON'T KNOW! I DON'T HAVE IT.
YOU'RE STILL ALIVE BECAUSE WE RESPECT YOUR HUSBAND'S MEMORY!
!!

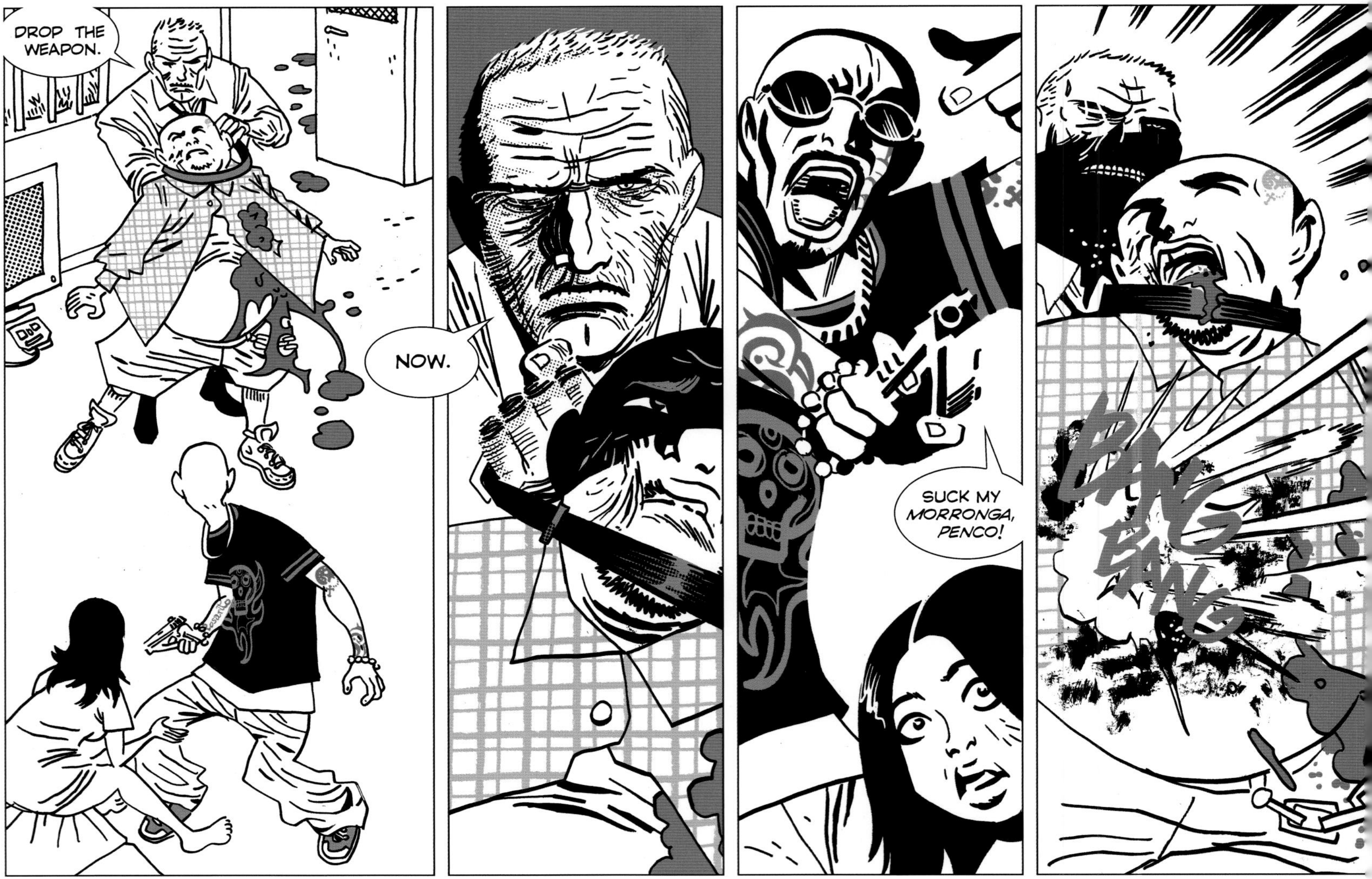
DROP THE WEAPON.
NOW.
SUCK MY *MORRONGA*, *PENCO*!
BANG BANG

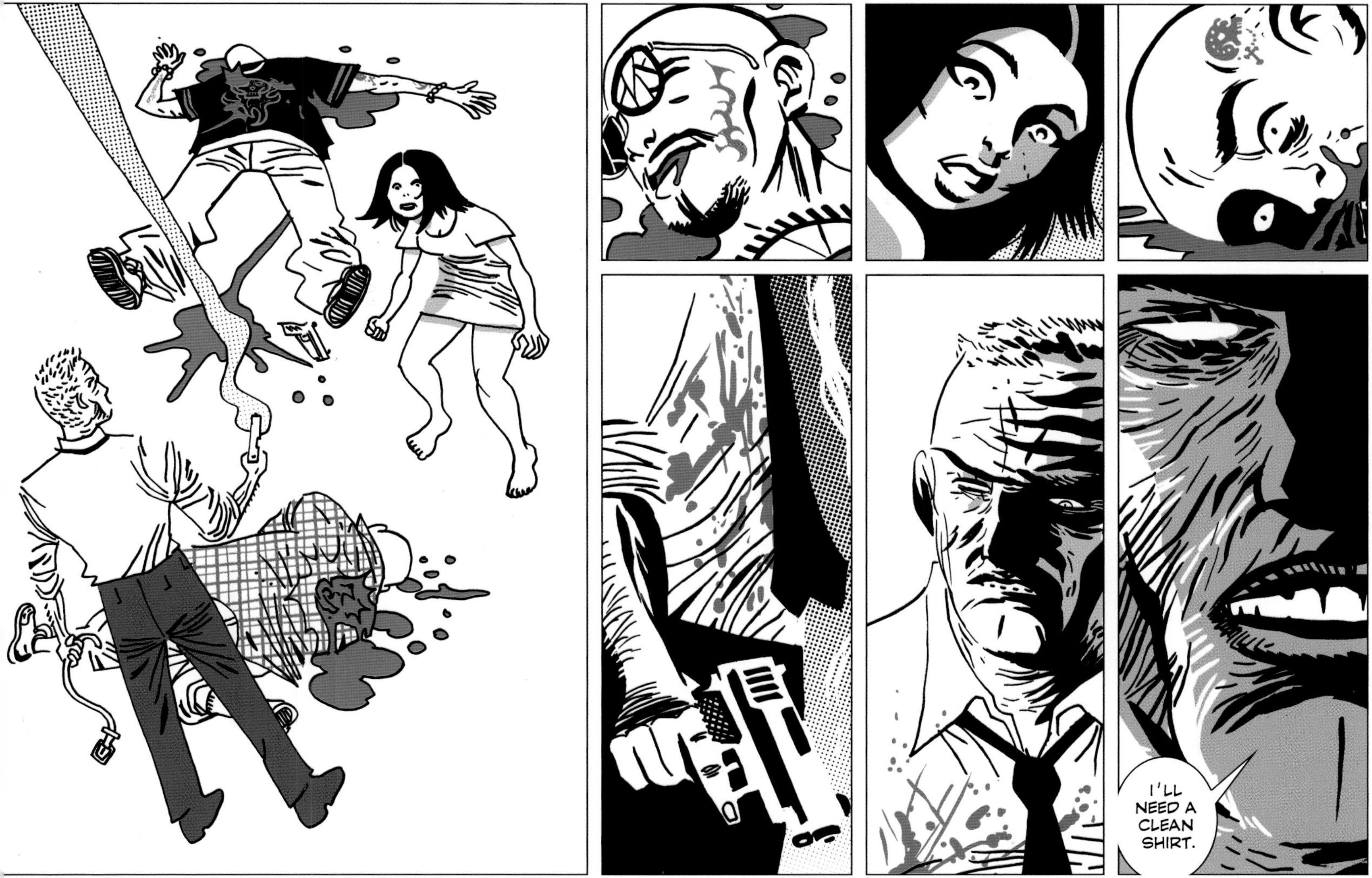
I'LL NEED A CLEAN SHIRT.

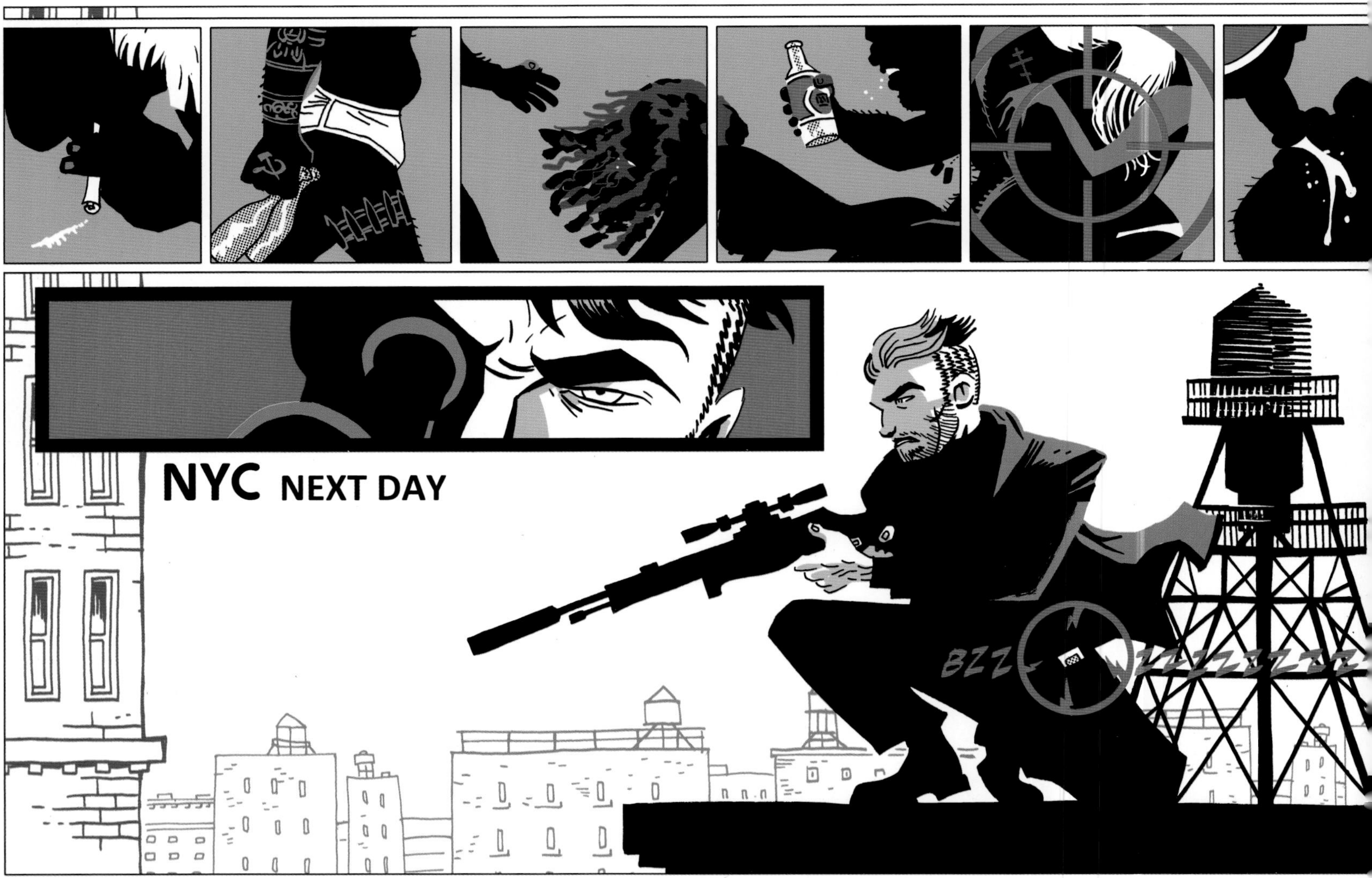
NYC NEXT DAY
BZZ
ZZZZZZZZZZ

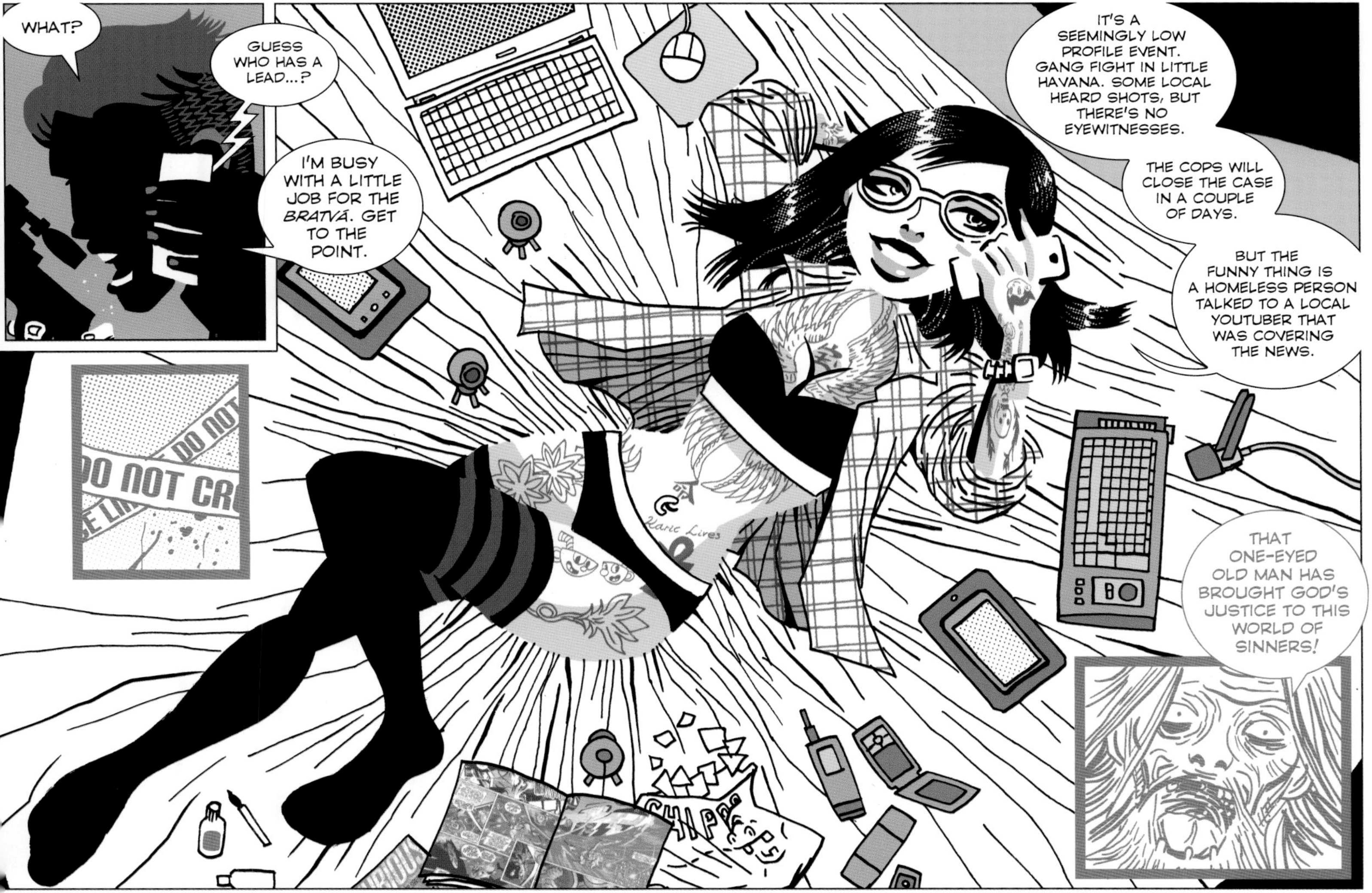
WHAT?
GUESS WHO HAS A LEAD...?
I'M BUSY WITH A LITTLE JOB FOR THE *BRATVÁ*. GET TO THE POINT.
IT'S A SEEMINGLY LOW PROFILE EVENT. GANG FIGHT IN LITTLE HAVANA. SOME LOCAL HEARD SHOTS, BUT THERE'S NO EYEWITNESSES.
THE COPS WILL CLOSE THE CASE IN A COUPLE OF DAYS.
BUT THE FUNNY THING IS A HOMELESS PERSON TALKED TO A LOCAL YOUTUBER THAT WAS COVERING THE NEWS.
THAT ONE-EYED OLD MAN HAS BROUGHT GOD'S JUSTICE TO THIS WORLD OF SINNERS!
DO NOT
DO NOT CR
Karic Lives
CHIPS

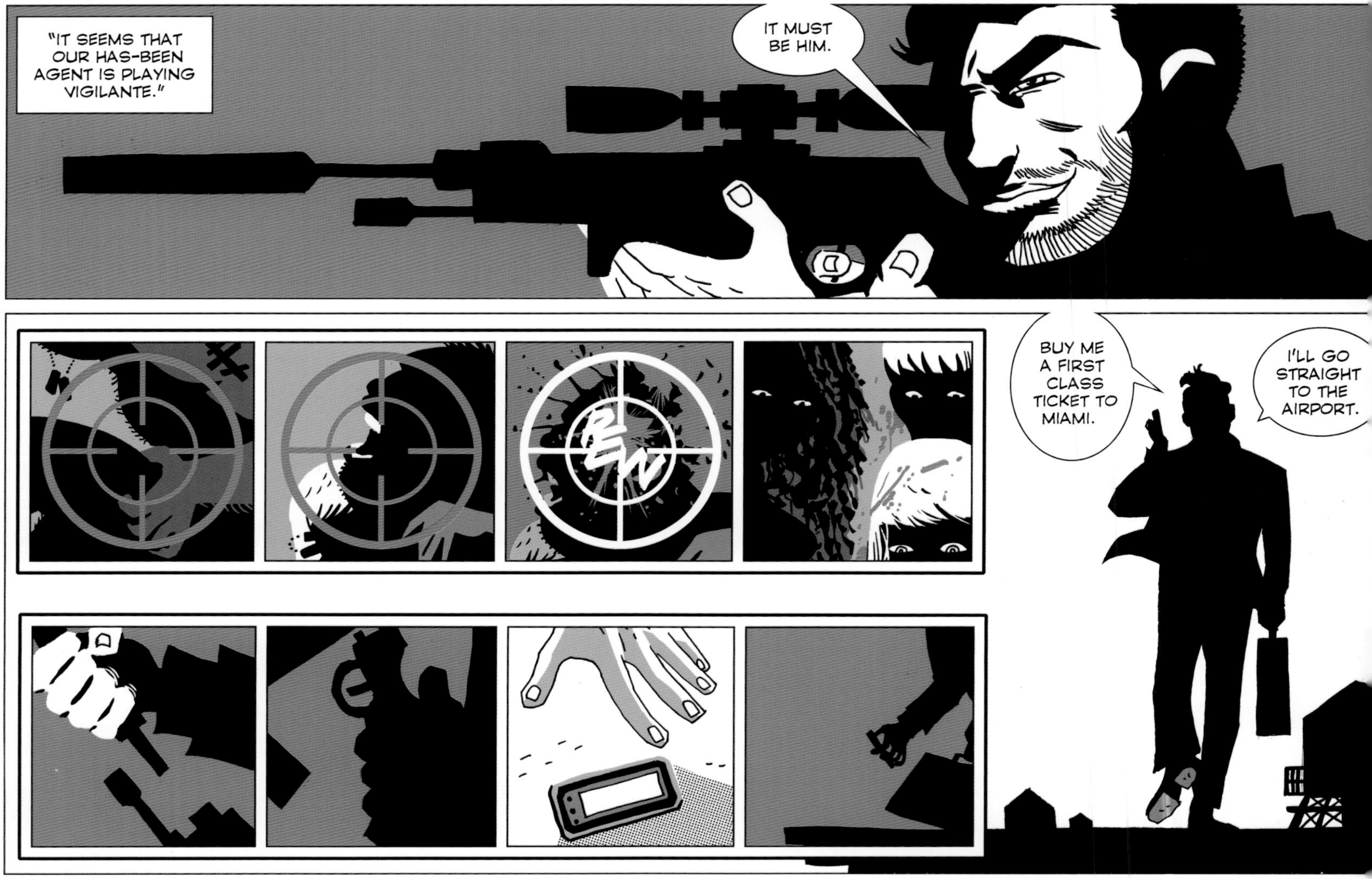
"IT SEEMS THAT OUR HAS-BEEN AGENT IS PLAYING VIGILANTE."
IT MUST BE HIM.
BUY ME A FIRST CLASS TICKET TO MIAMI.
I'LL GO STRAIGHT TO THE AIRPORT.

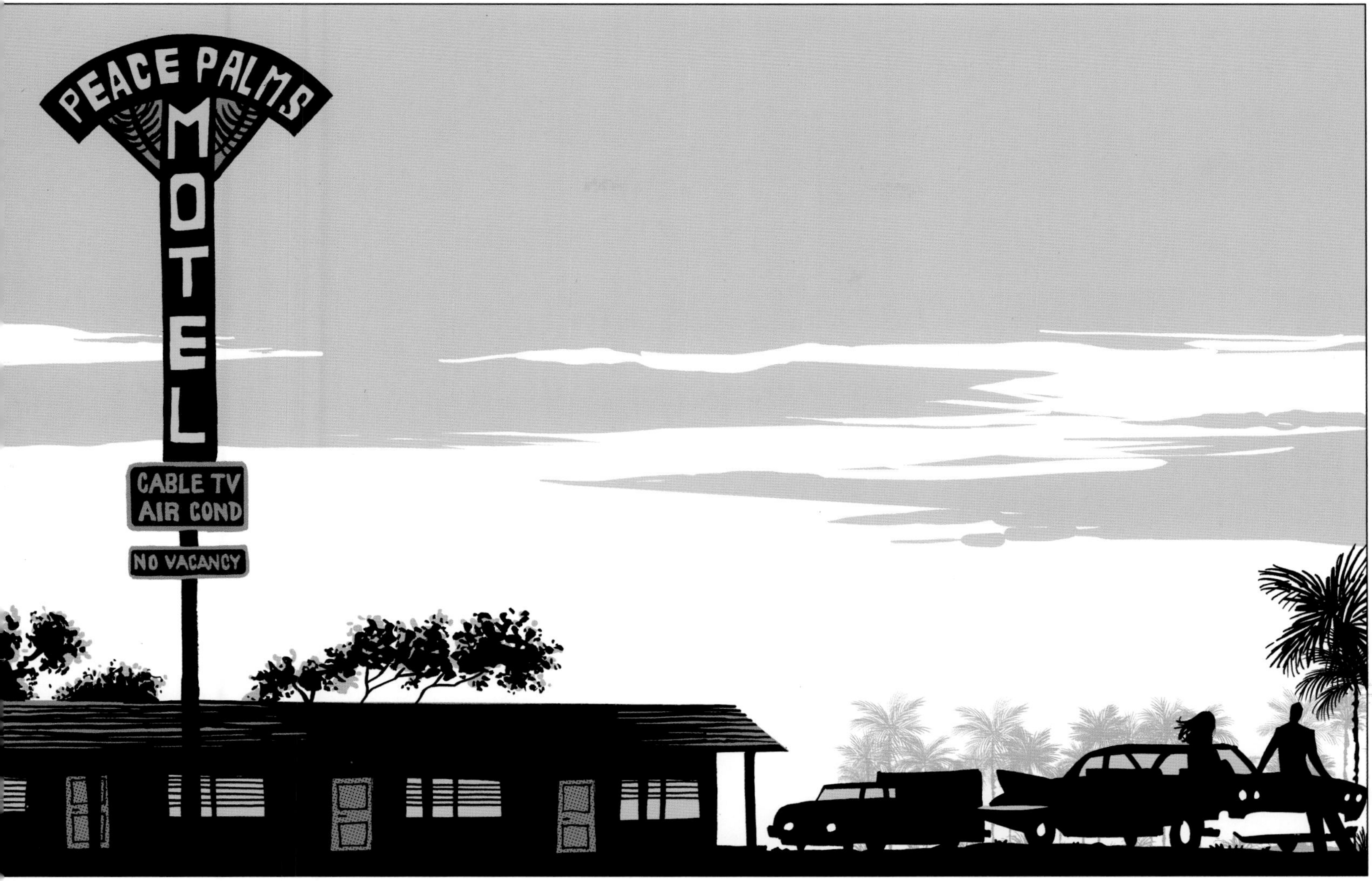
PEACE PALMS
MOTEL
CABLE TV
AIR COND
NO VACANCY

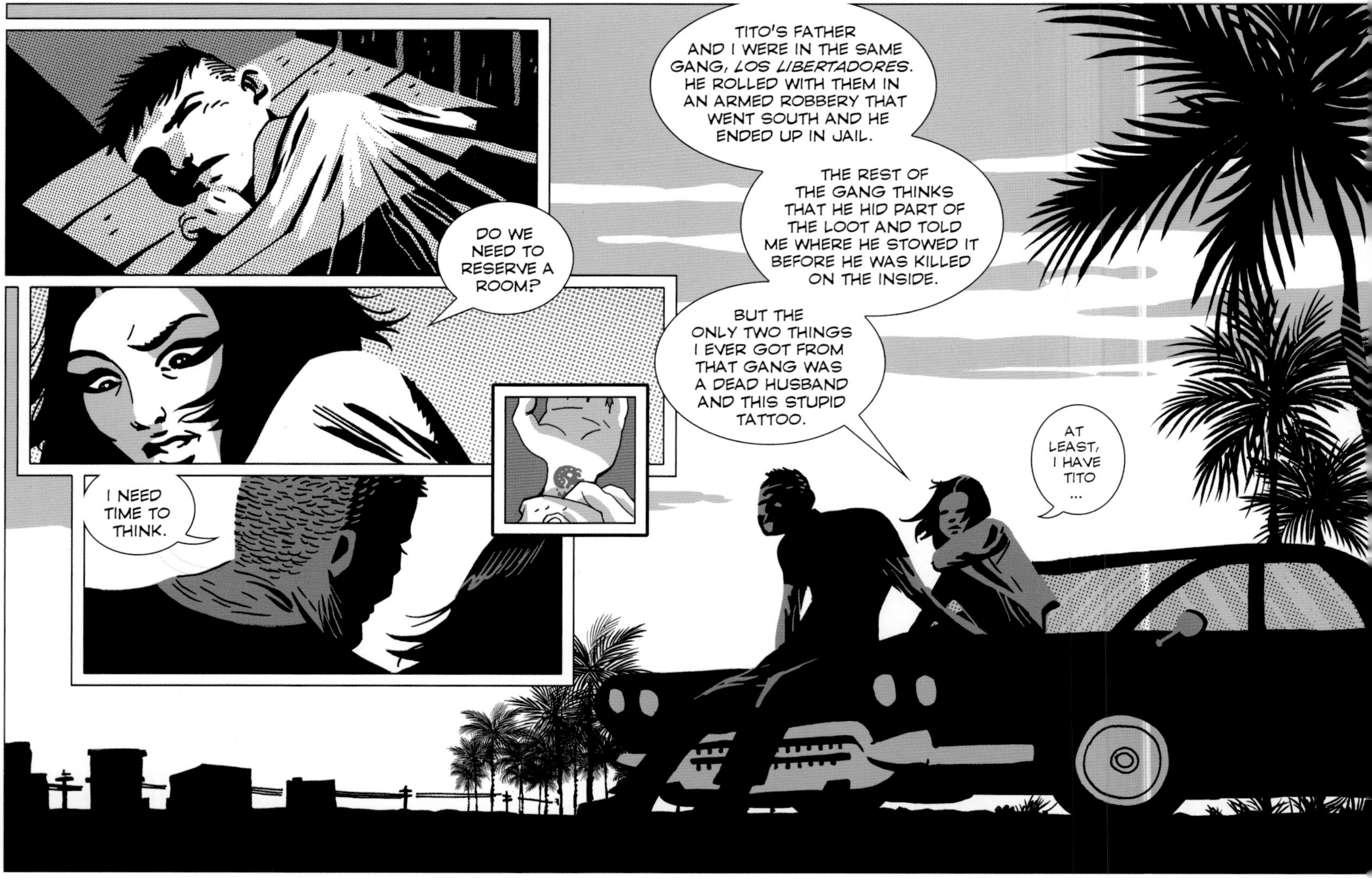

DO WE NEED TO RESERVE A ROOM?
I NEED TIME TO THINK.
TITO'S FATHER AND I WERE IN THE SAME GANG, *LOS LIBERTADORES*. HE ROLLED WITH THEM IN AN ARMED ROBBERY THAT WENT SOUTH AND HE ENDED UP IN JAIL.
THE REST OF THE GANG THINKS THAT HE HID PART OF THE LOOT AND TOLD ME WHERE HE STOWED IT BEFORE HE WAS KILLED ON THE INSIDE.
BUT THE ONLY TWO THINGS I EVER GOT FROM THAT GANG WAS A DEAD HUSBAND AND THIS STUPID TATTOO.
AT LEAST, I HAVE TITO ...

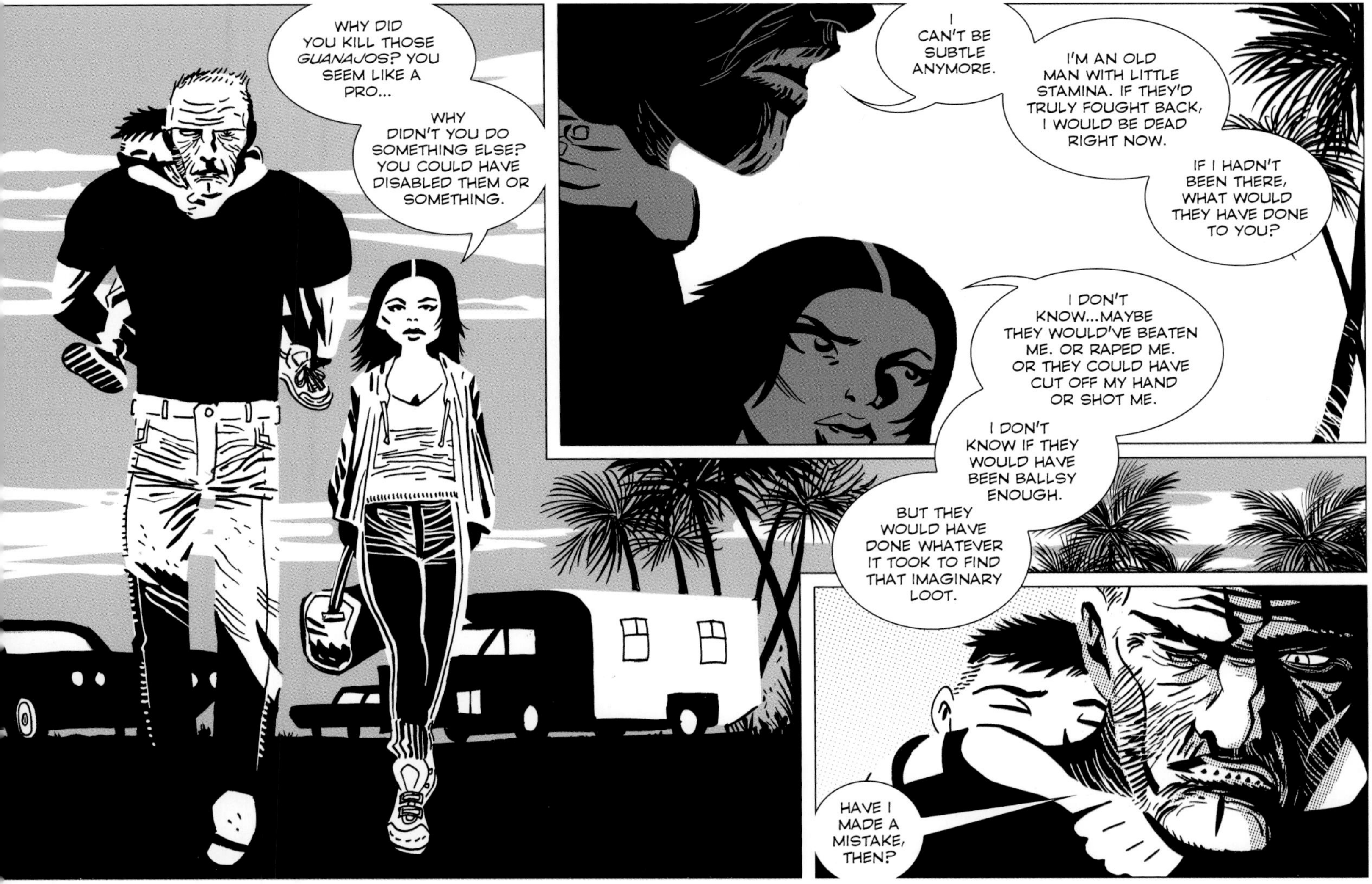
WHY DID YOU KILL THOSE *GUANAJOS*? YOU SEEM LIKE A PRO...
WHY DIDN'T YOU DO SOMETHING ELSE? YOU COULD HAVE DISABLED THEM OR SOMETHING.
I CAN'T BE SUBTLE ANYMORE.
I'M AN OLD MAN WITH LITTLE STAMINA. IF THEY'D TRULY FOUGHT BACK, I WOULD BE DEAD RIGHT NOW.
IF I HADN'T BEEN THERE, WHAT WOULD THEY HAVE DONE TO YOU?
I DON'T KNOW...MAYBE THEY WOULD'VE BEATEN ME. OR RAPED ME. OR THEY COULD HAVE CUT OFF MY HAND OR SHOT ME.
I DON'T KNOW IF THEY WOULD HAVE BEEN BALLSY ENOUGH.
BUT THEY WOULD HAVE DONE WHATEVER IT TOOK TO FIND THAT IMAGINARY LOOT.
HAVE I MADE A MISTAKE, THEN?

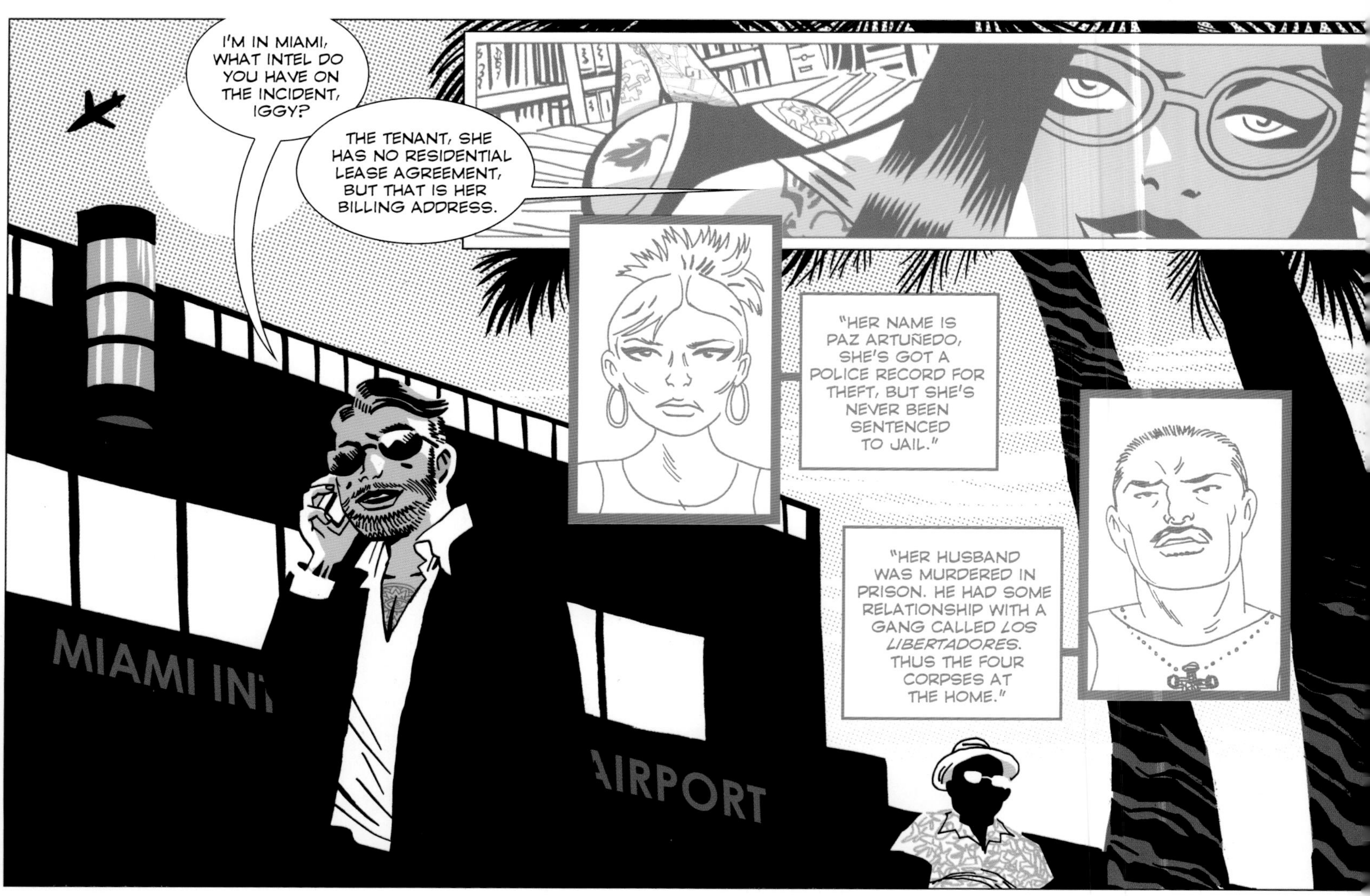
I'M IN MIAMI, WHAT INTEL DO YOU HAVE ON THE INCIDENT, IGGY?
THE TENANT, SHE HAS NO RESIDENTIAL LEASE AGREEMENT, BUT THAT IS HER BILLING ADDRESS.
"HER NAME IS PAZ ARTUÑEDO, SHE'S GOT A POLICE RECORD FOR THEFT, BUT SHE'S NEVER BEEN SENTENCED TO JAIL."
"HER HUSBAND WAS MURDERED IN PRISON. HE HAD SOME RELATIONSHIP WITH A GANG CALLED *LOS LIBERTADORES*. THUS THE FOUR CORPSES AT THE HOME."
MIAMI INT
AIRPORT

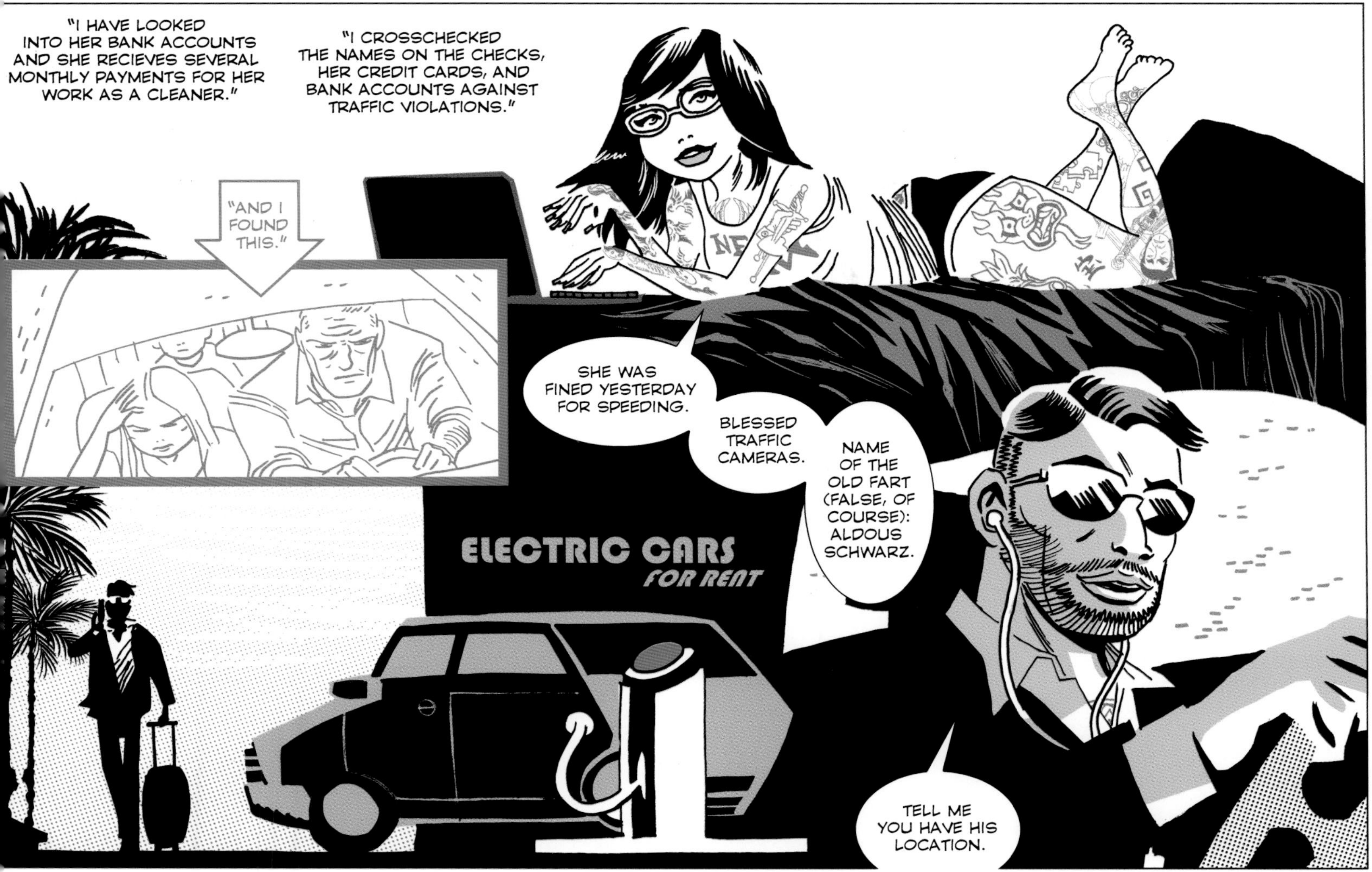
"I HAVE LOOKED INTO HER BANK ACCOUNTS AND SHE RECIEVES SEVERAL MONTHLY PAYMENTS FOR HER WORK AS A CLEANER."
"I CROSSCHECKED THE NAMES ON THE CHECKS, HER CREDIT CARDS, AND BANK ACCOUNTS AGAINST TRAFFIC VIOLATIONS."
"AND I FOUND THIS."
SHE WAS FINED YESTERDAY FOR SPEEDING.
BLESSED TRAFFIC CAMERAS.
NAME OF THE OLD FART (FALSE, OF COURSE): ALDOUS SCHWARZ.
ELECTRIC CARS FOR RENT
TELL ME YOU HAVE HIS LOCATION.

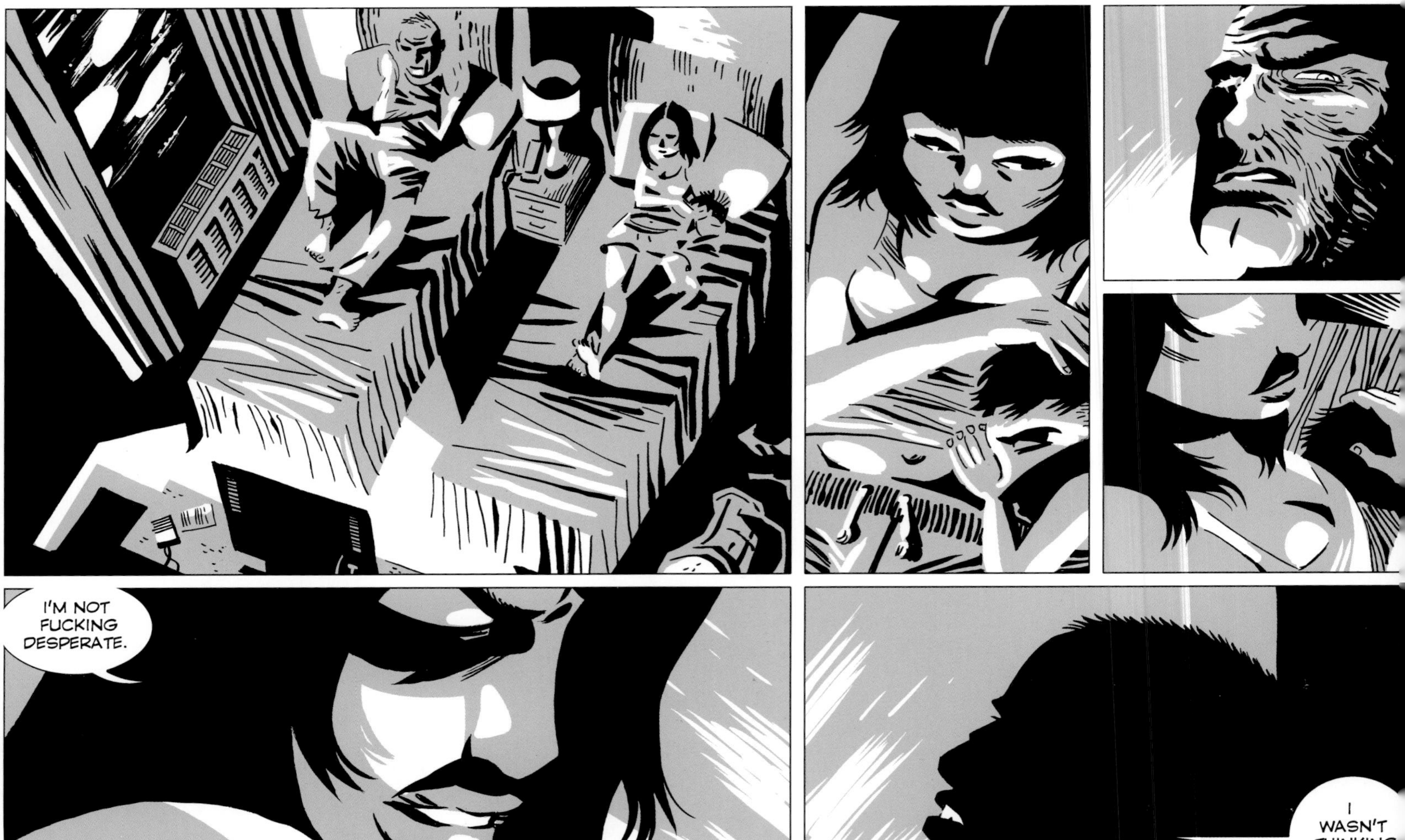
I'M NOT FUCKING DESPERATE.
I WASN'T THINKING THAT.

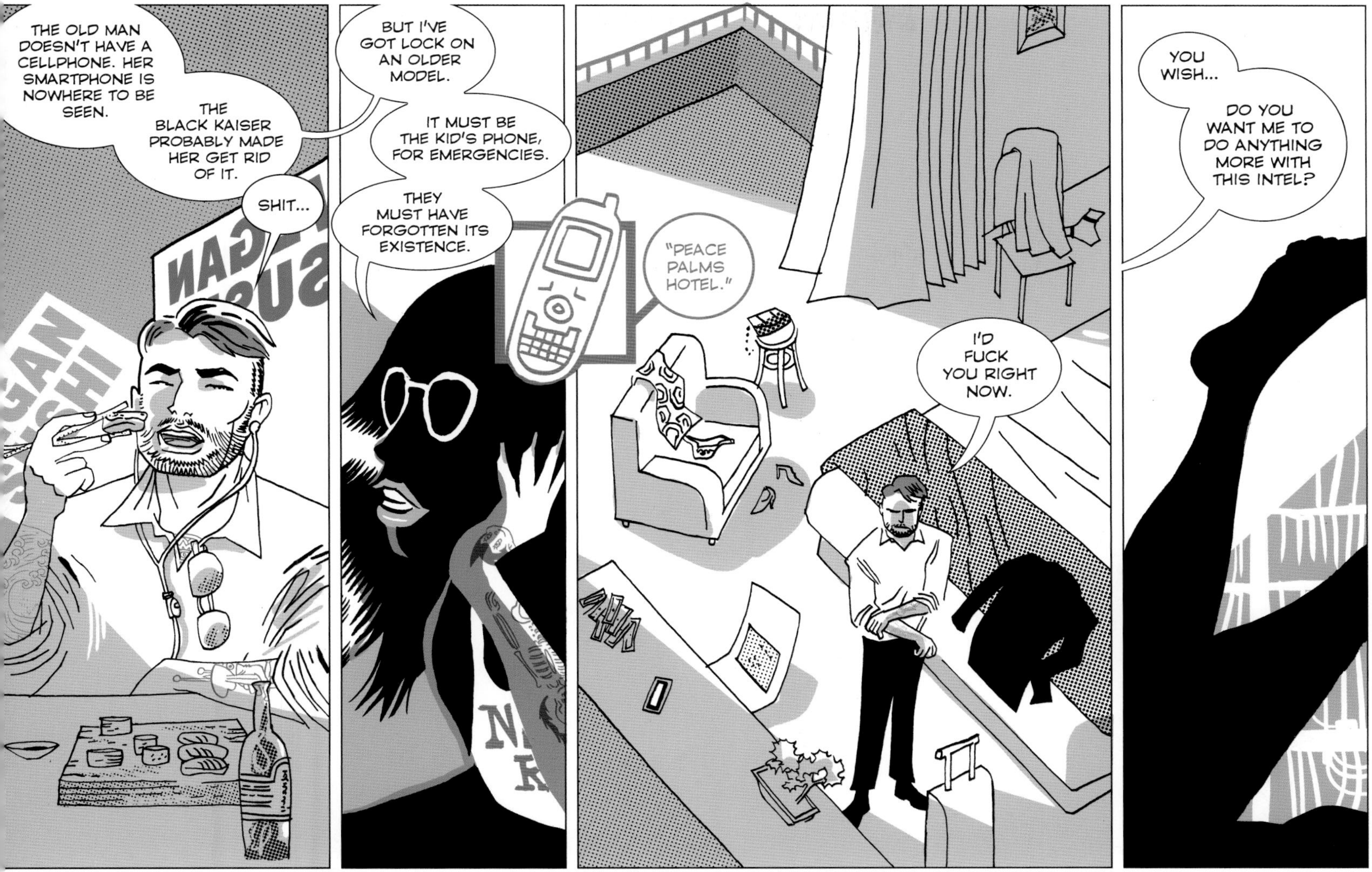
THE OLD MAN DOESN'T HAVE A CELLPHONE. HER SMARTPHONE IS NOWHERE TO BE SEEN.
THE BLACK KAISER PROBABLY MADE HER GET RID OF IT.
SHIT...
BUT I'VE GOT LOCK ON AN OLDER MODEL.
IT MUST BE THE KID'S PHONE, FOR EMERGENCIES.
THEY MUST HAVE FORGOTTEN ITS EXISTENCE.
"PEACE PALMS HOTEL."
I'D FUCK YOU RIGHT NOW.
YOU WISH...
DO YOU WANT ME TO DO ANYTHING MORE WITH THIS INTEL?

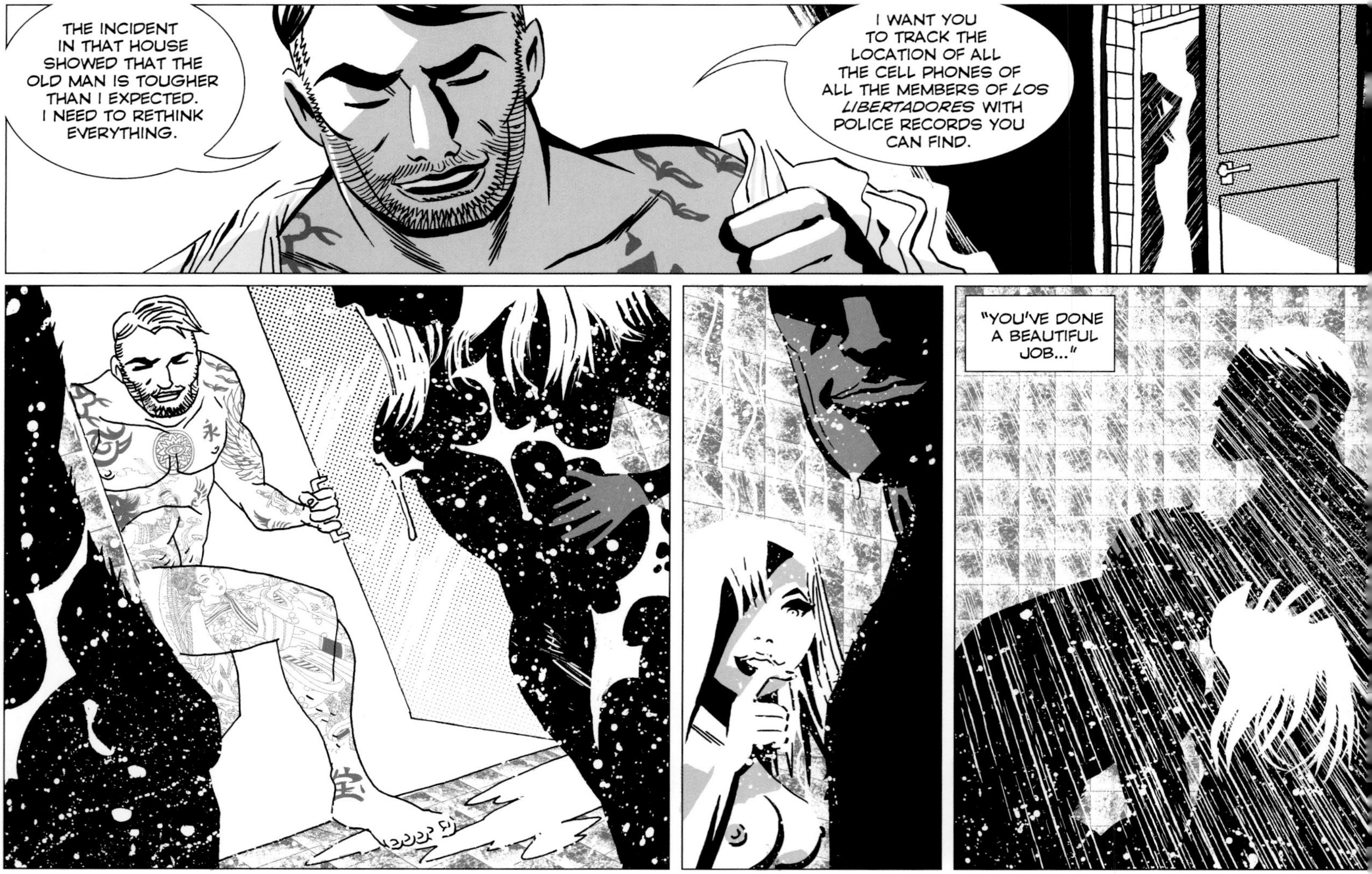
THE INCIDENT IN THAT HOUSE SHOWED THAT THE OLD MAN IS TOUGHER THAN I EXPECTED. I NEED TO RETHINK EVERYTHING.
I WANT YOU TO TRACK THE LOCATION OF ALL THE CELL PHONES OF ALL THE MEMBERS OF *LOS LIBERTADORES* WITH POLICE RECORDS YOU CAN FIND.
"YOU'VE DONE A BEAUTIFUL JOB..."

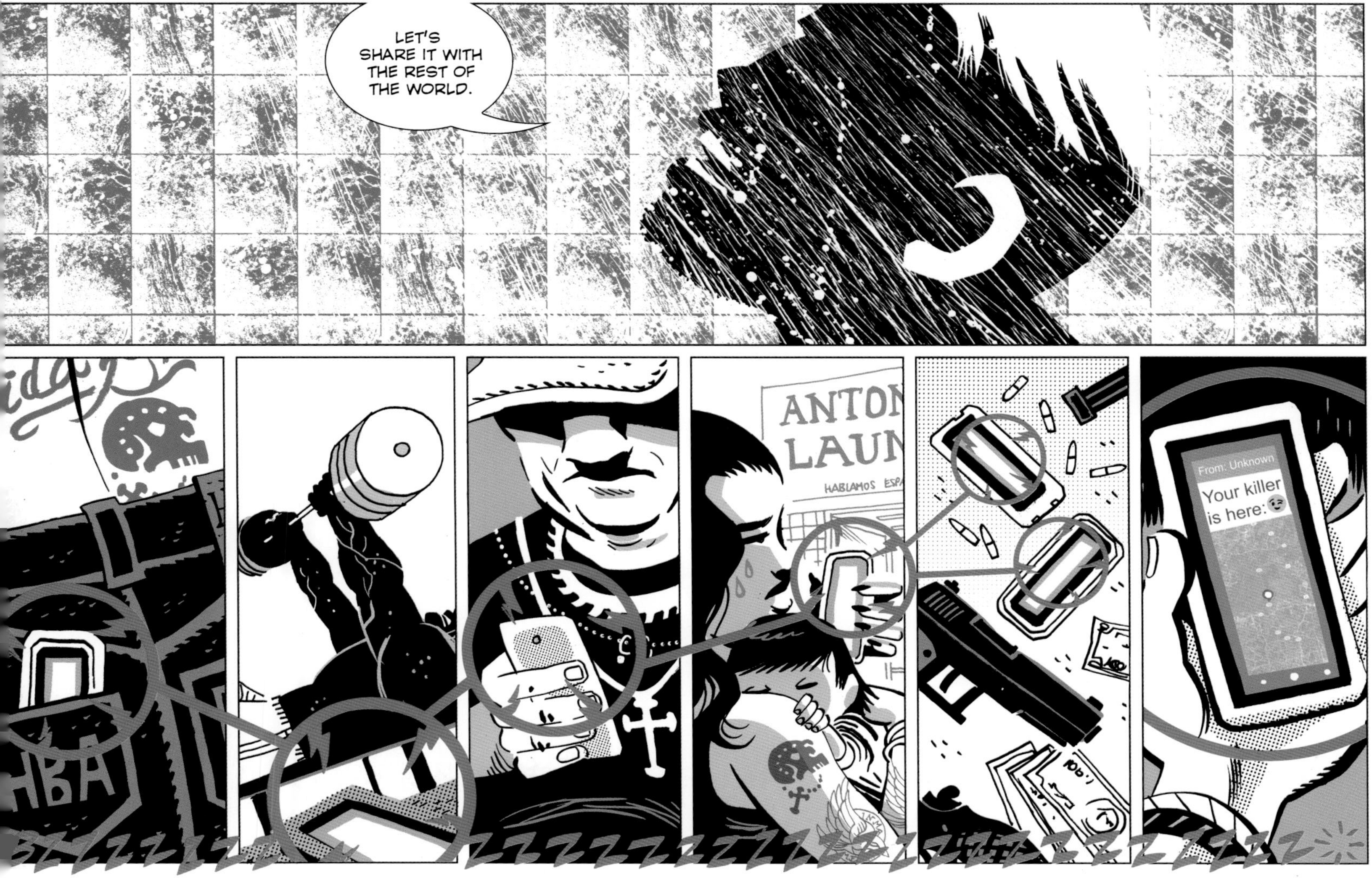
LET'S SHARE IT WITH THE REST OF THE WORLD.
ANTON
LAUN
HABLAMOS ESPA
From: Unknown
Your killer is here:

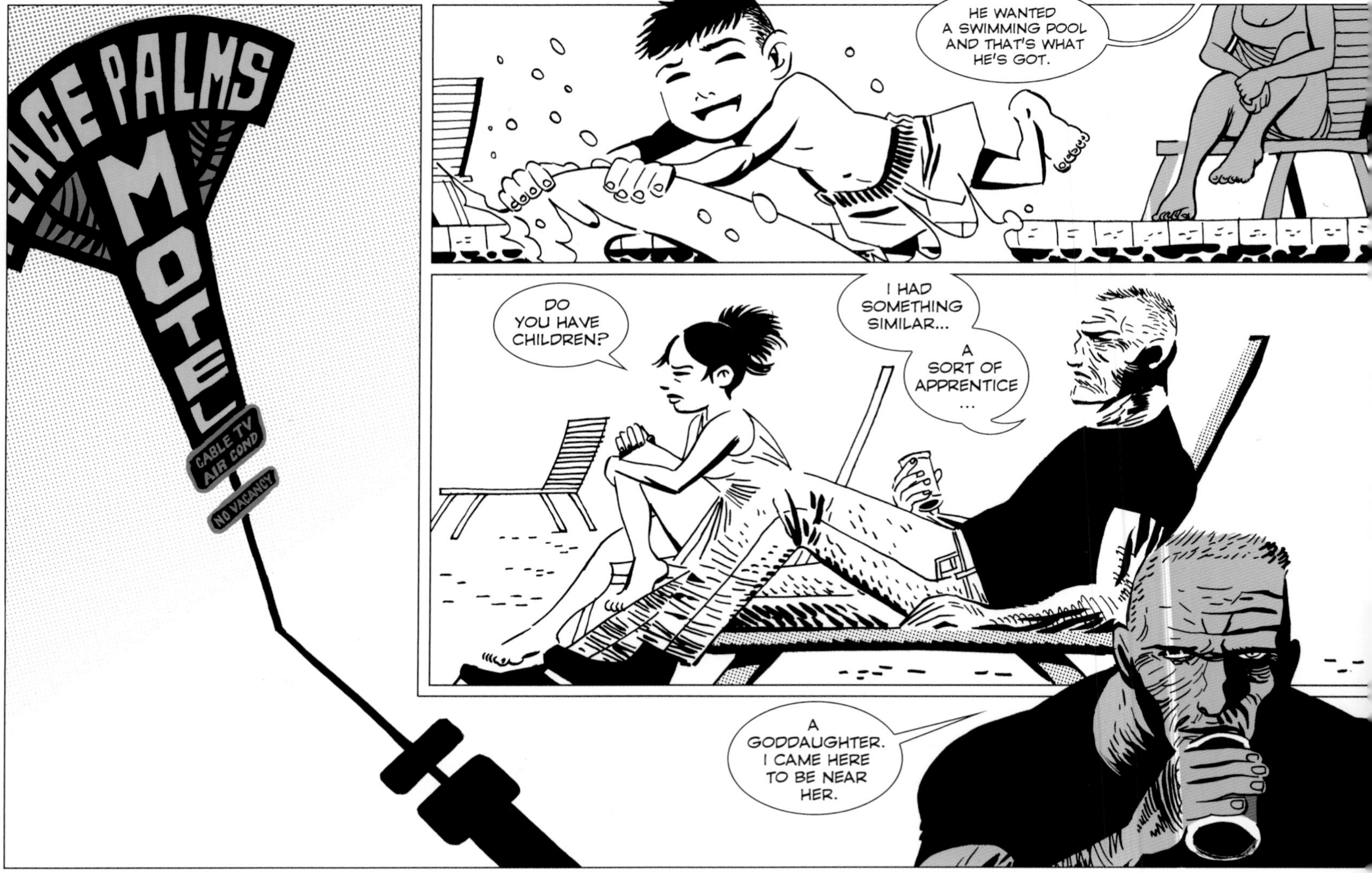

ACE PALMS
MOTEL
CABLE TV
AIR COND
NO VACANCY
HE WANTED A SWIMMING POOL AND THAT'S WHAT HE'S GOT.
DO YOU HAVE CHILDREN?
I HAD SOMETHING SIMILAR...
A SORT OF APPRENTICE ...
A GODDAUGHTER. I CAME HERE TO BE NEAR HER.

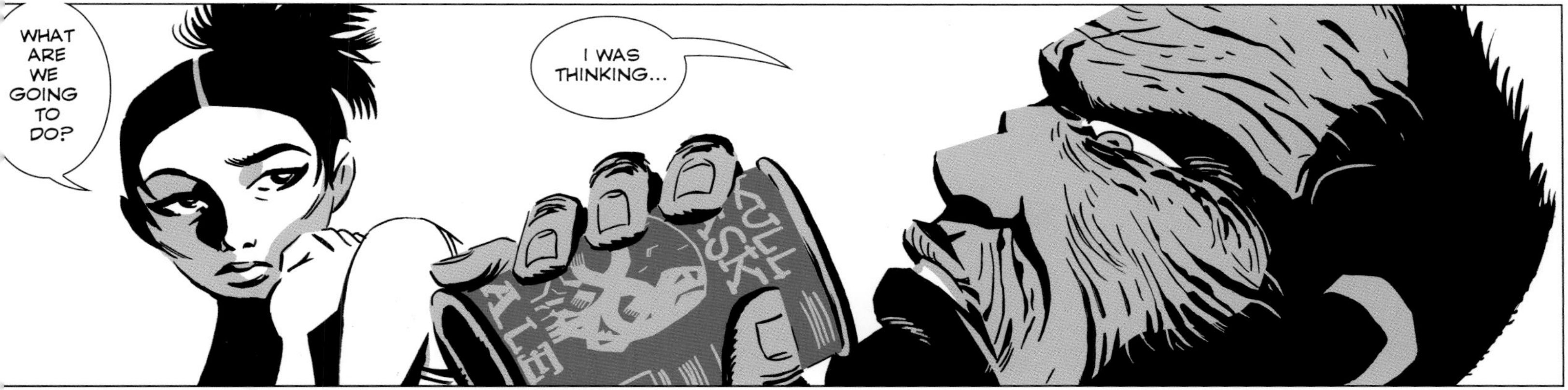
WHAT ARE WE GOING TO DO?
I WAS THINKING...
SKULL TUSK ALE

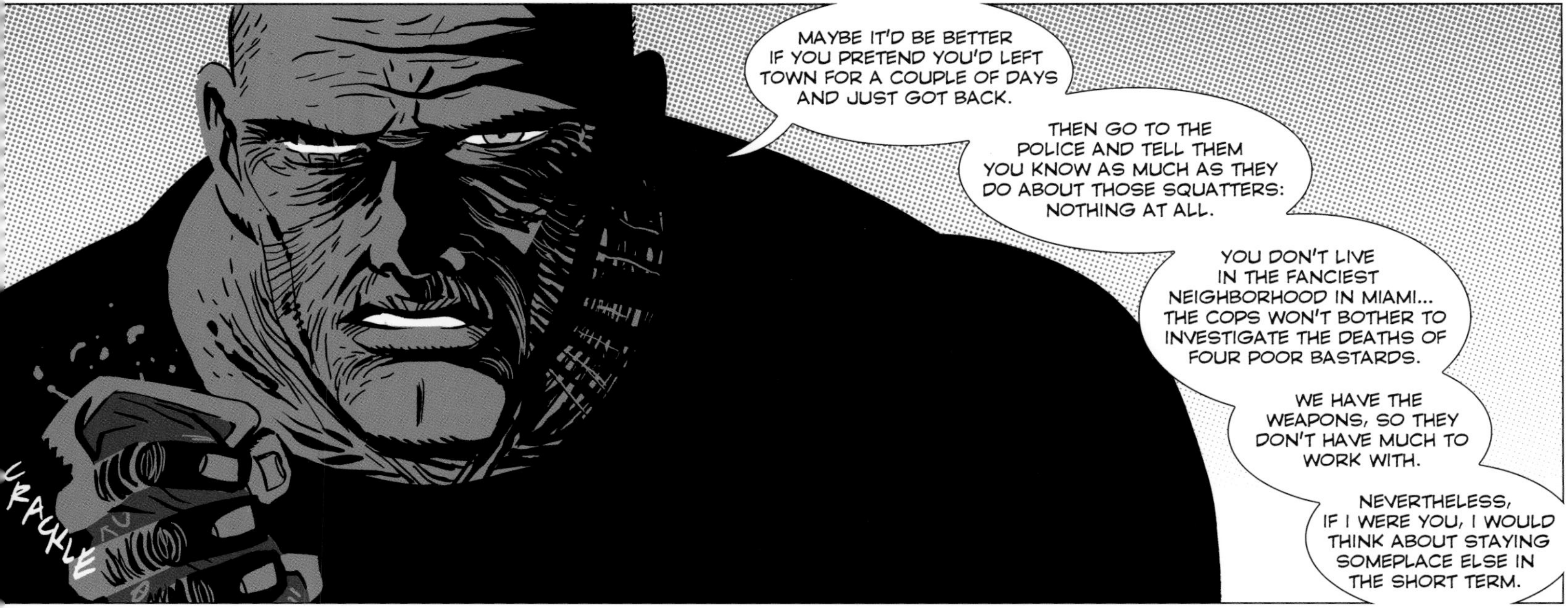
MAYBE IT'D BE BETTER IF YOU PRETEND YOU'D LEFT TOWN FOR A COUPLE OF DAYS AND JUST GOT BACK.
THEN GO TO THE POLICE AND TELL THEM YOU KNOW AS MUCH AS THEY DO ABOUT THOSE SQUATTERS: NOTHING AT ALL.
YOU DON'T LIVE IN THE FANCIEST NEIGHBORHOOD IN MIAMI... THE COPS WON'T BOTHER TO INVESTIGATE THE DEATHS OF FOUR POOR BASTARDS.
WE HAVE THE WEAPONS, SO THEY DON'T HAVE MUCH TO WORK WITH.
NEVERTHELESS, IF I WERE YOU, I WOULD THINK ABOUT STAYING SOMEPLACE ELSE IN THE SHORT TERM.
CRACKLE

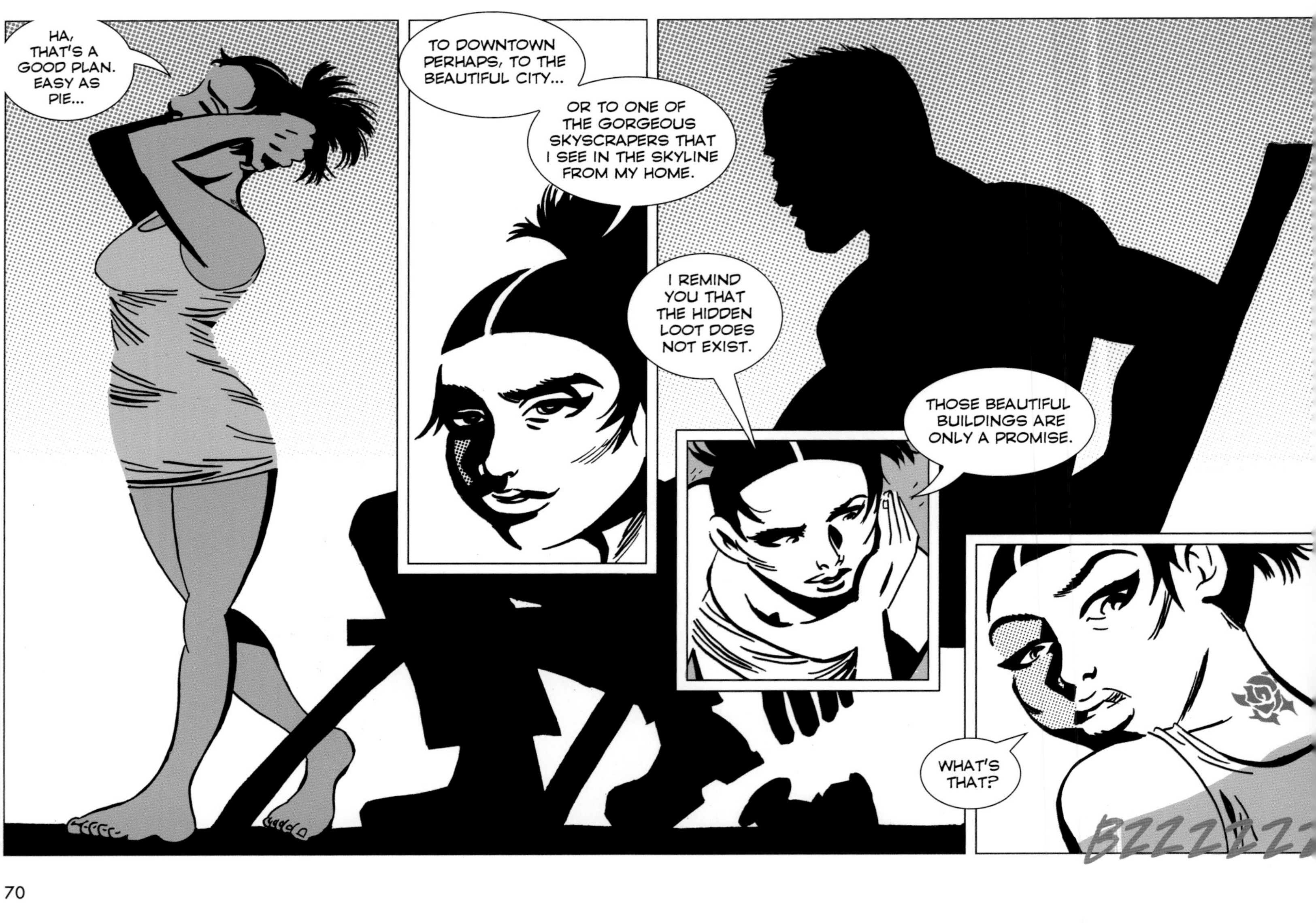
HA, THAT'S A GOOD PLAN. EASY AS PIE...
TO DOWNTOWN PERHAPS, TO THE BEAUTIFUL CITY...
OR TO ONE OF THE GORGEOUS SKYSCRAPERS THAT I SEE IN THE SKYLINE FROM MY HOME.
I REMIND YOU THAT THE HIDDEN LOOT DOES NOT EXIST.
THOSE BEAUTIFUL BUILDINGS ARE ONLY A PROMISE.
WHAT'S THAT?
BZZZZZZ

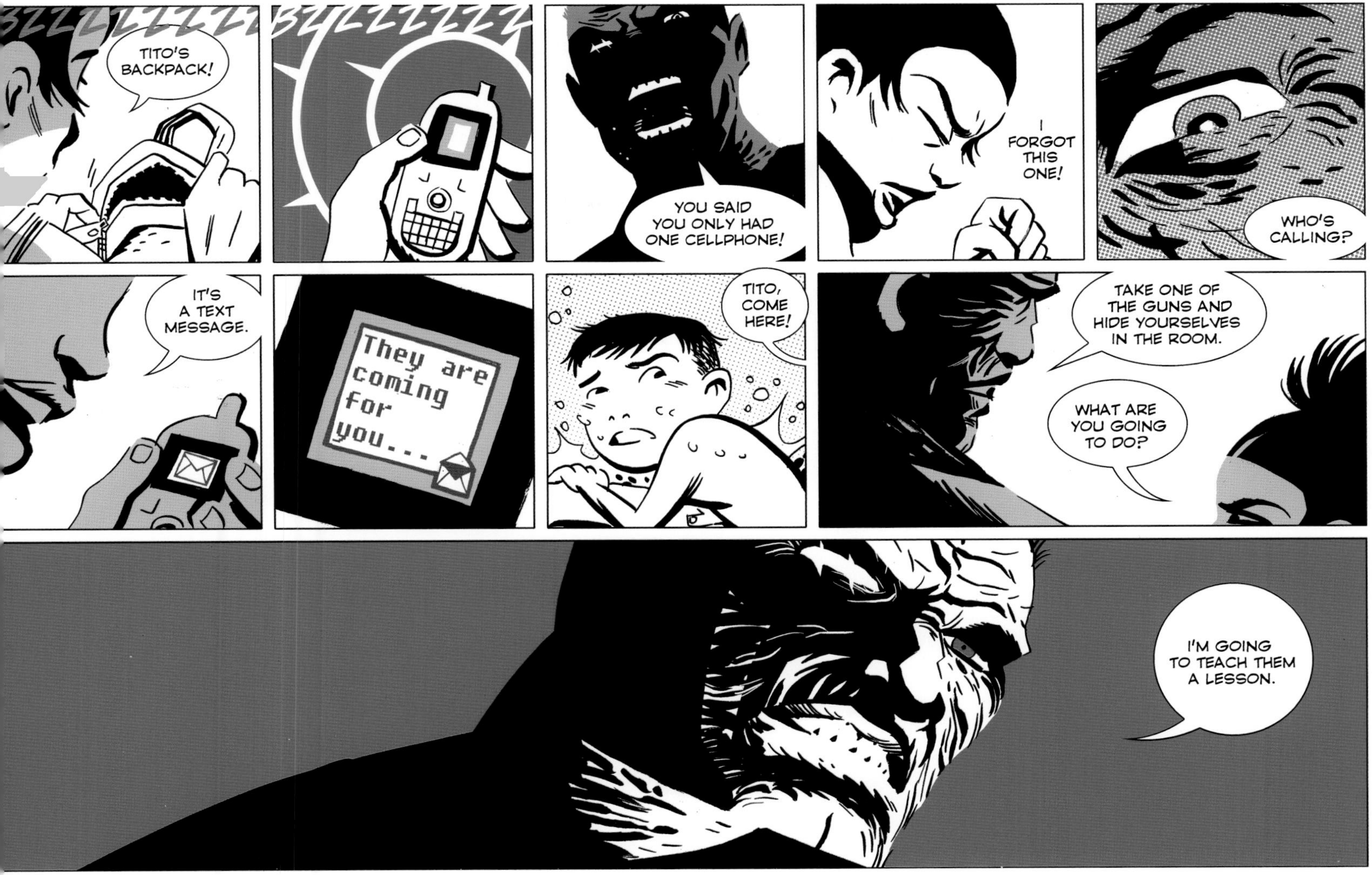
TITO'S BACKPACK!
YOU SAID YOU ONLY HAD ONE CELLPHONE!
I FORGOT THIS ONE!
WHO'S CALLING?
IT'S A TEXT MESSAGE.
They are coming for you...
TITO, COME HERE!
TAKE ONE OF THE GUNS AND HIDE YOURSELVES IN THE ROOM.
WHAT ARE YOU GOING TO DO?
I'M GOING TO TEACH THEM A LESSON.

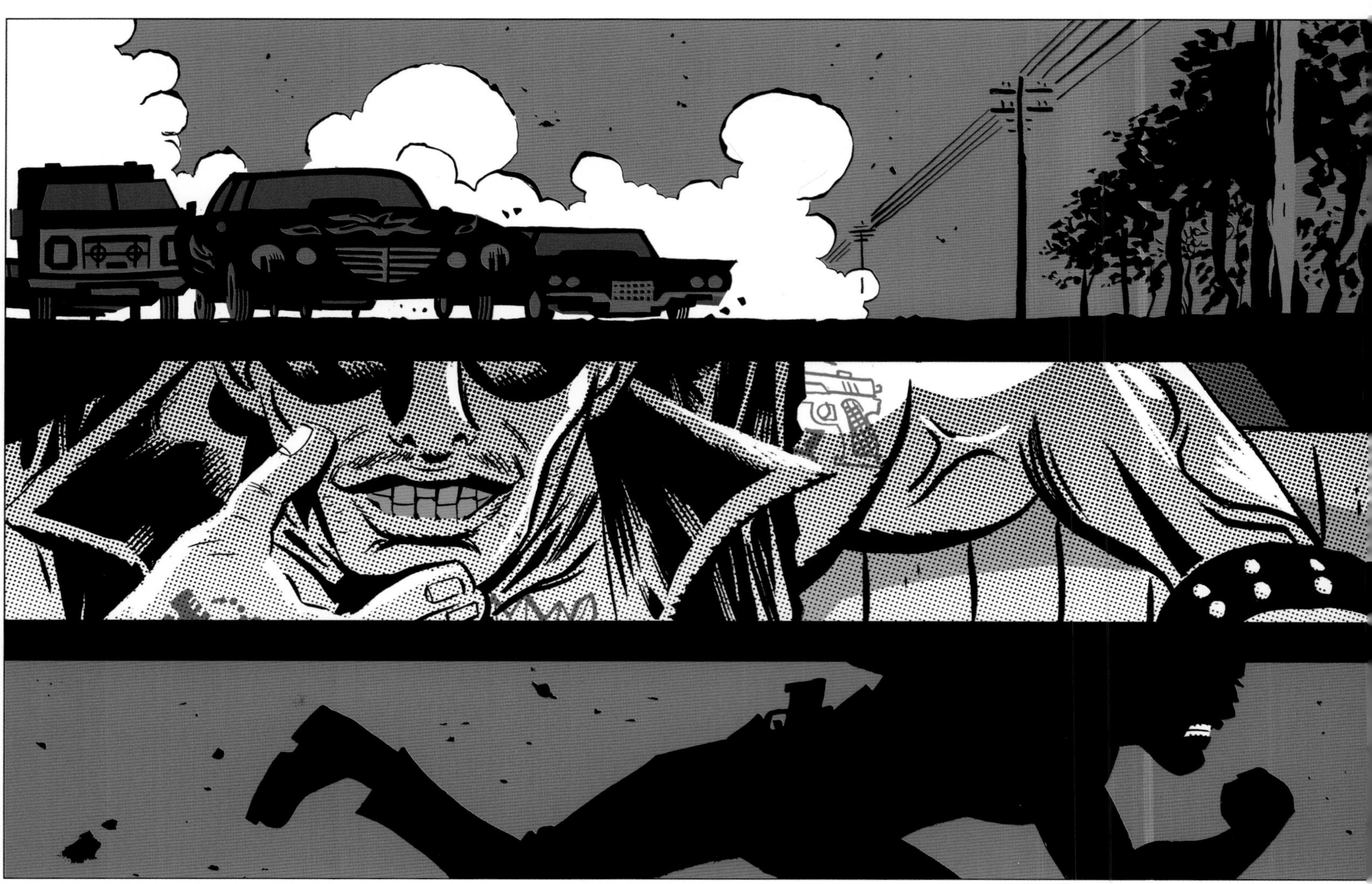

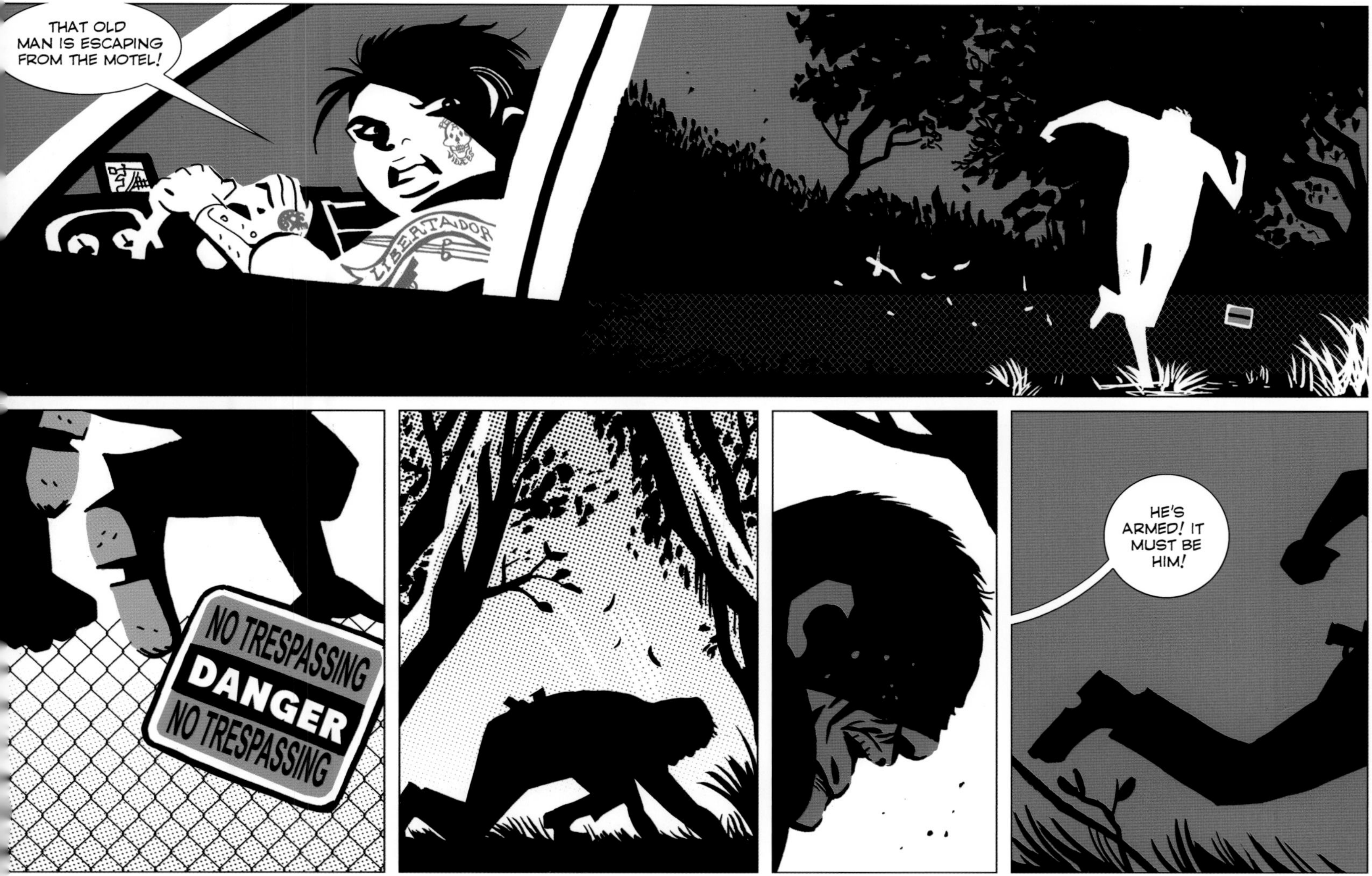
THAT OLD MAN IS ESCAPING FROM THE MOTEL!
LIBERTADOR
NO TRESPASSING
DANGER
NO TRESPASSING
HE'S ARMED! IT MUST BE HIM!

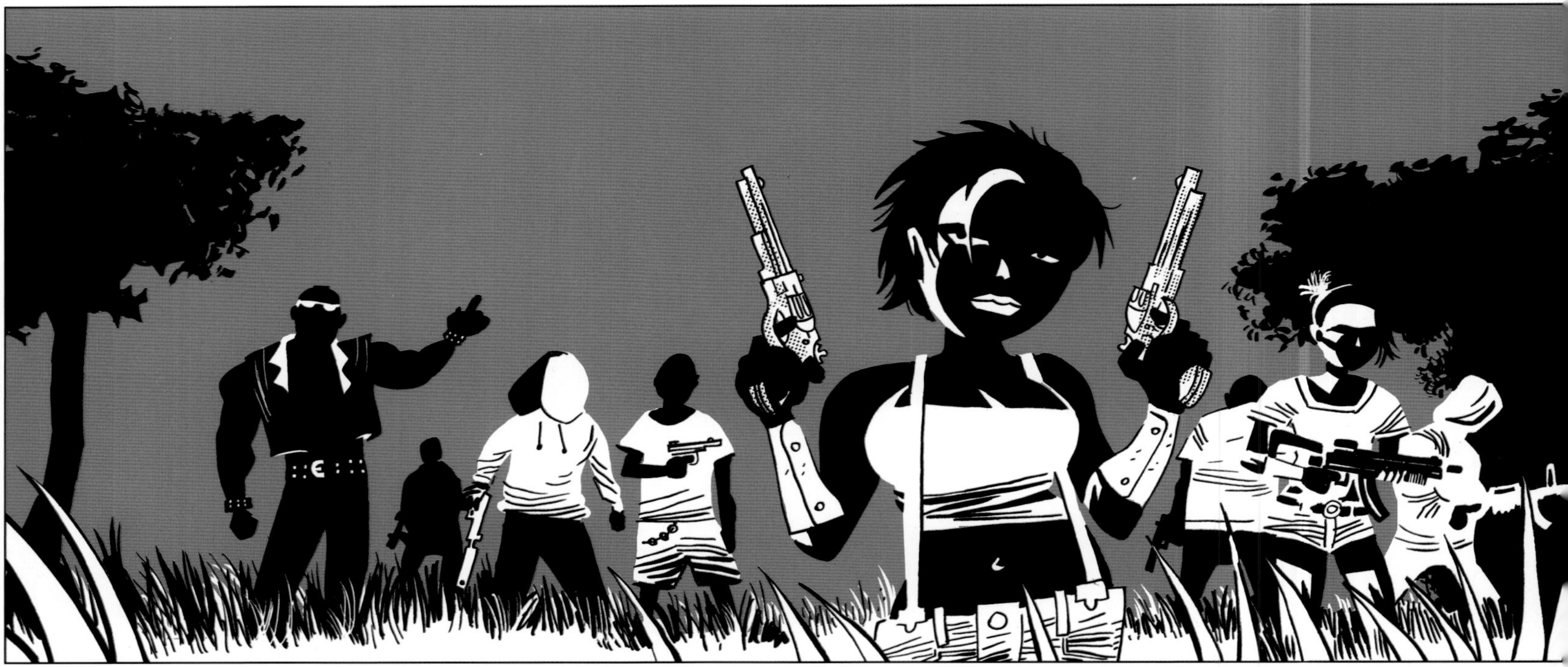

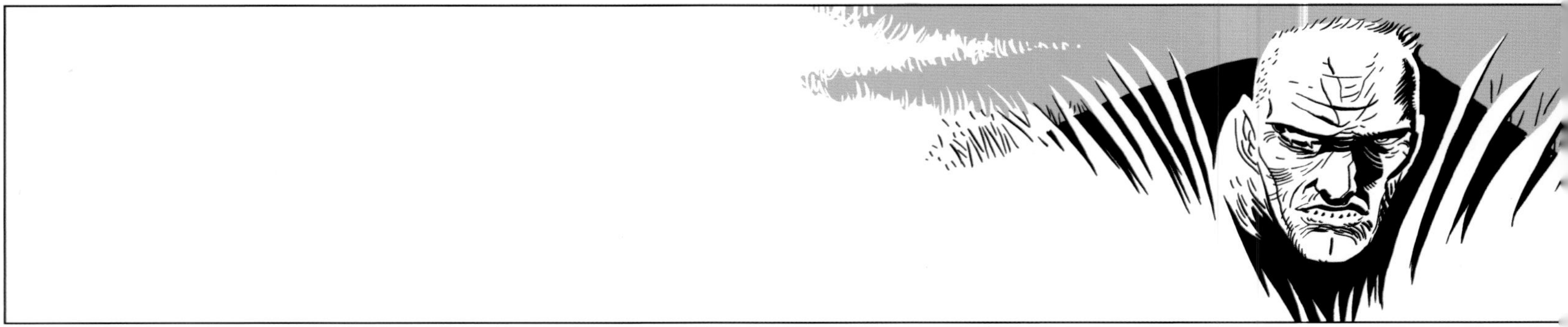

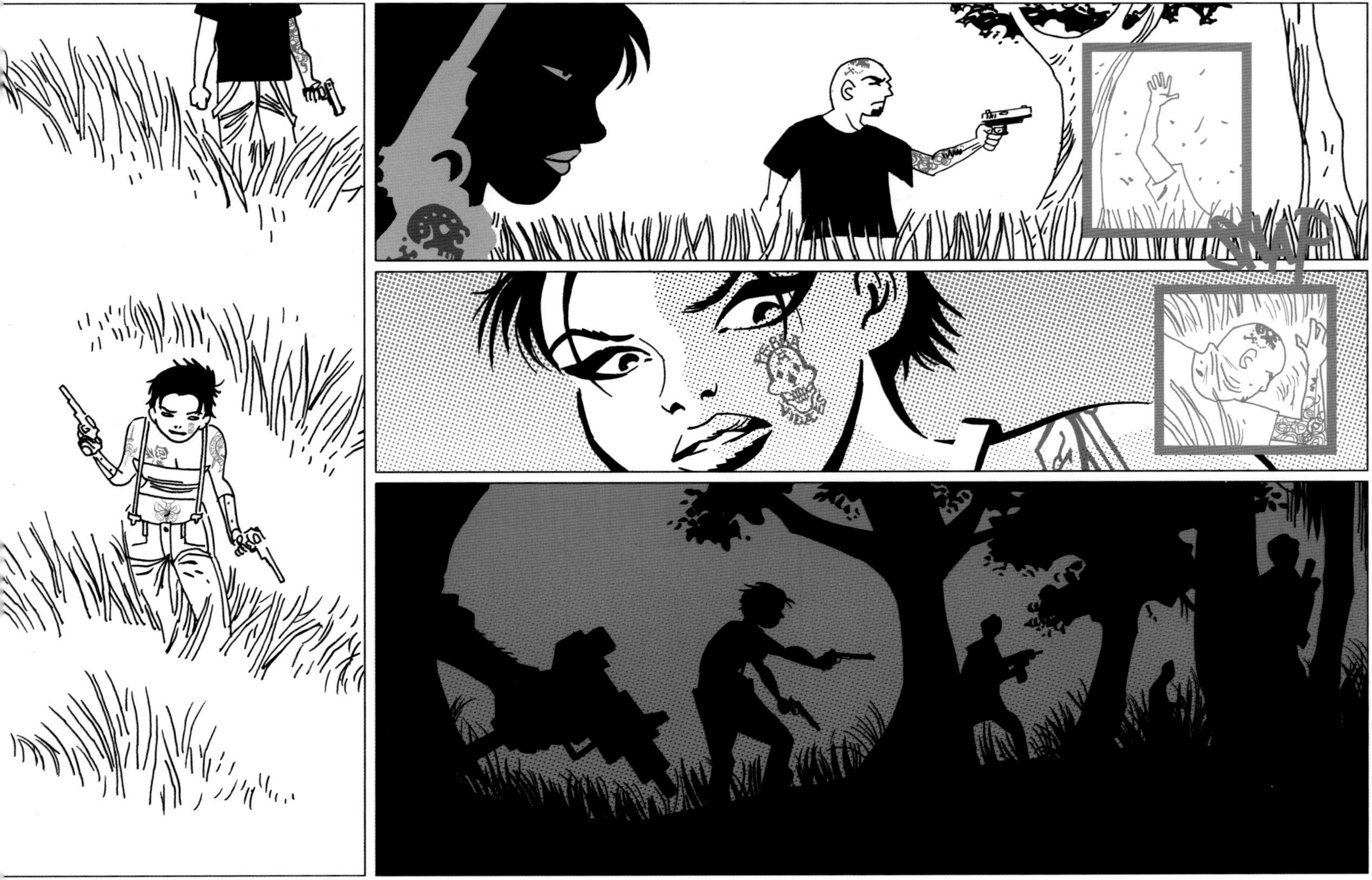
SNAP

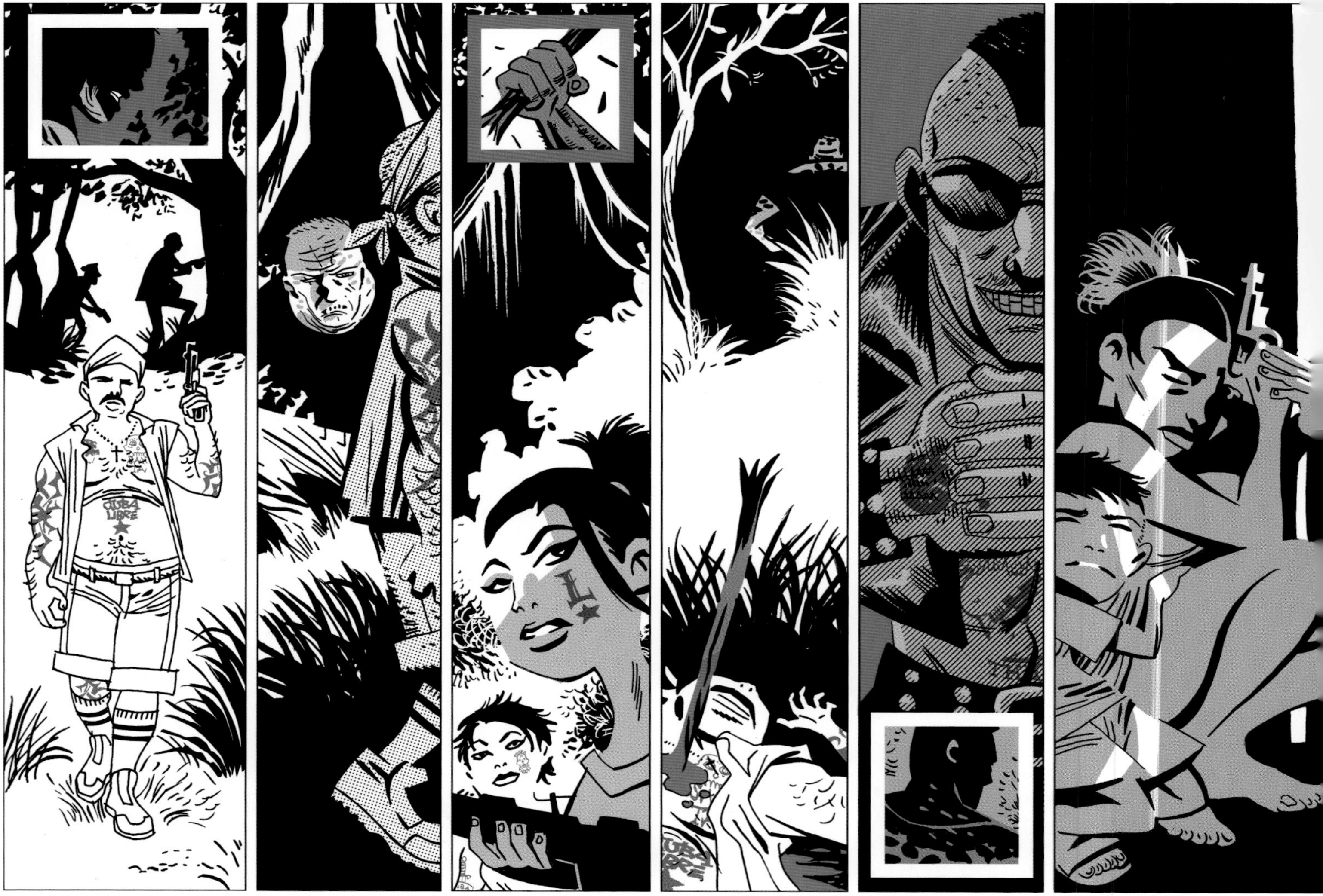
CUBA LIBRE

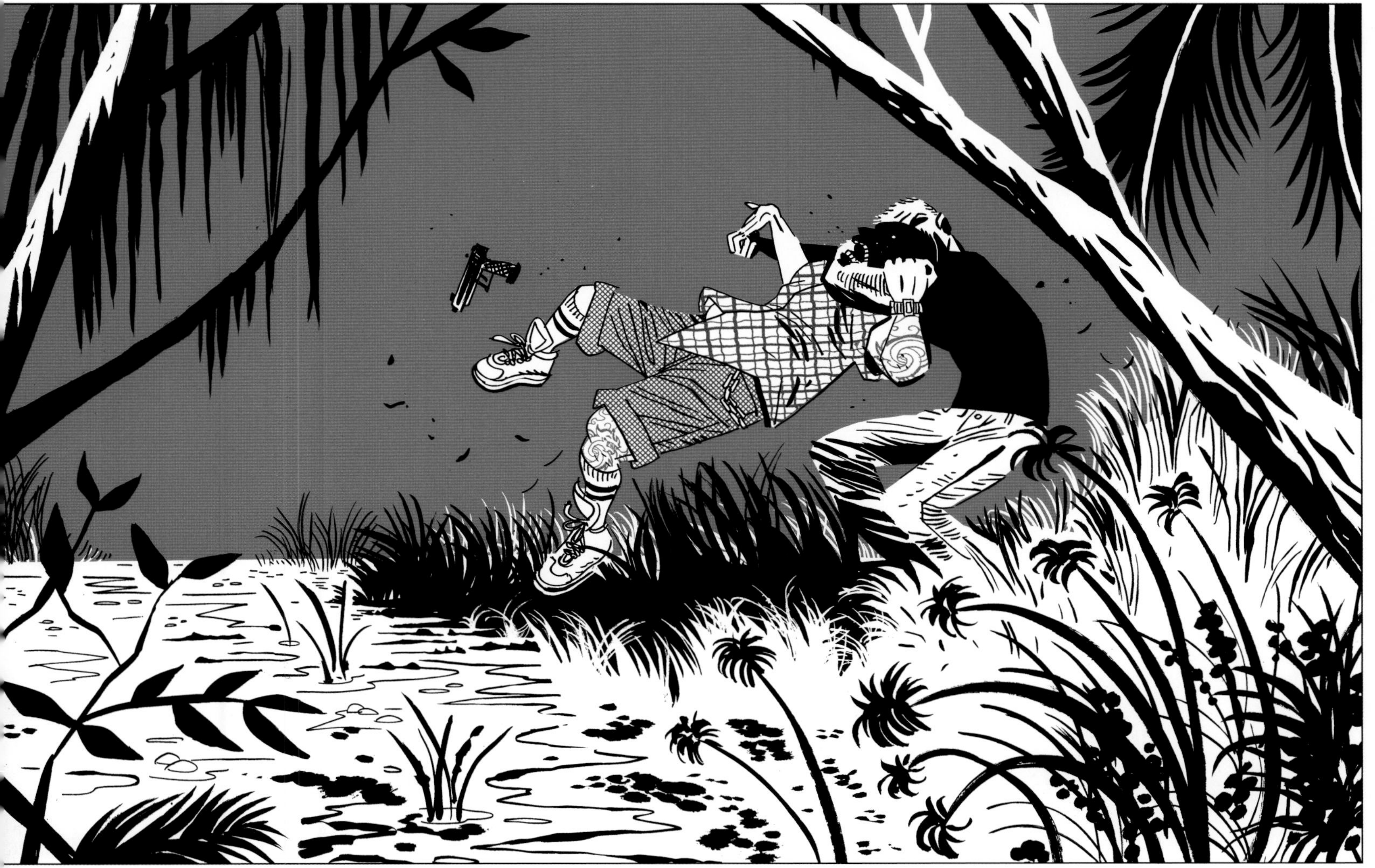

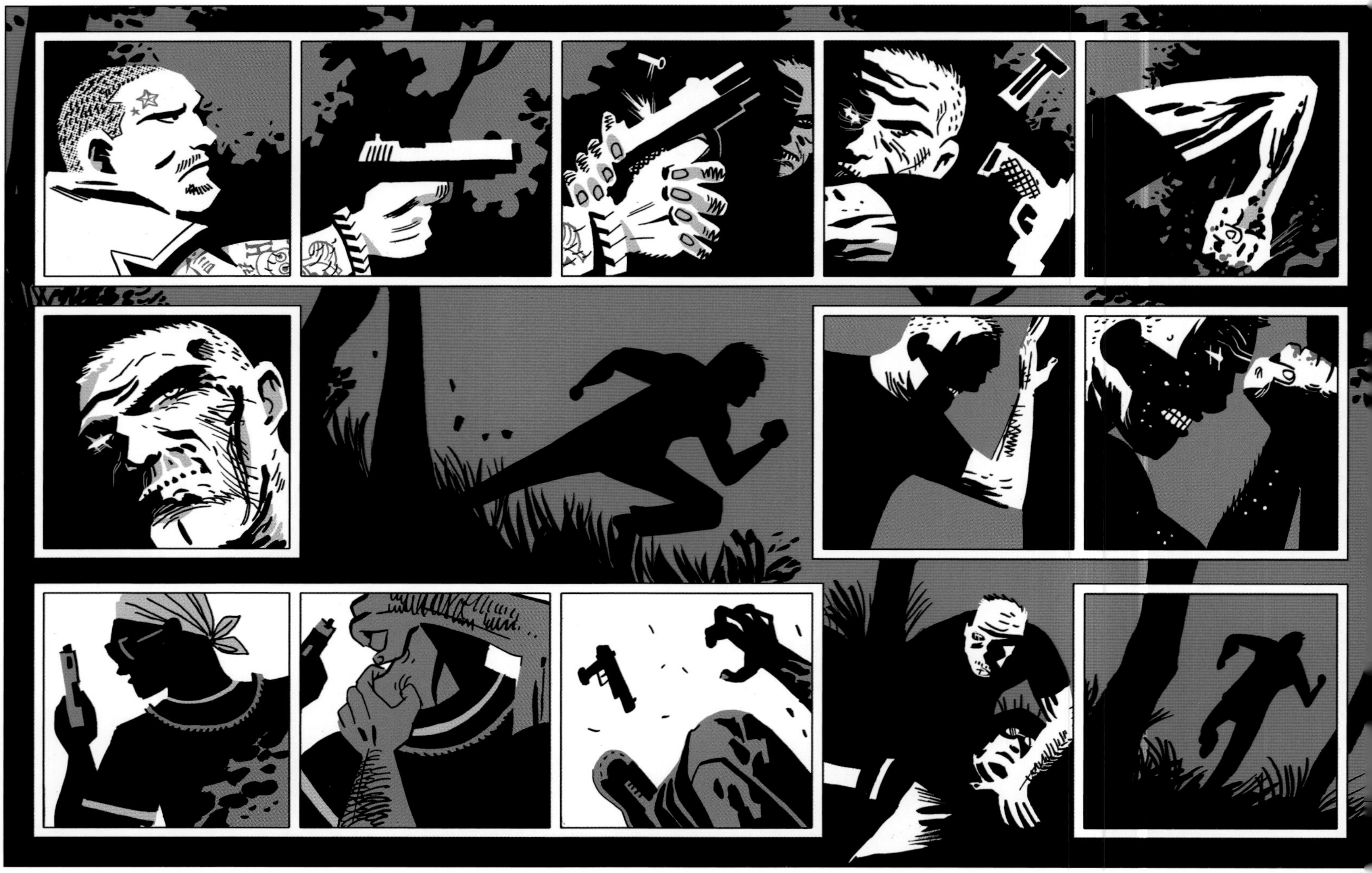

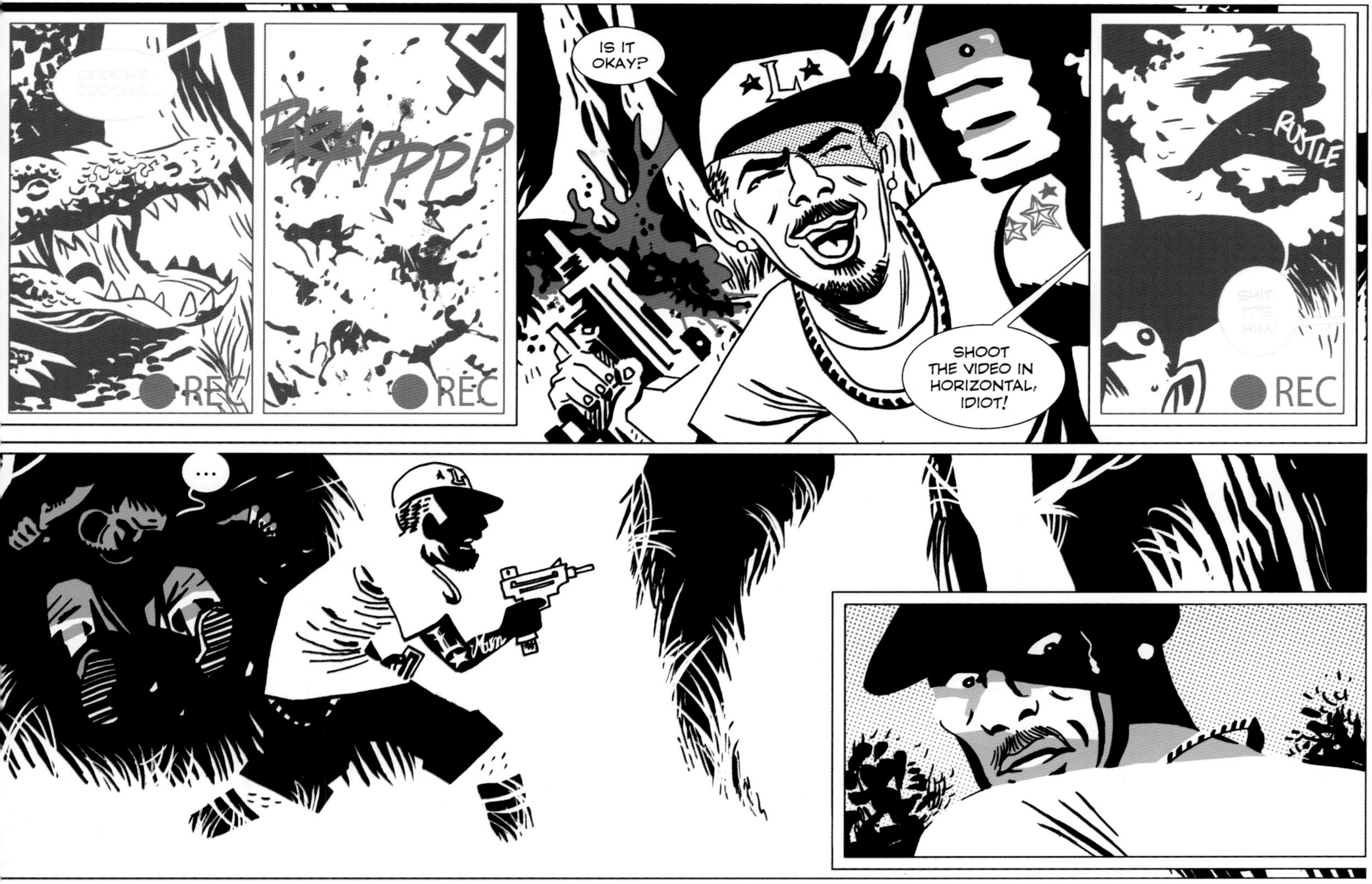
COOCHIE, COOCHIE...
REC
REC
IS IT OKAY?
SHOOT THE VIDEO IN HORIZONTAL, IDIOT!
RUSTLE
SHIT, IT'S HIM!
REC
...

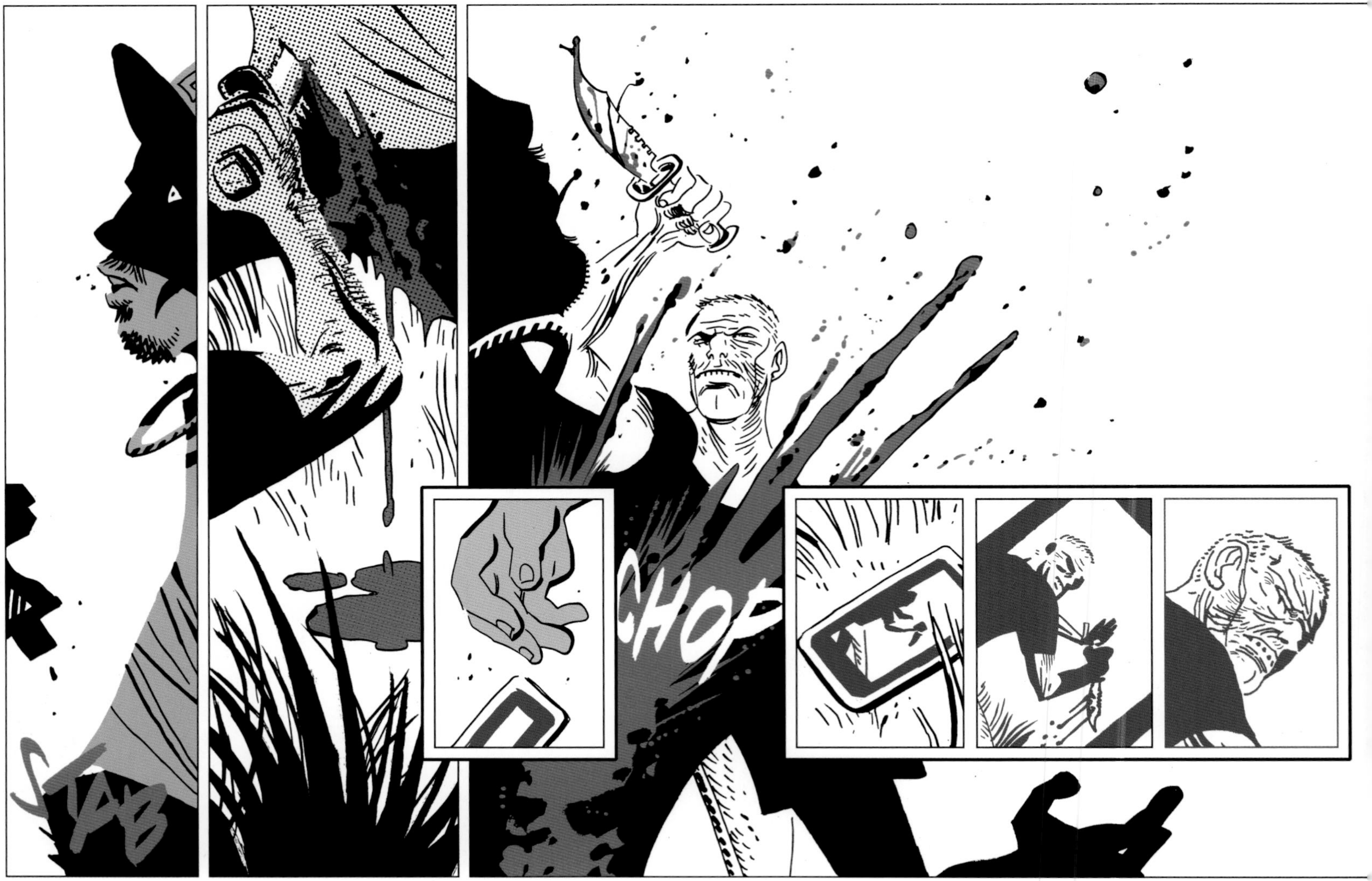
STAB
CHOP

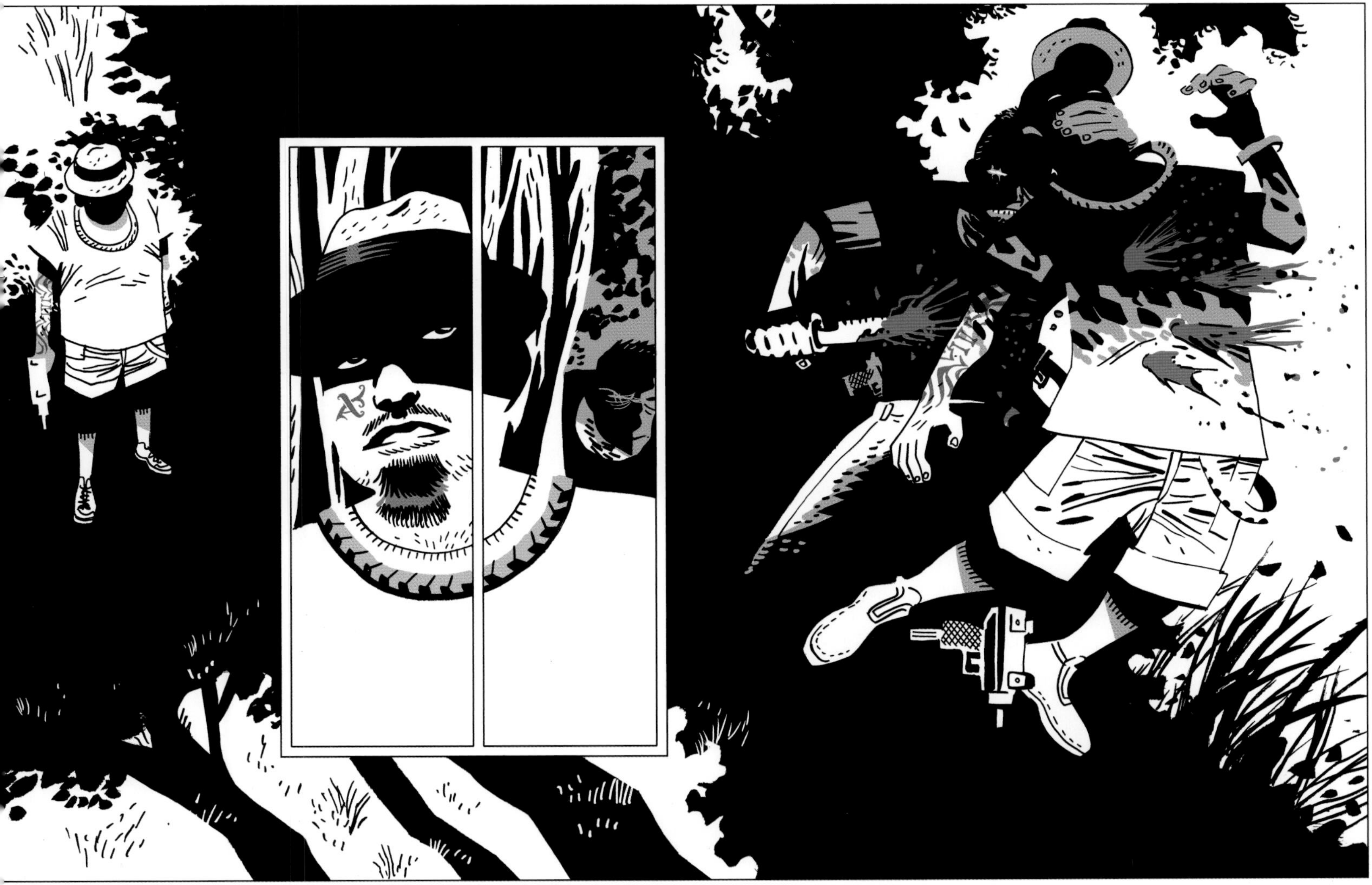

CHOMP
CHOMP
CHOMP
CHOMP
CHOMP
CHOMP
CHOMP

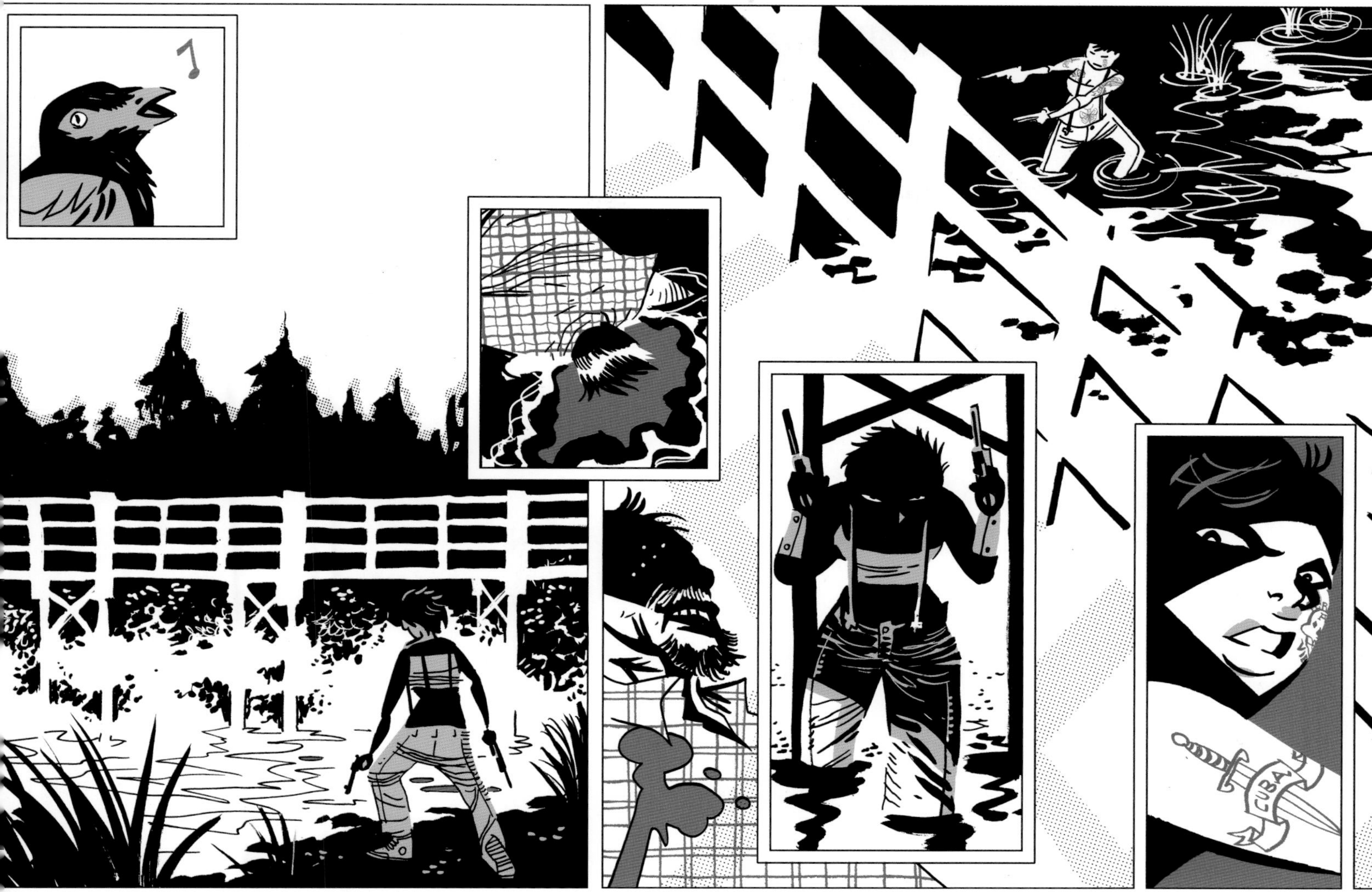
CUBA

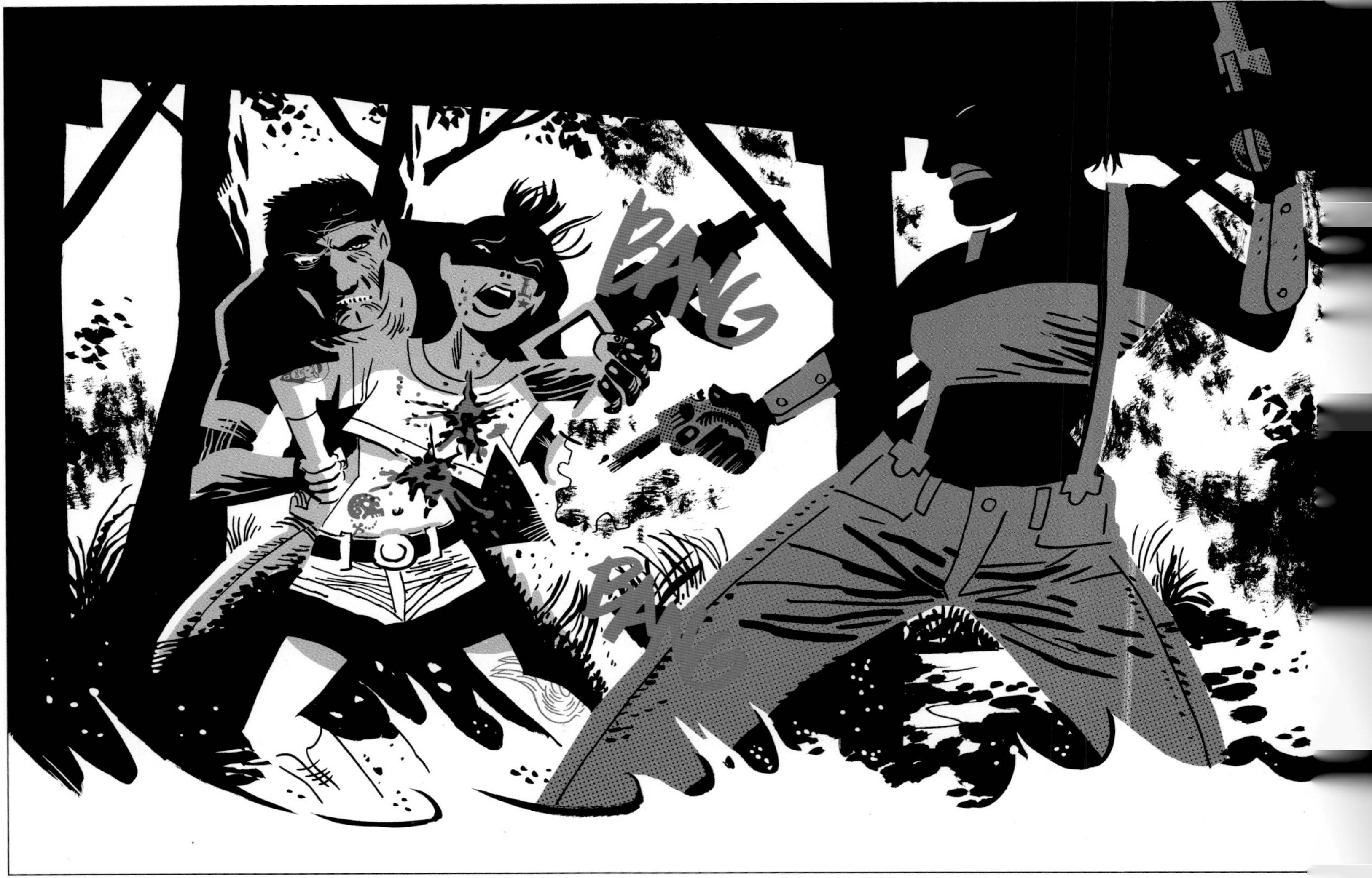
BANG
BANG

BRAPP
BRAPPP
BRAPPPP

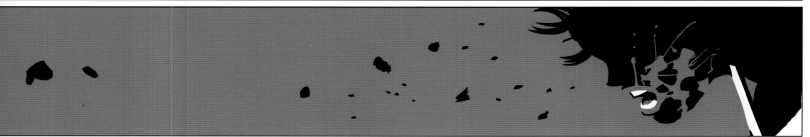

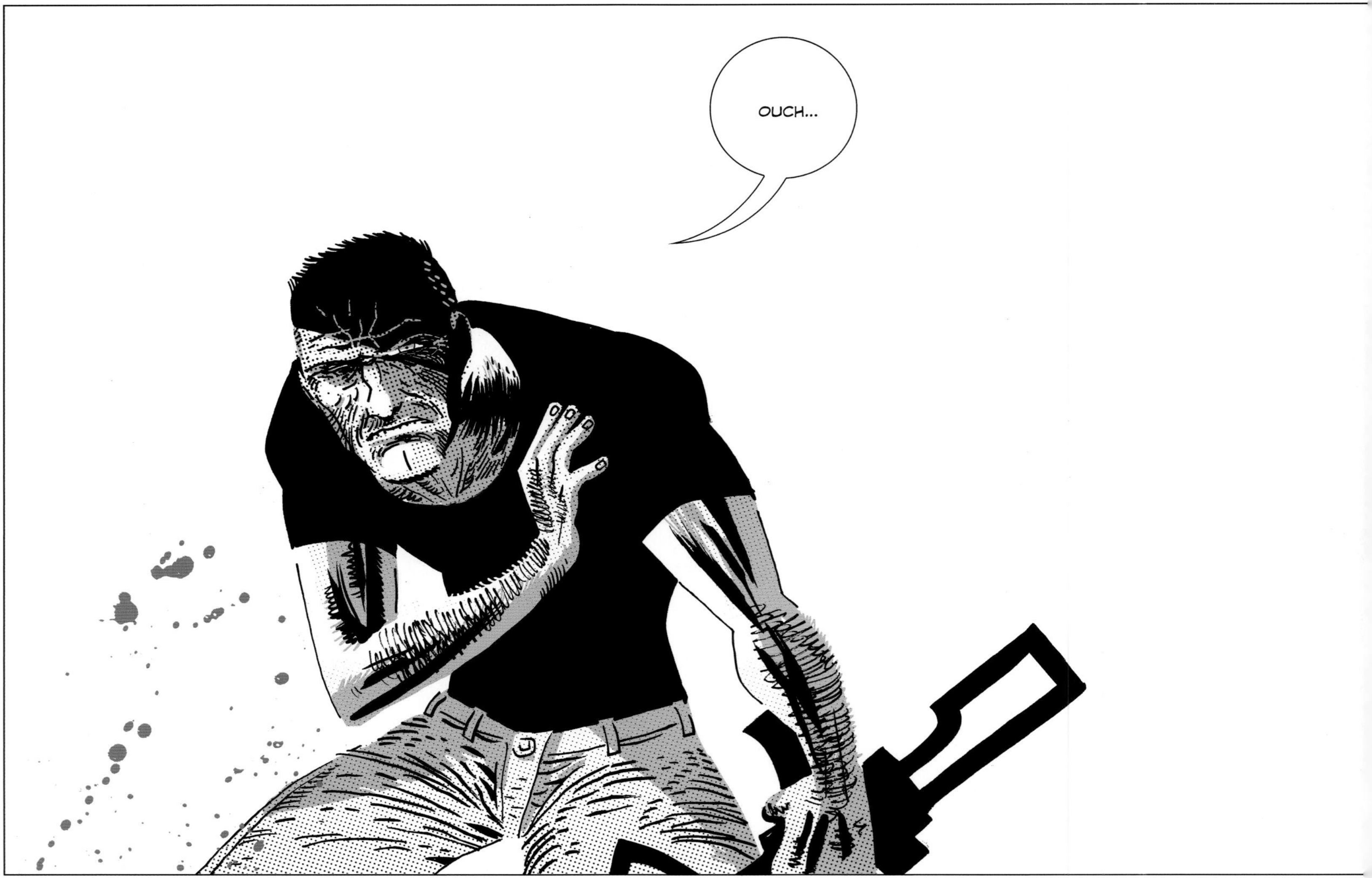
OUCH...

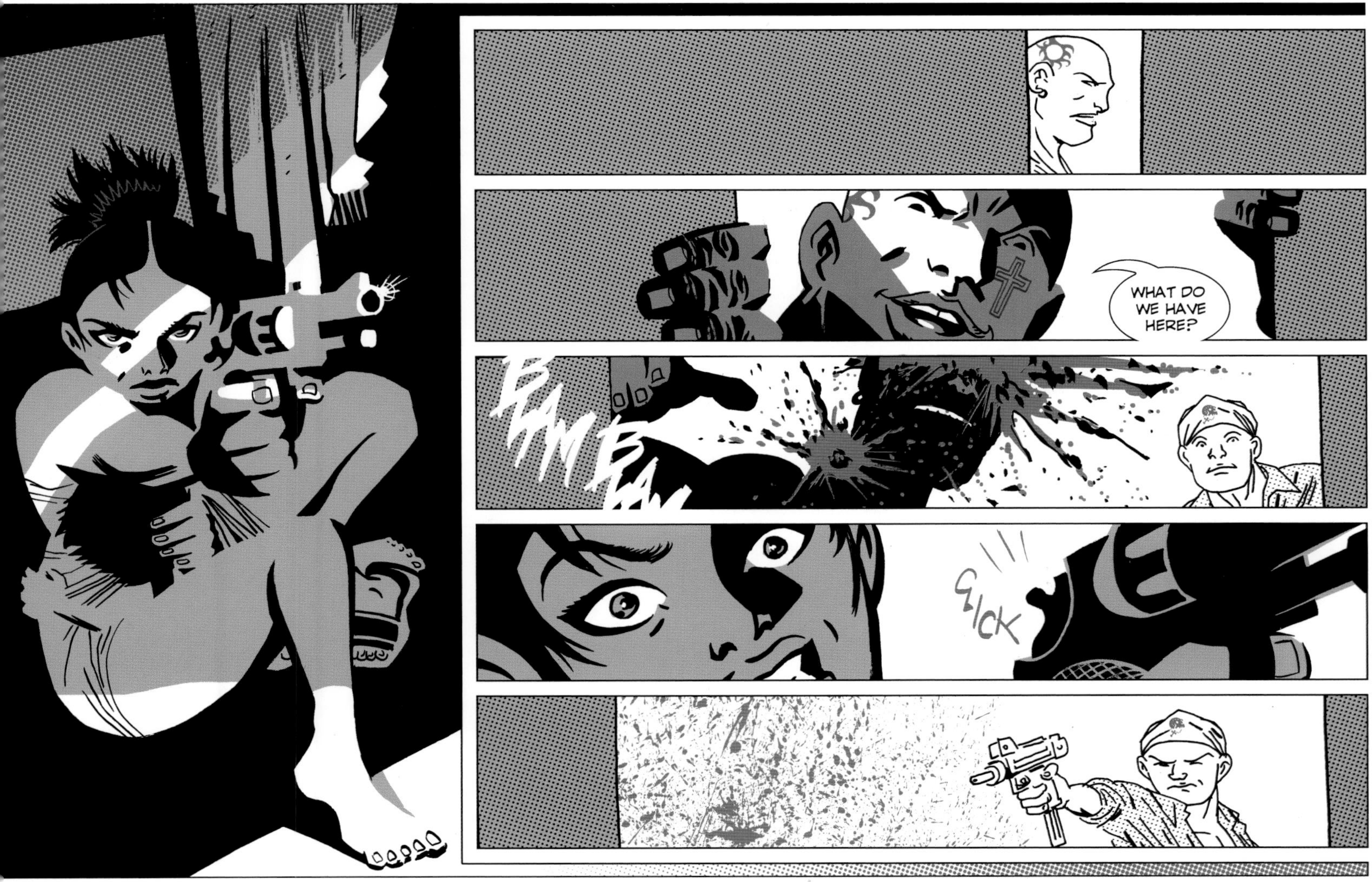
WHAT DO WE HAVE HERE?
BLAM BLAM
CLICK

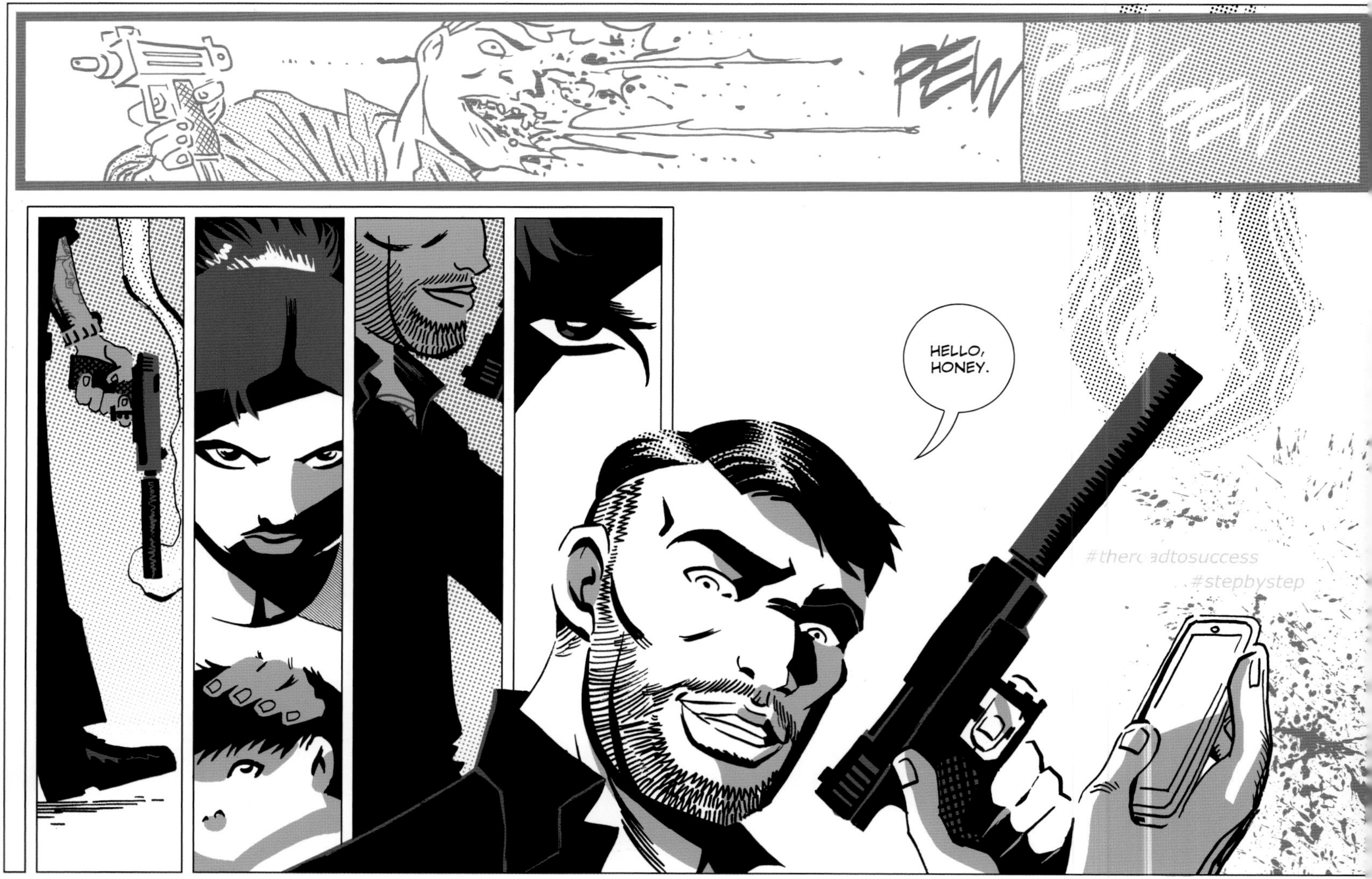
PEW
HELLO, HONEY.
#stepbystep

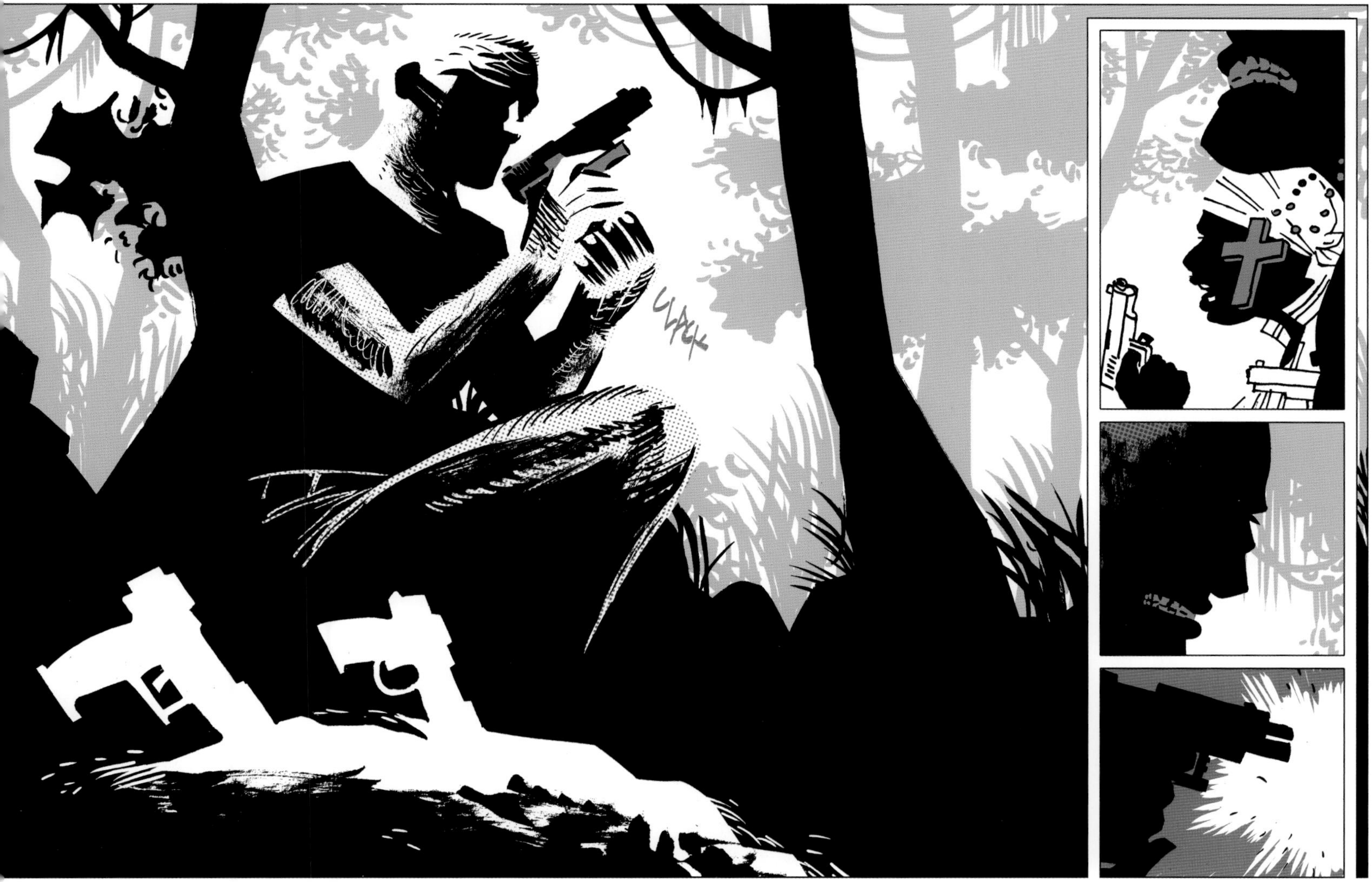
CLACK

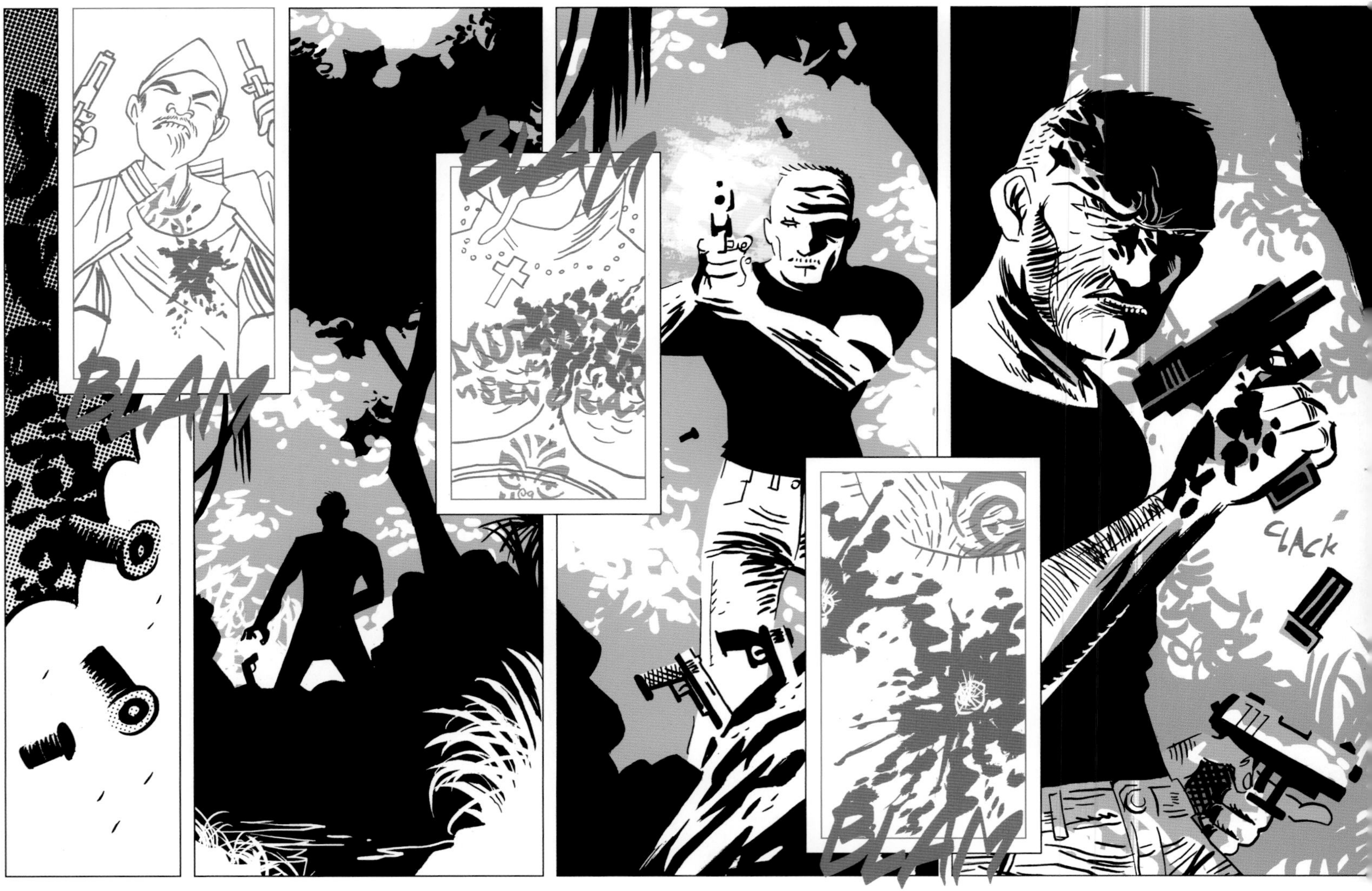
BLAM
BLAM
BLAM
CLACK

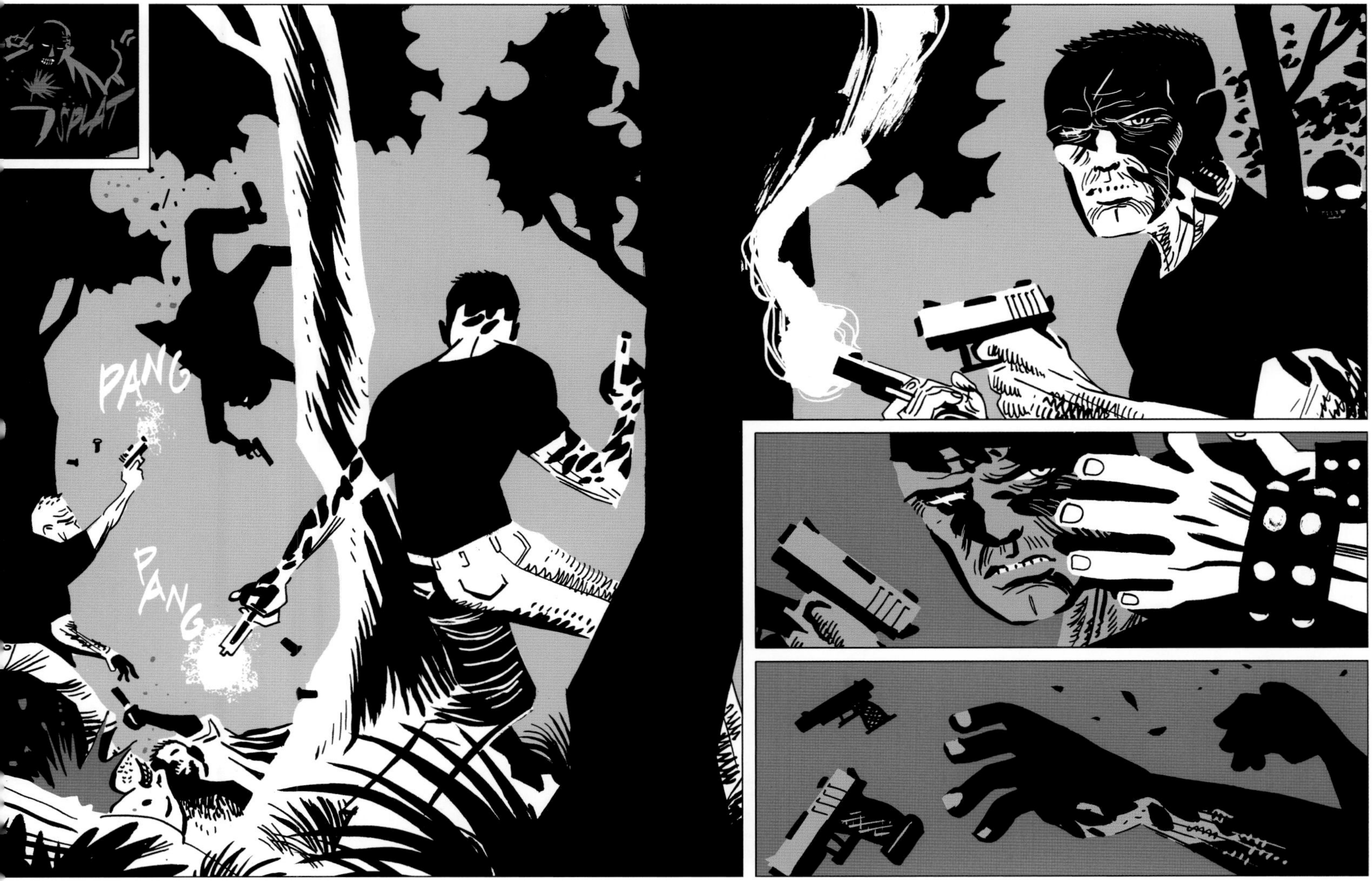
SPLAT
PANG
PANG

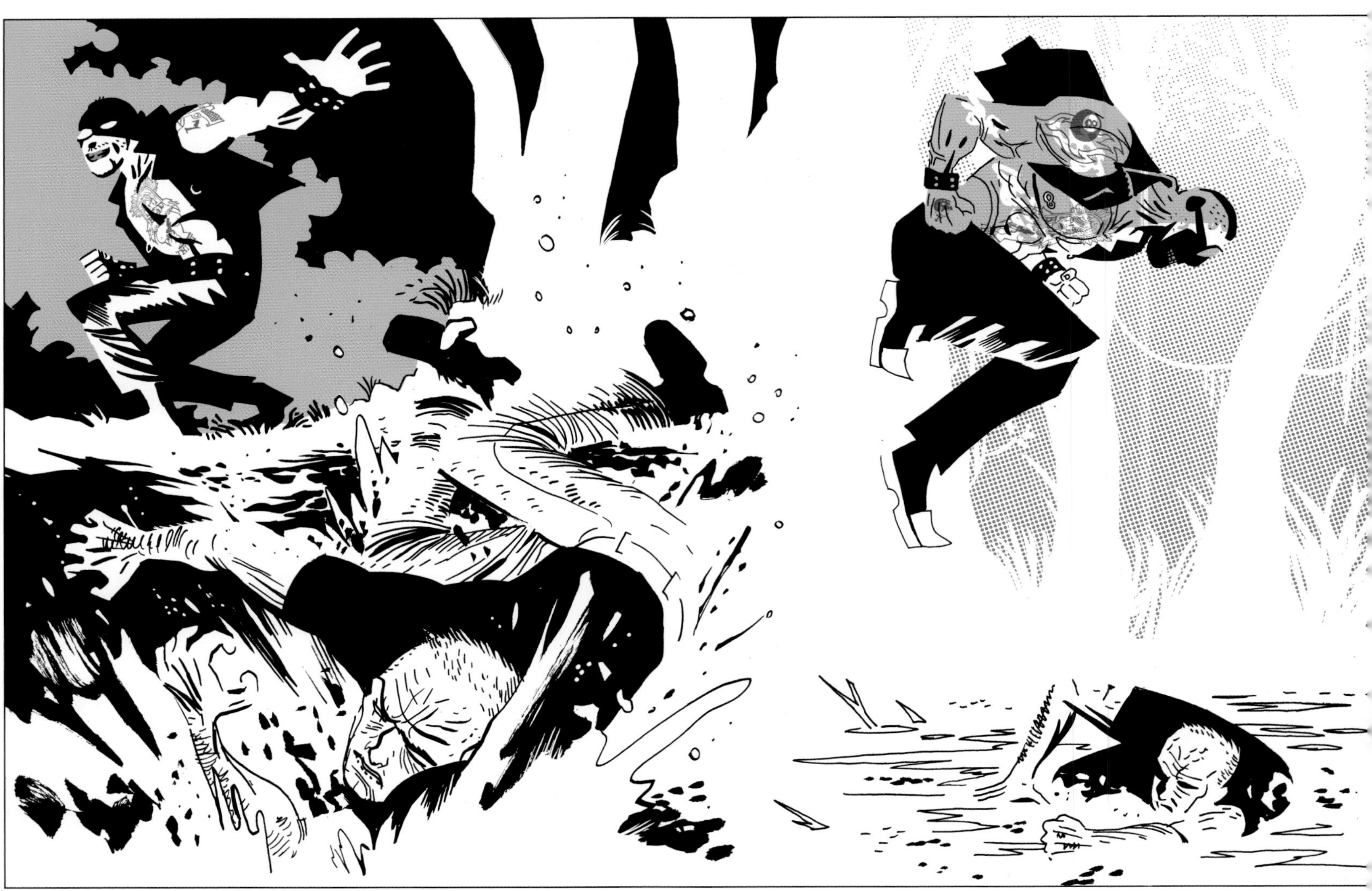

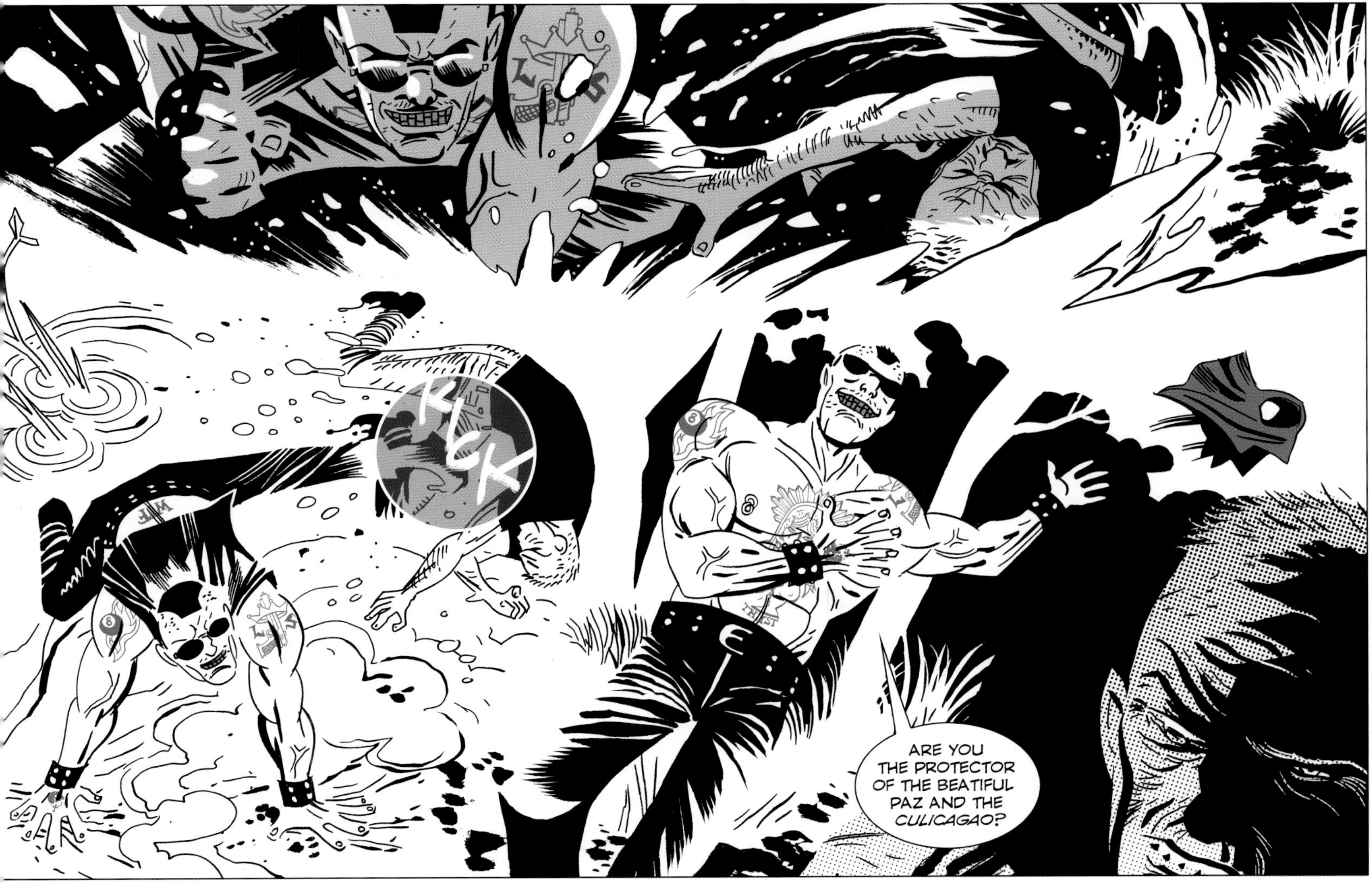
KICK
ARE YOU THE PROTECTOR OF THE BEATIFUL PAZ AND THE *CULICAGAO*?

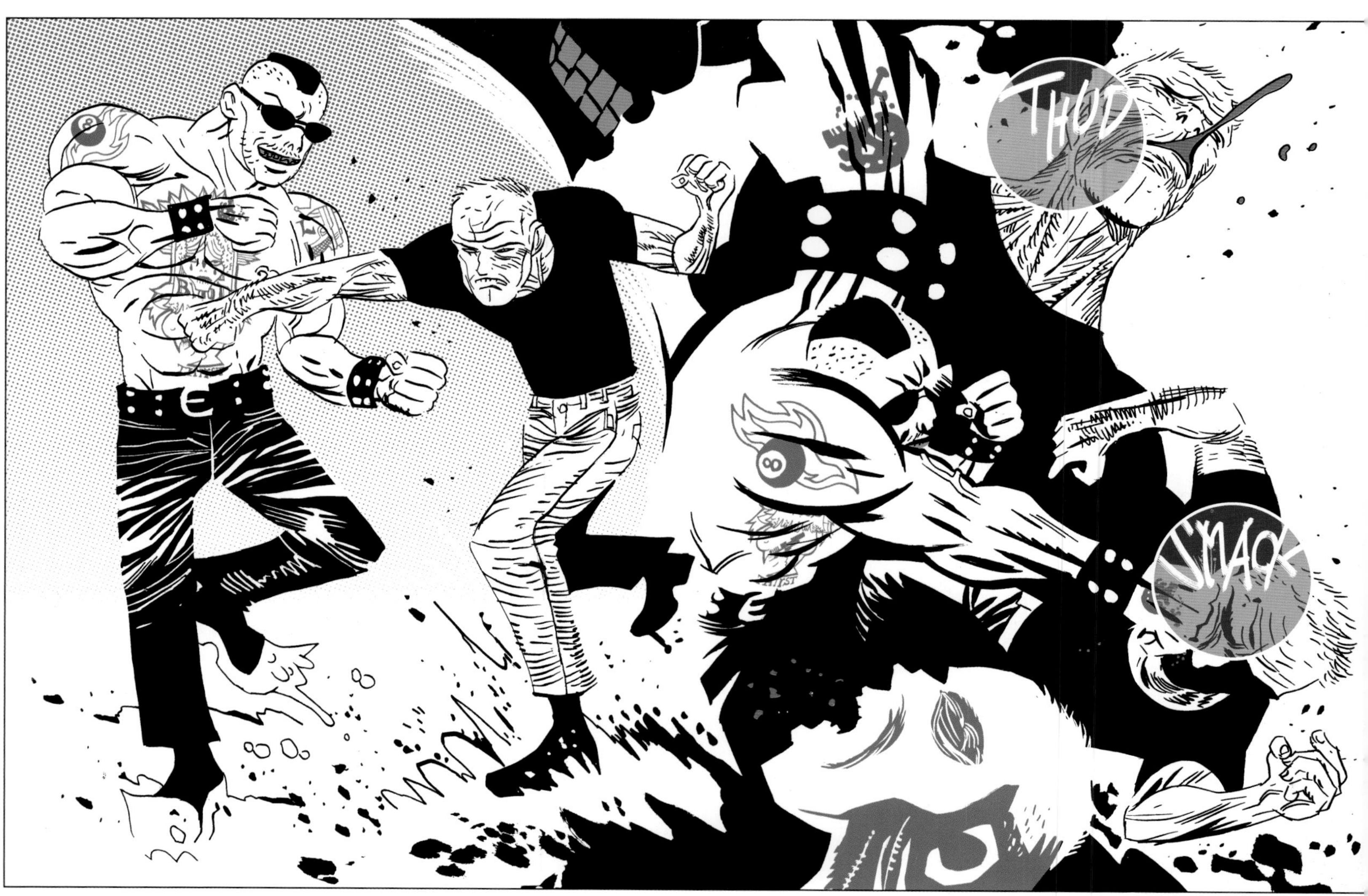
THUD
SMACK

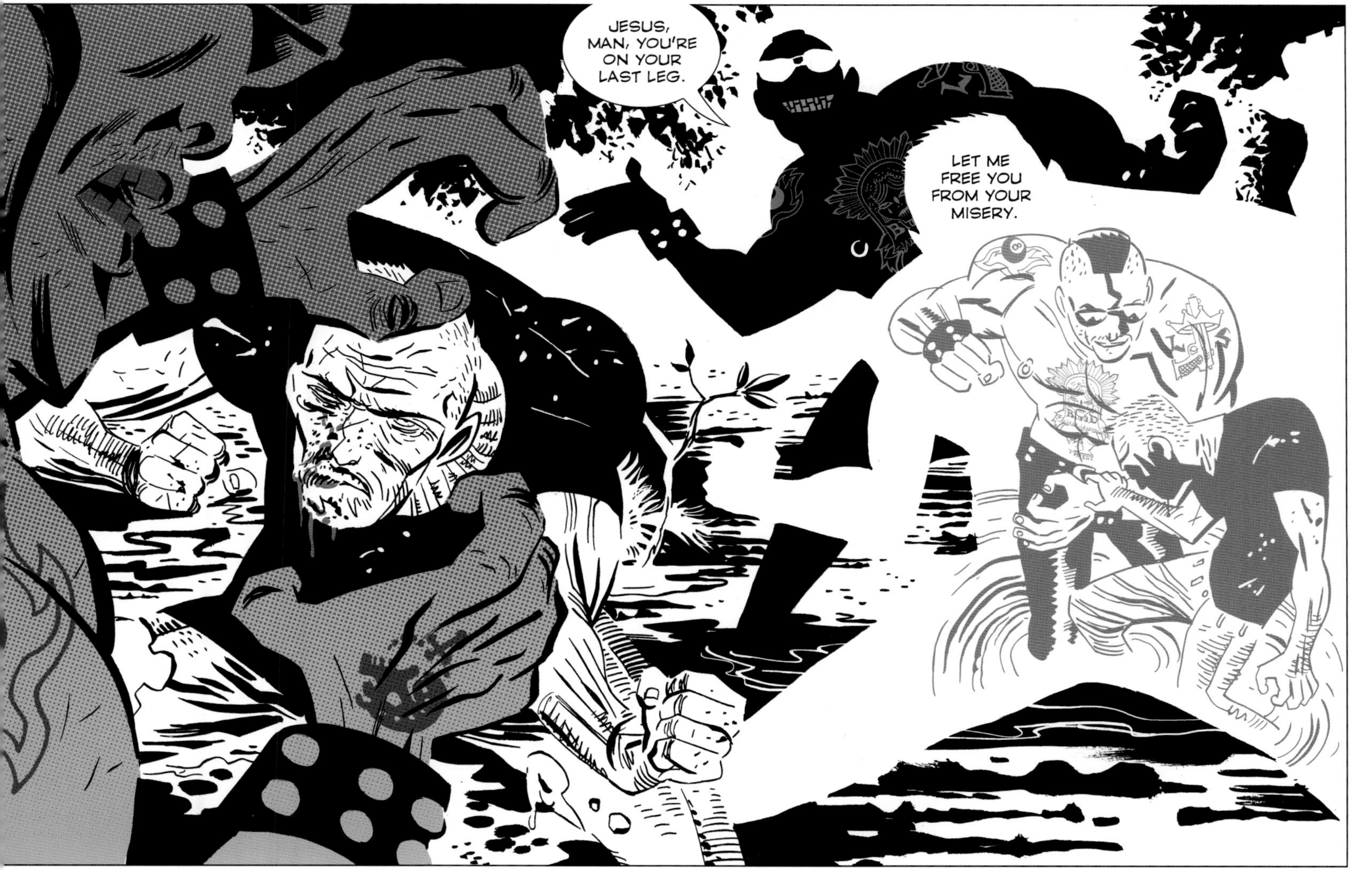
JESUS, MAN, YOU'RE ON YOUR LAST LEG.
LET ME FREE YOU FROM YOUR MISERY.

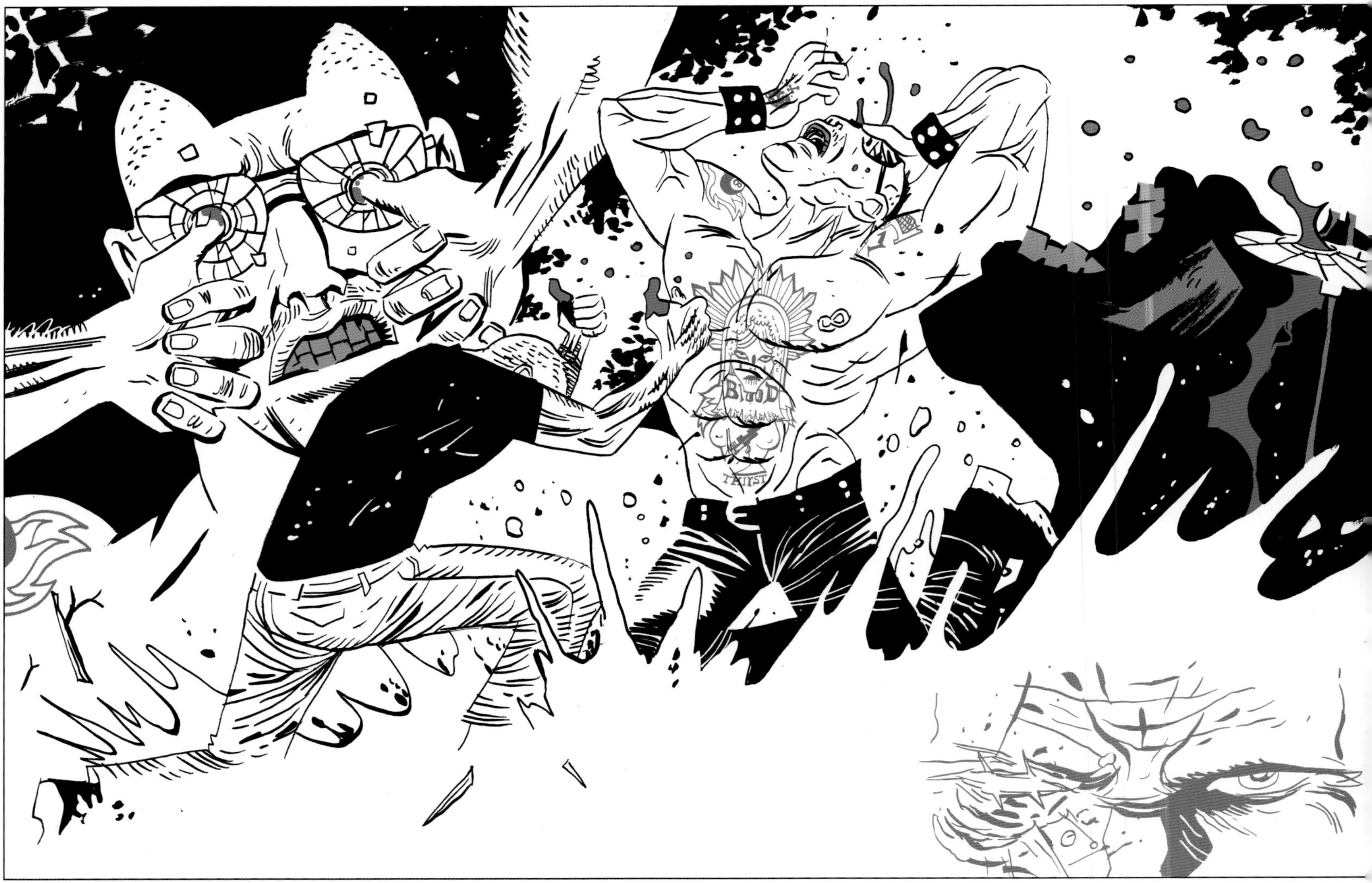

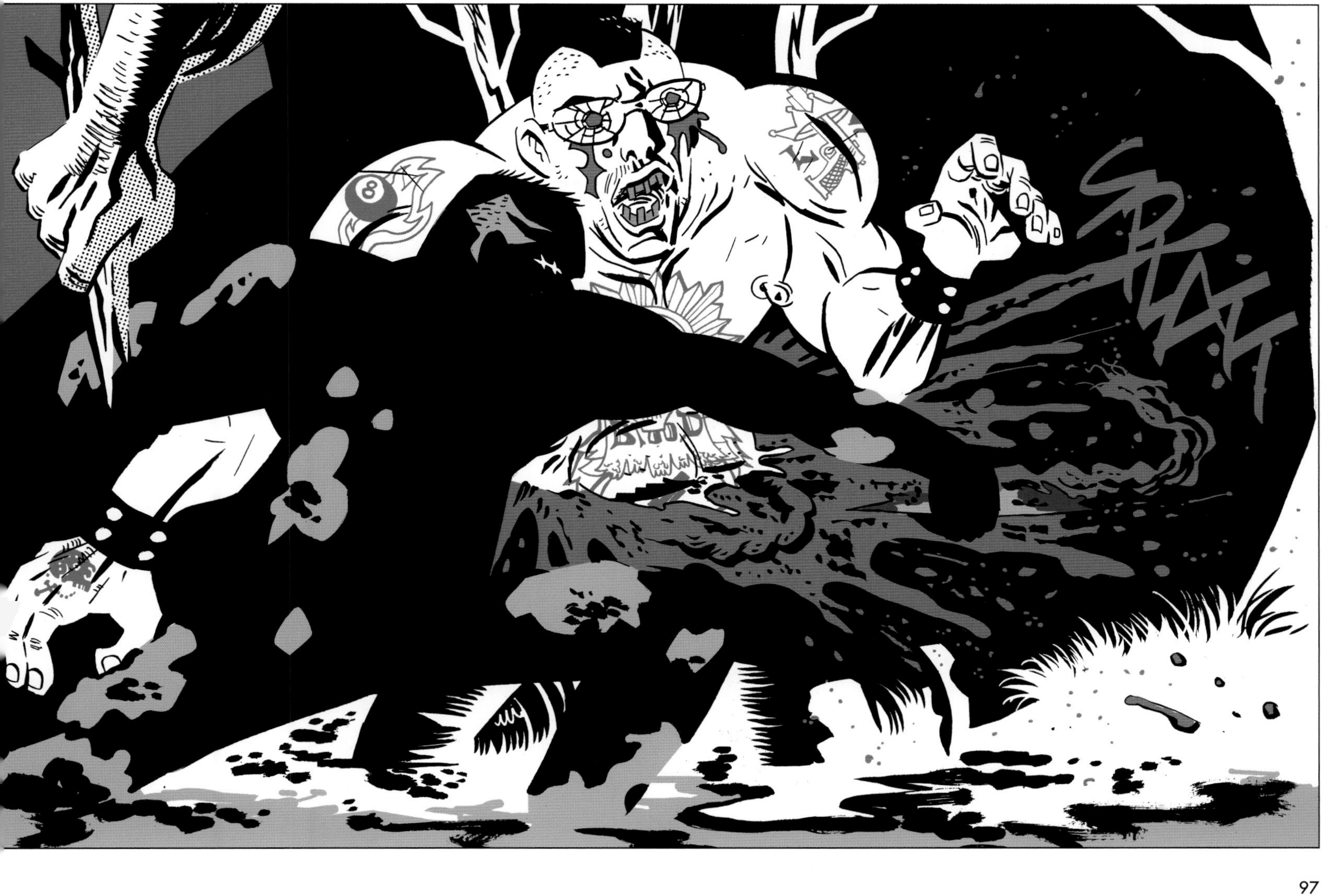

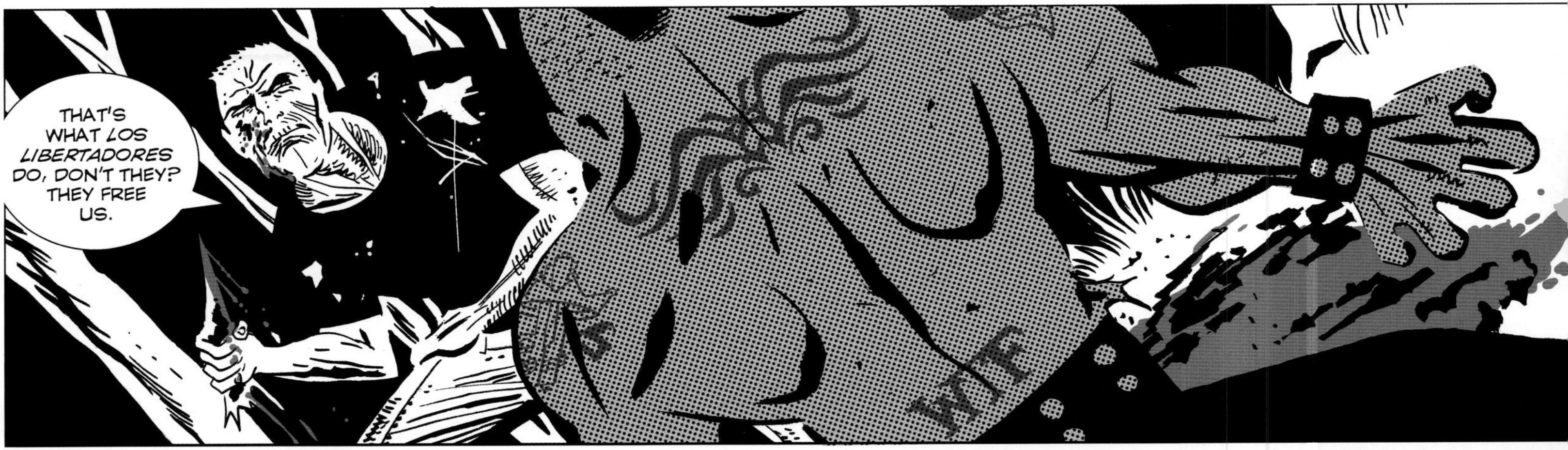
THAT'S WHAT *LOS LIBERTADORES* DO, DON'T THEY? THEY FREE US.

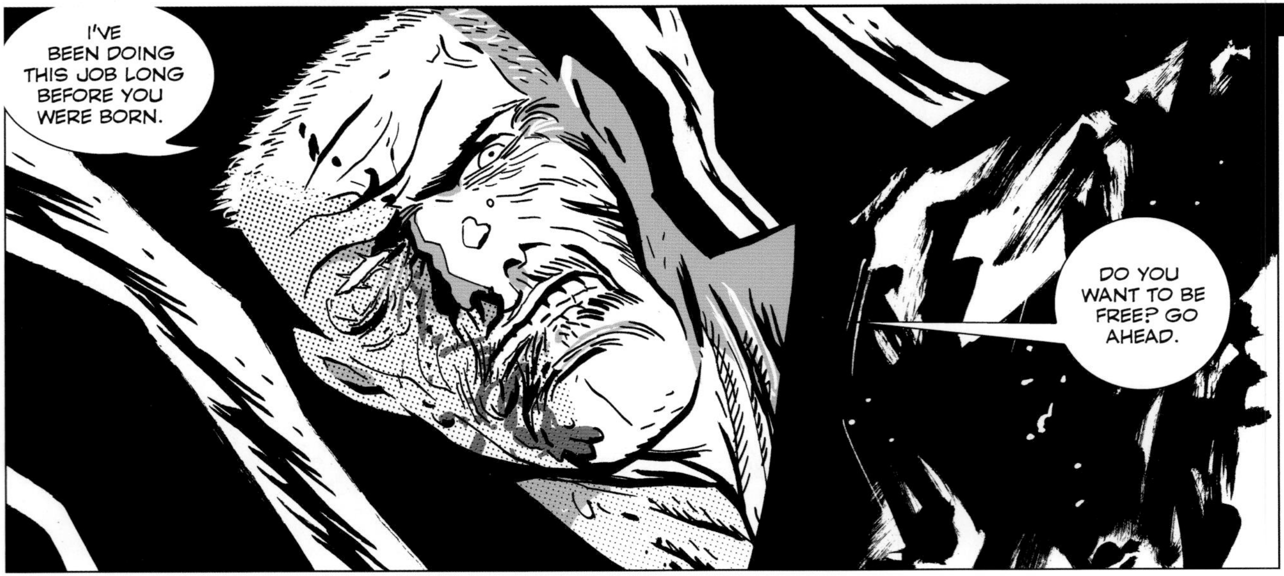
I'VE BEEN DOING THIS JOB LONG BEFORE YOU WERE BORN.
DO YOU WANT TO BE FREE? GO AHEAD.

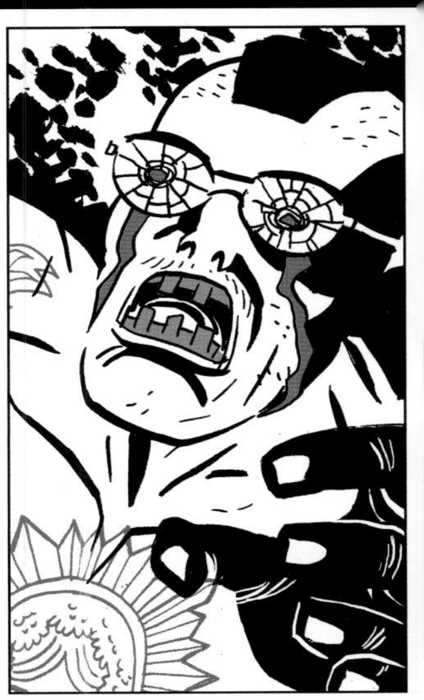

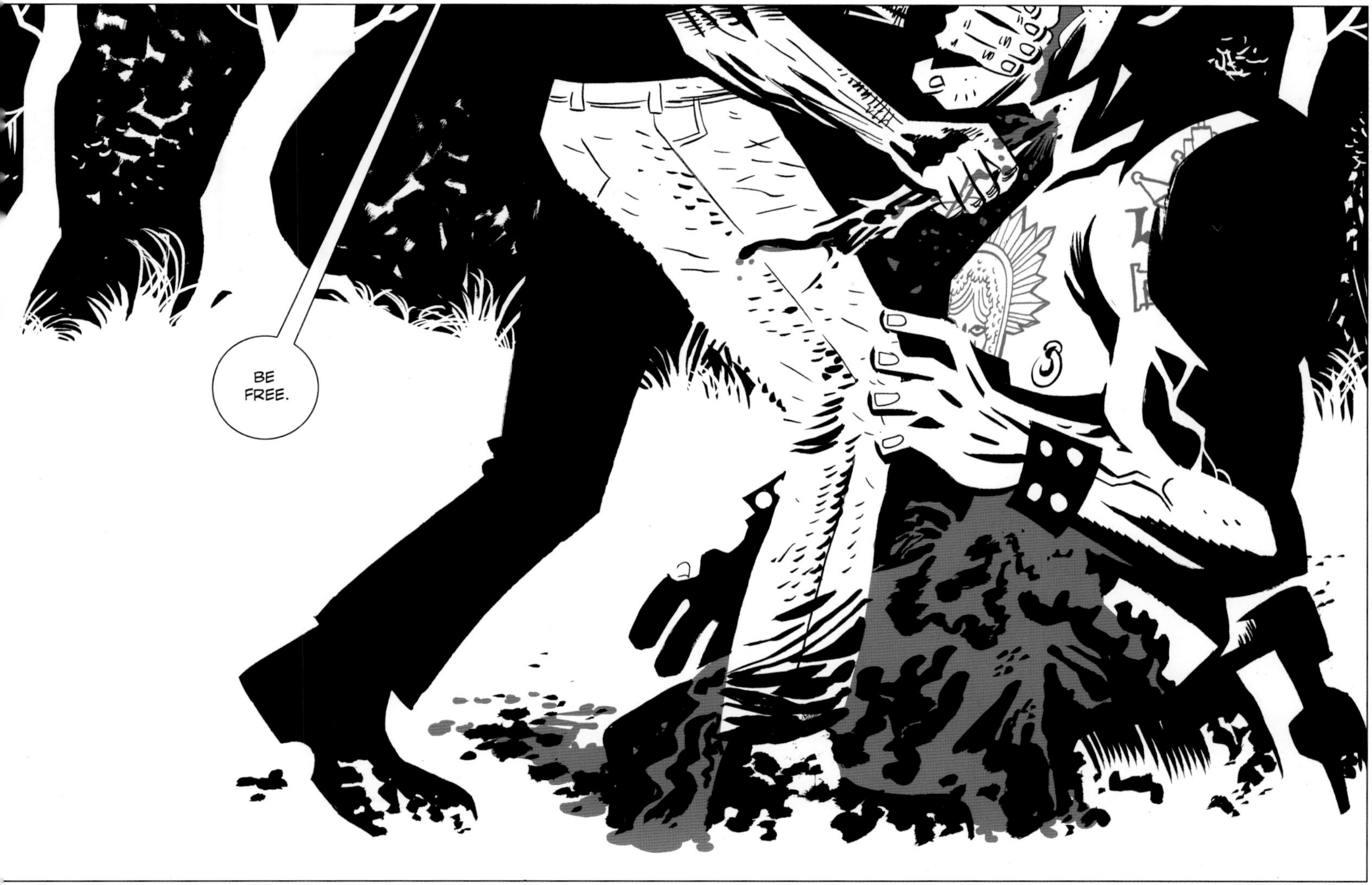
BE FREE.

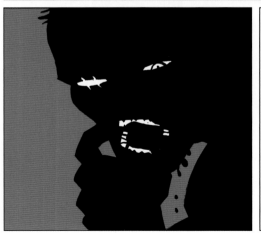

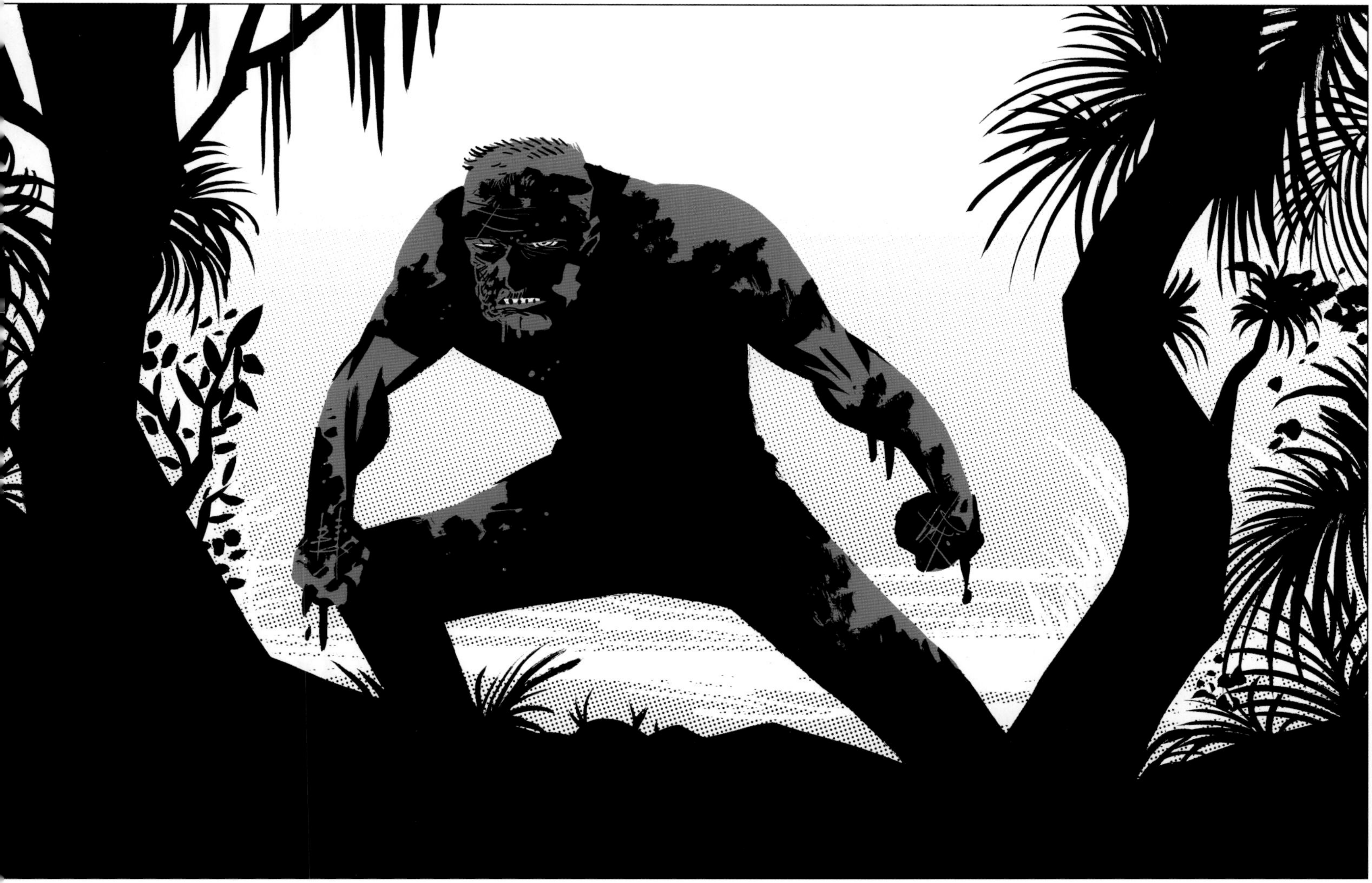

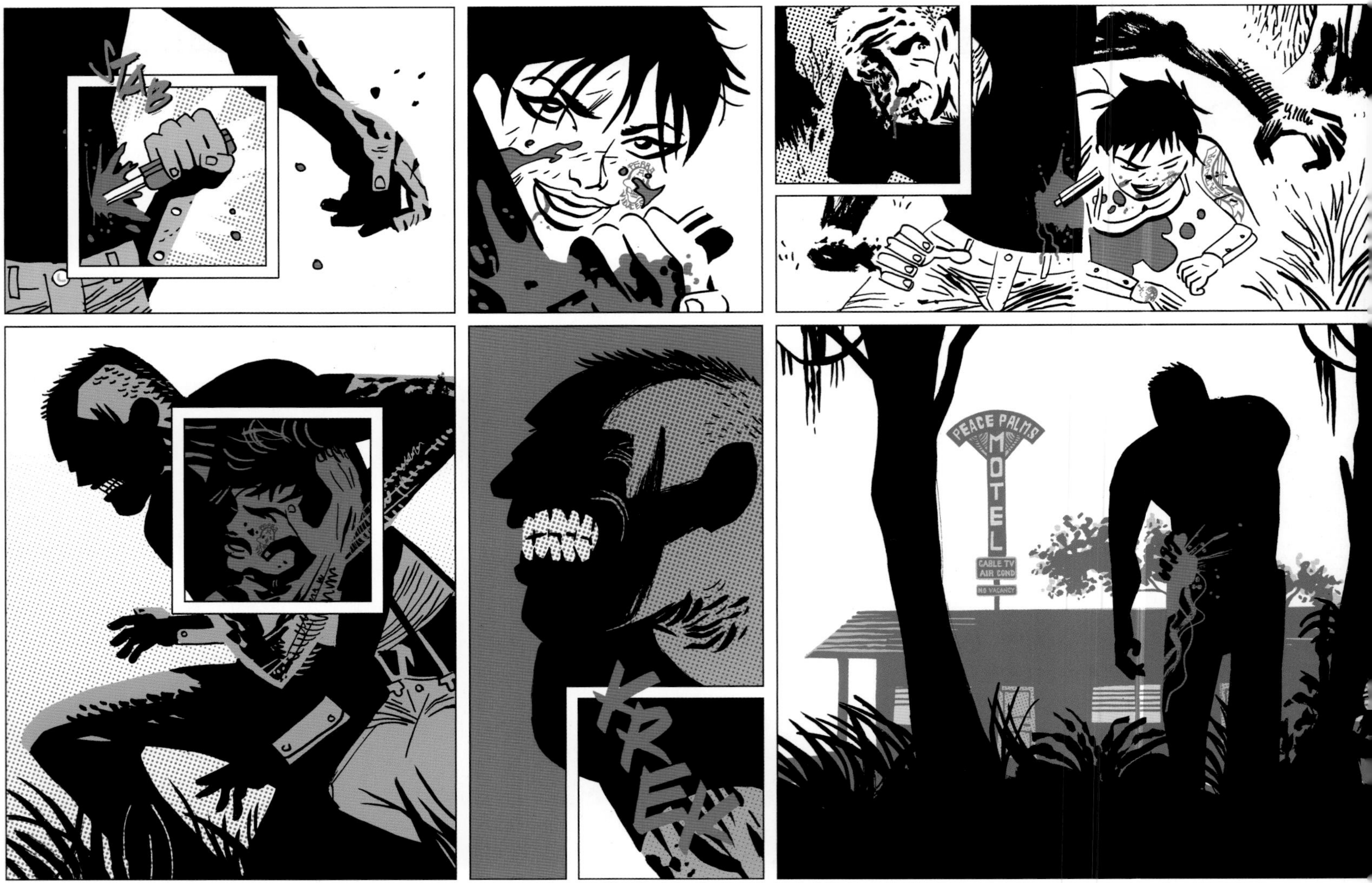
STAB
KREK
PEACE PALMS MOTEL
CABLE TV
AIR COND
NO VACANCY

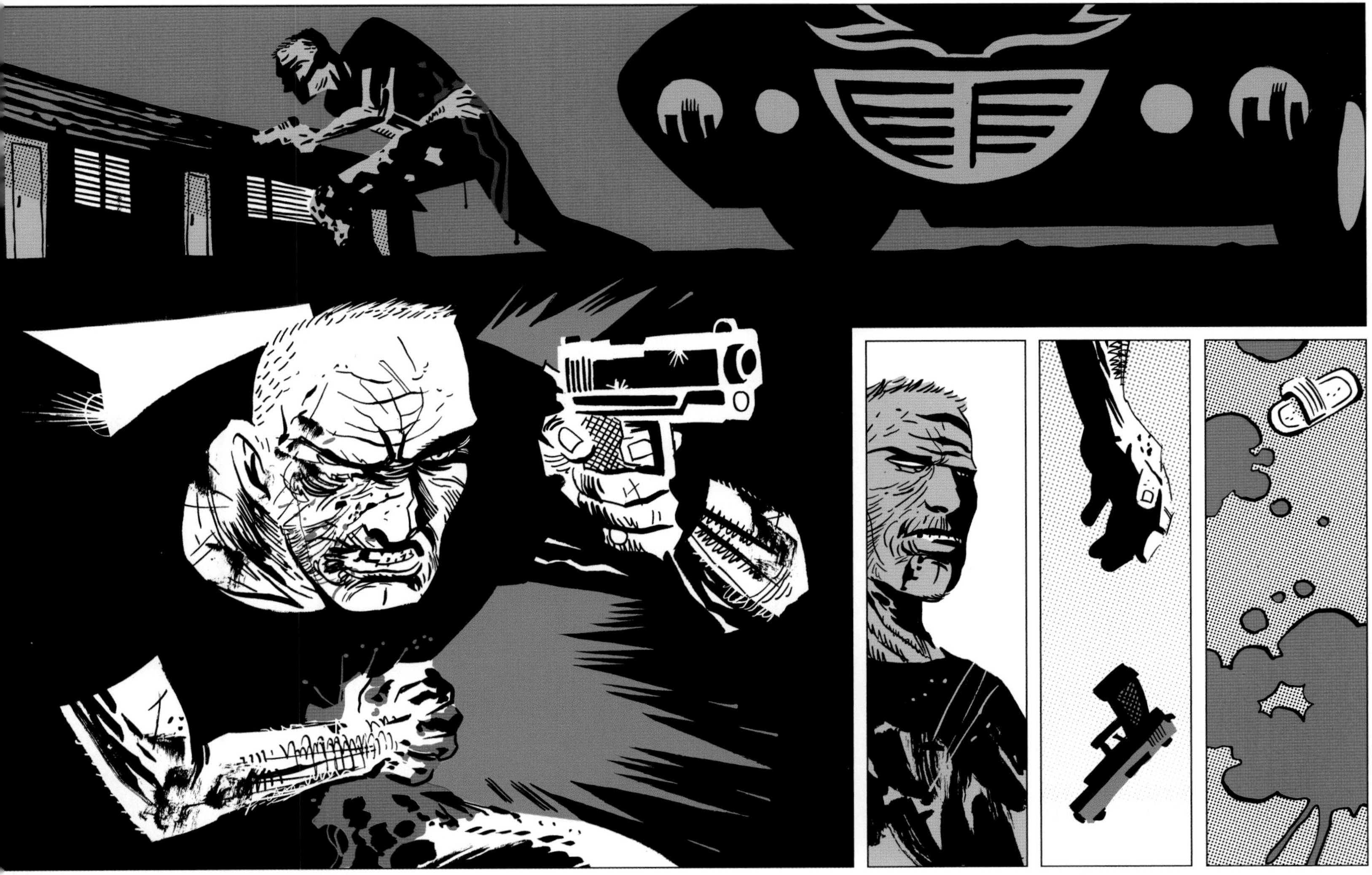

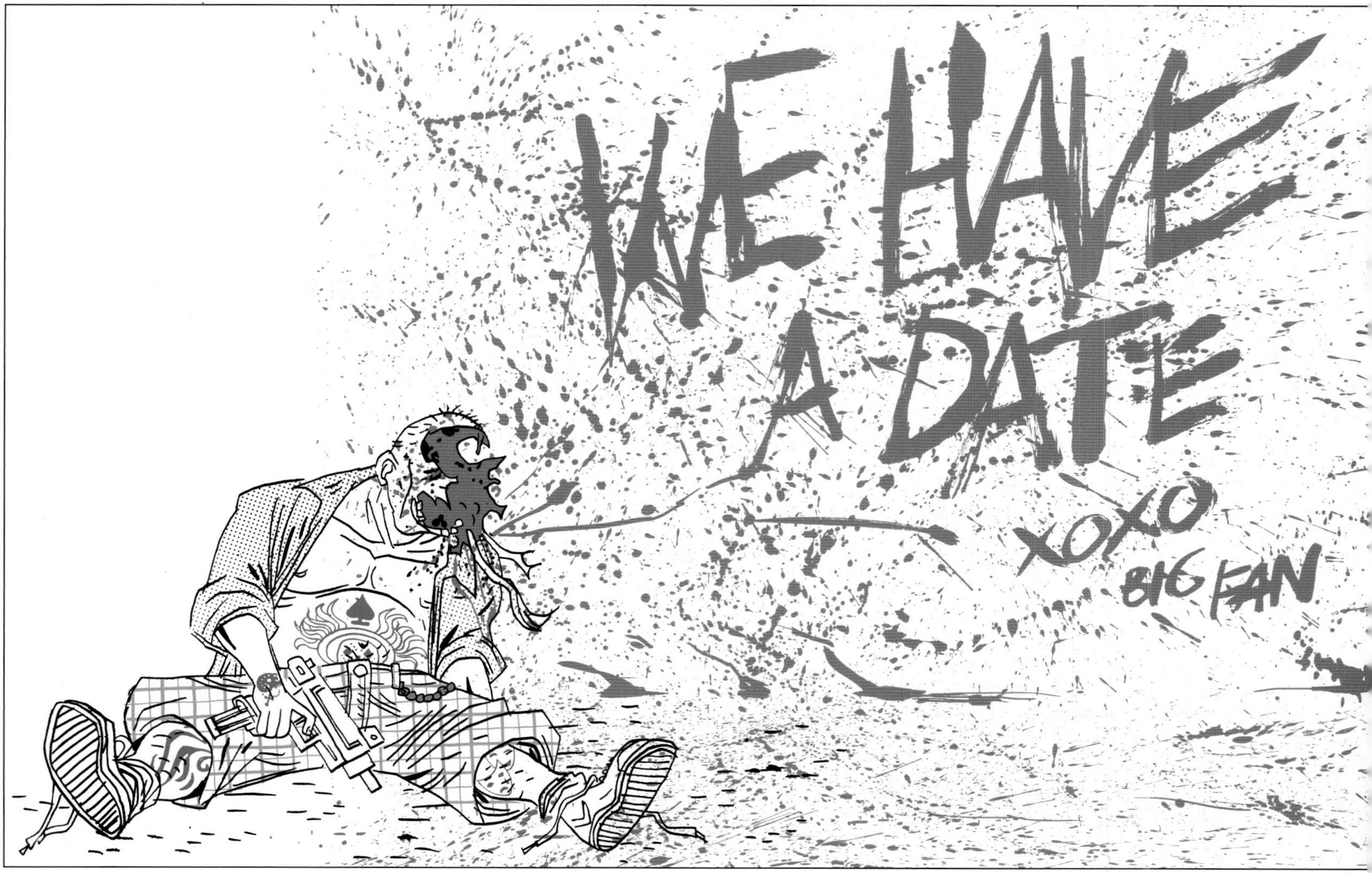
WE HAVE
A DATE
XOXO
BIG FAN

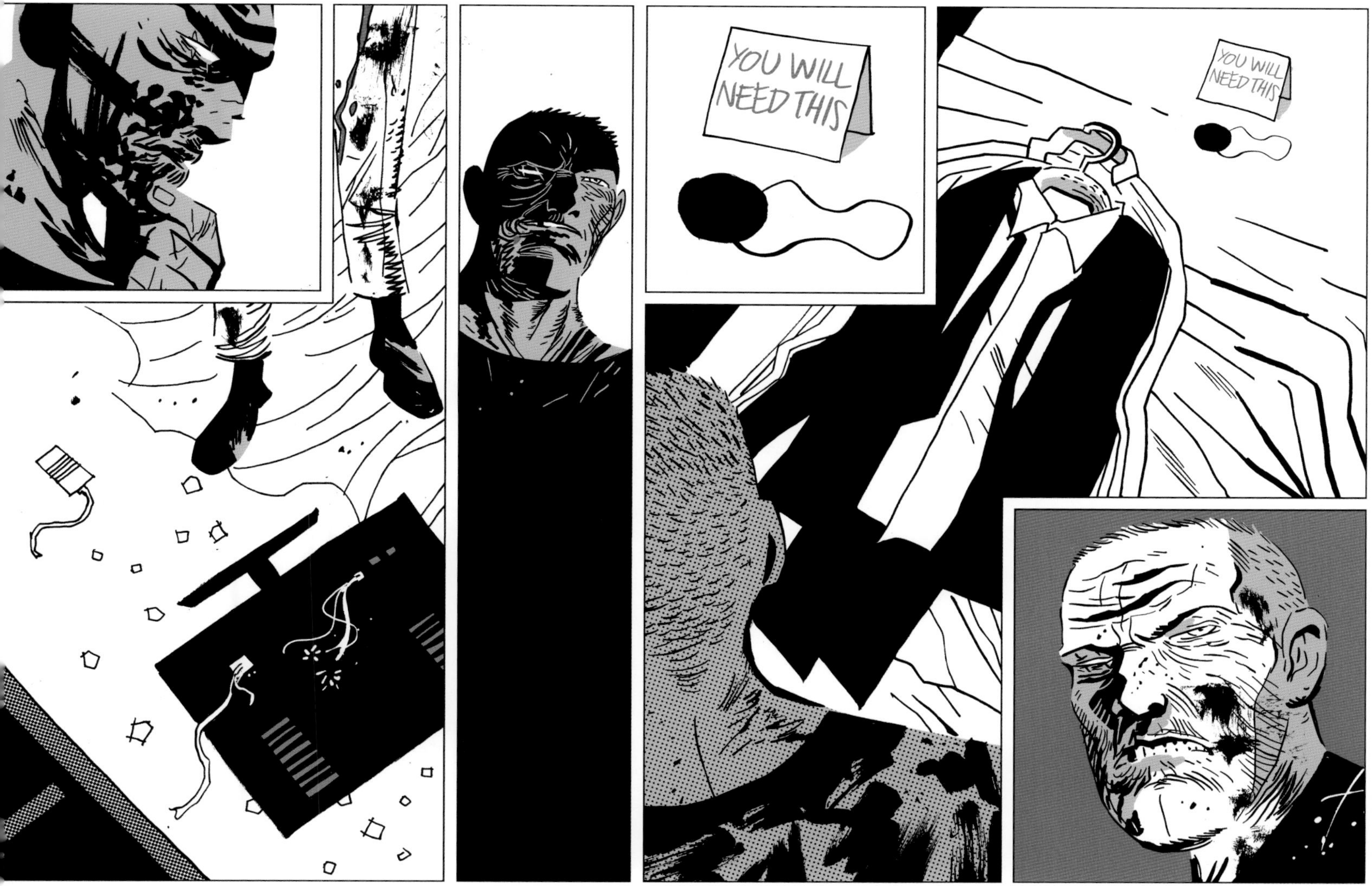
YOU WILL NEED THIS
YOU WILL NEED THIS

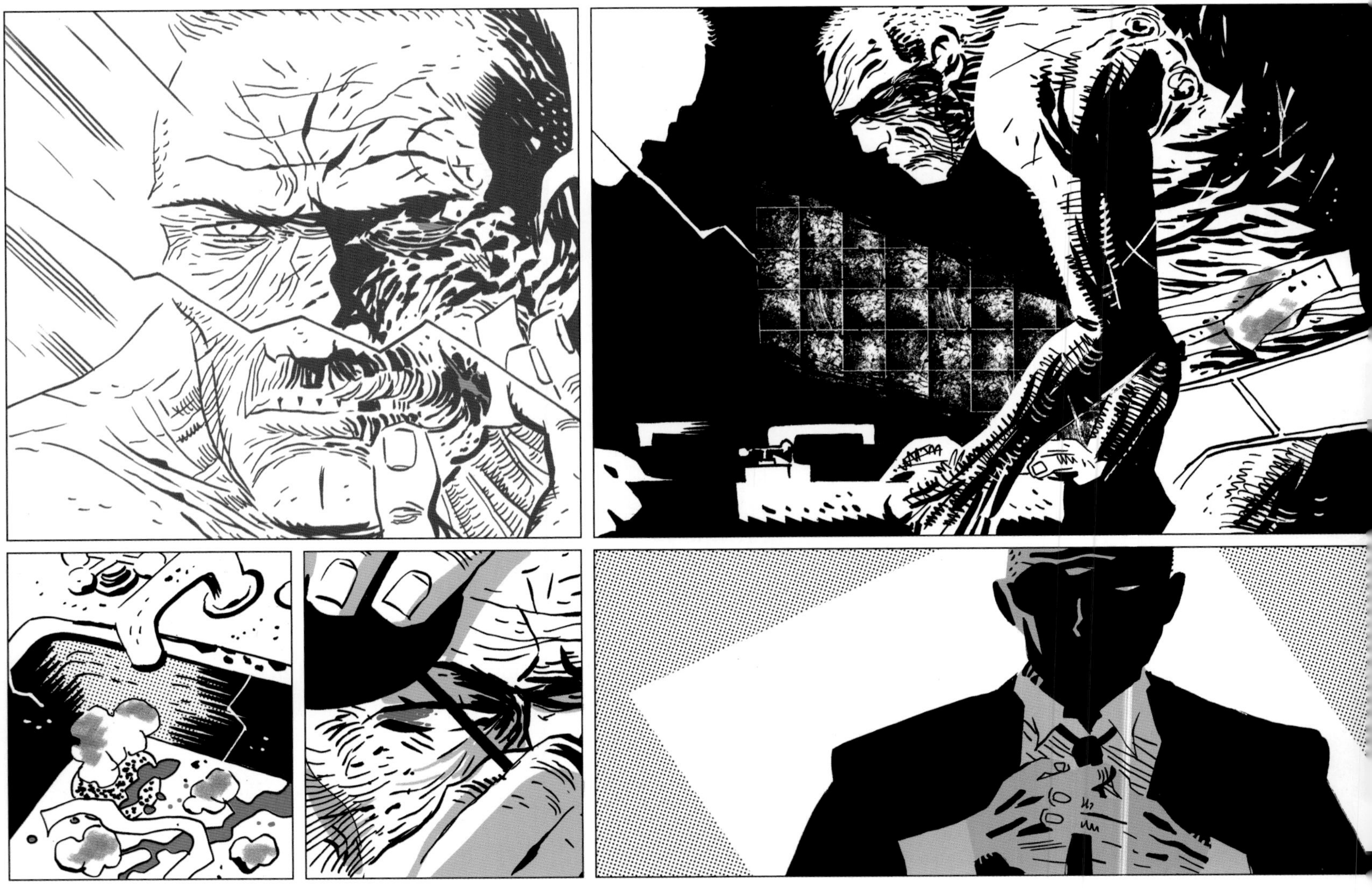

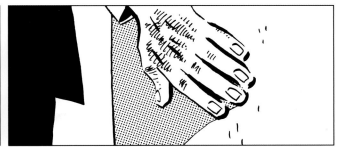

IT WILL BE GREAT, IGGY. ABSOLUTELY VINTAGE.

COME WITH THE GANG.

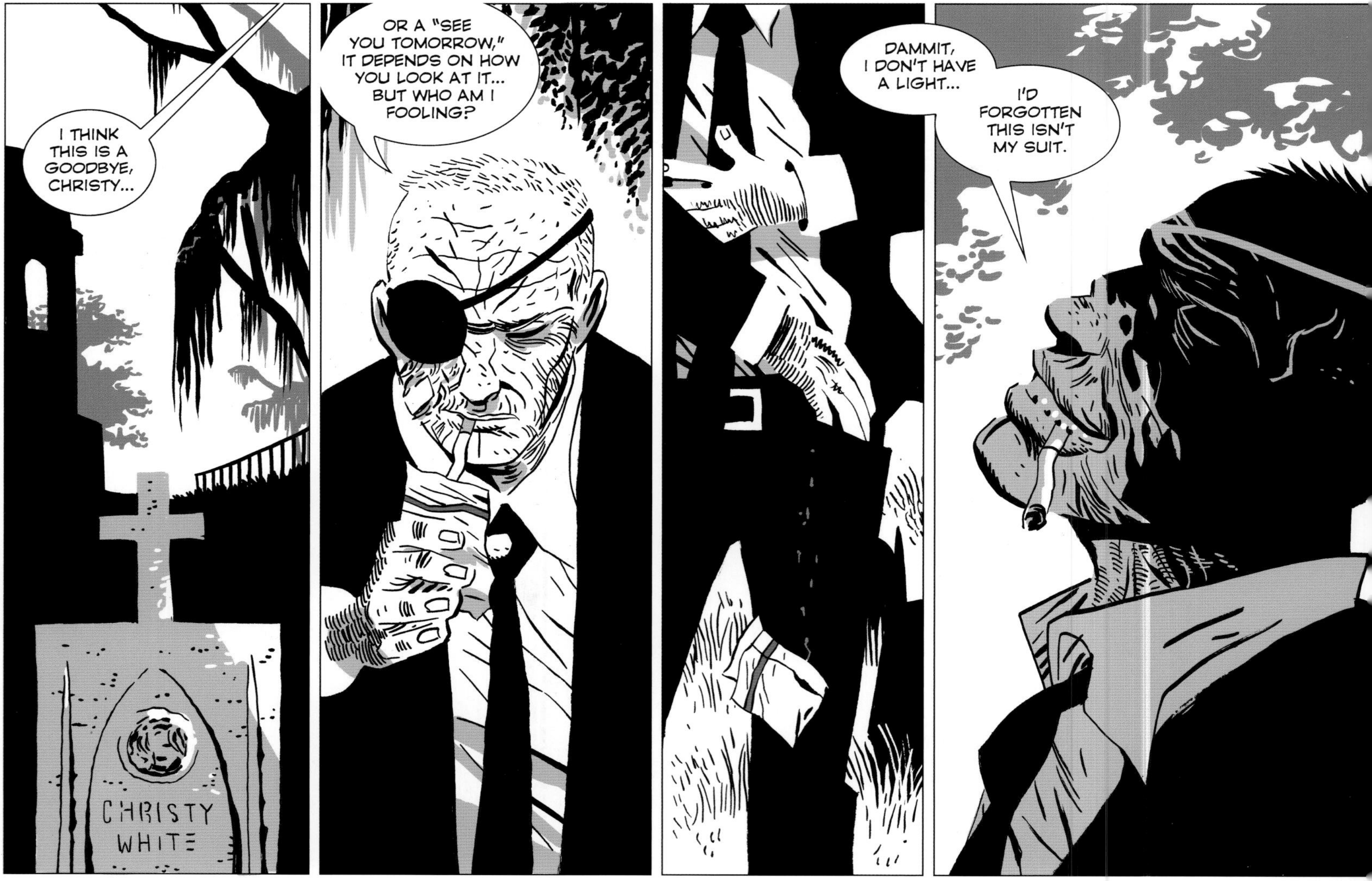
I THINK THIS IS A GOODBYE, CHRISTY...
CHRISTY WHITE
OR A "SEE YOU TOMORROW," IT DEPENDS ON HOW YOU LOOK AT IT... BUT WHO AM I FOOLING?
DAMMIT, I DON'T HAVE A LIGHT...
I'D FORGOTTEN THIS ISN'T MY SUIT.

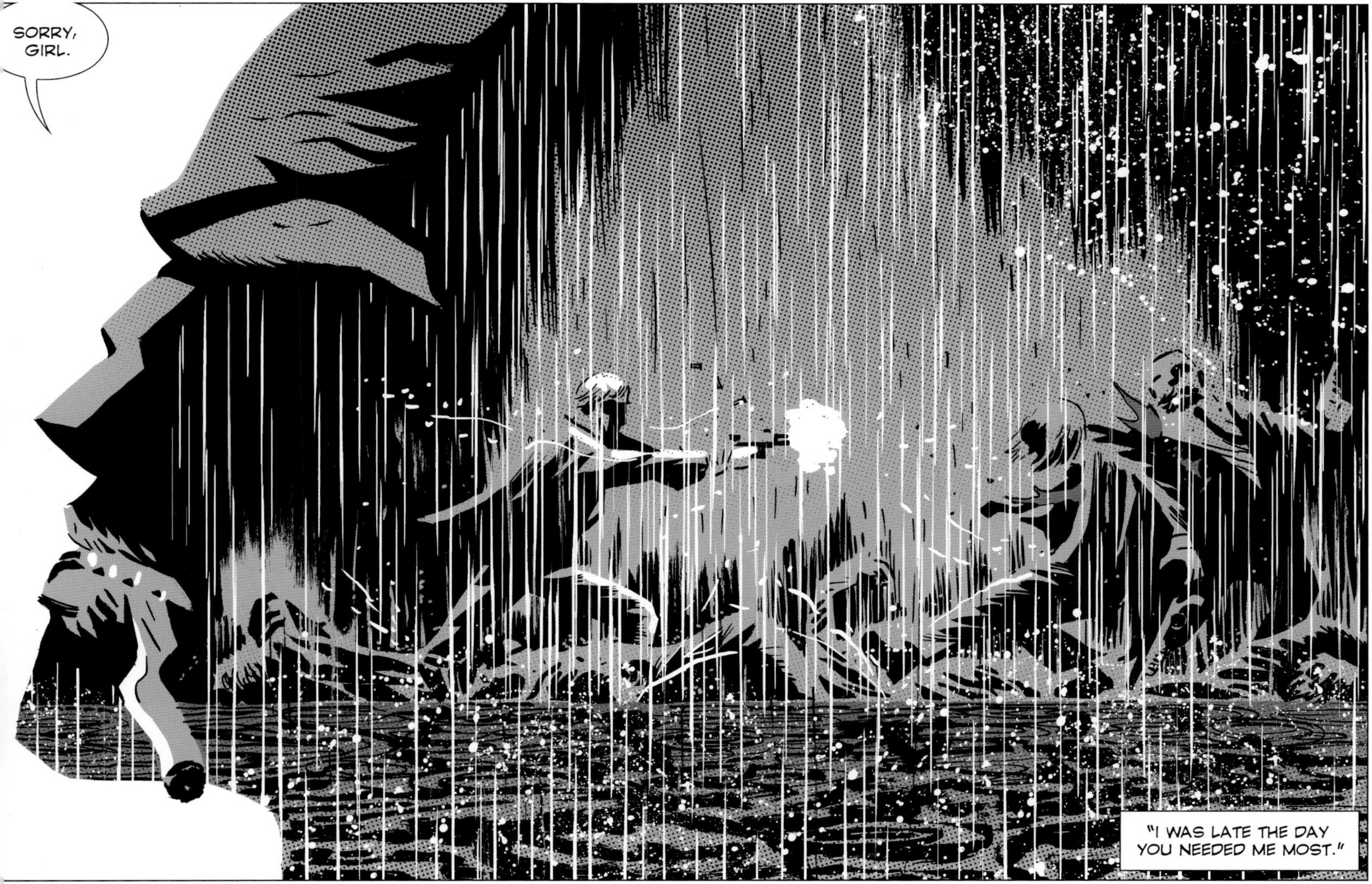
SORRY, GIRL.
"I WAS LATE THE DAY YOU NEEDED ME MOST."

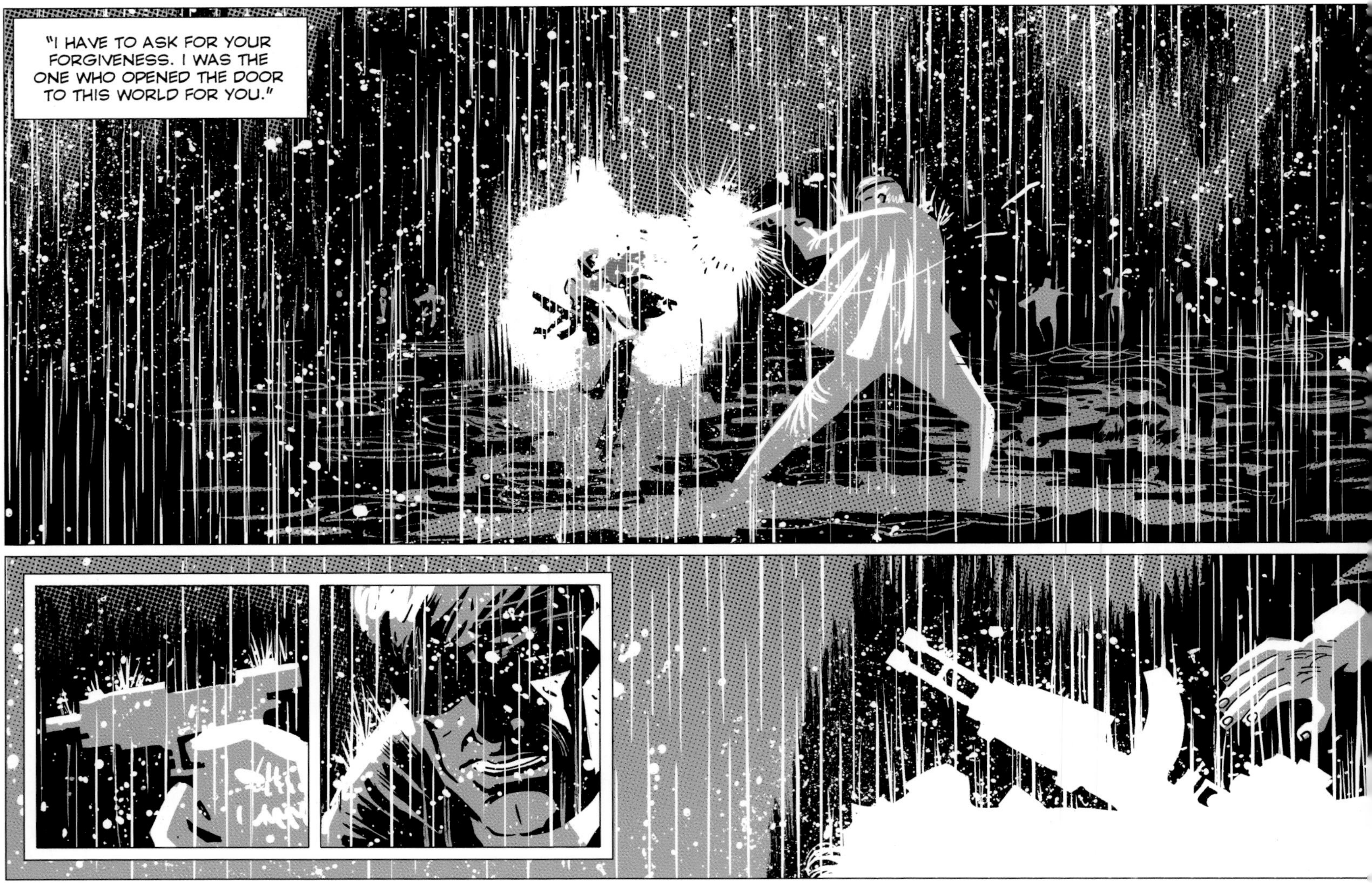
"I HAVE TO ASK FOR YOUR FORGIVENESS. I WAS THE ONE WHO OPENED THE DOOR TO THIS WORLD FOR YOU."

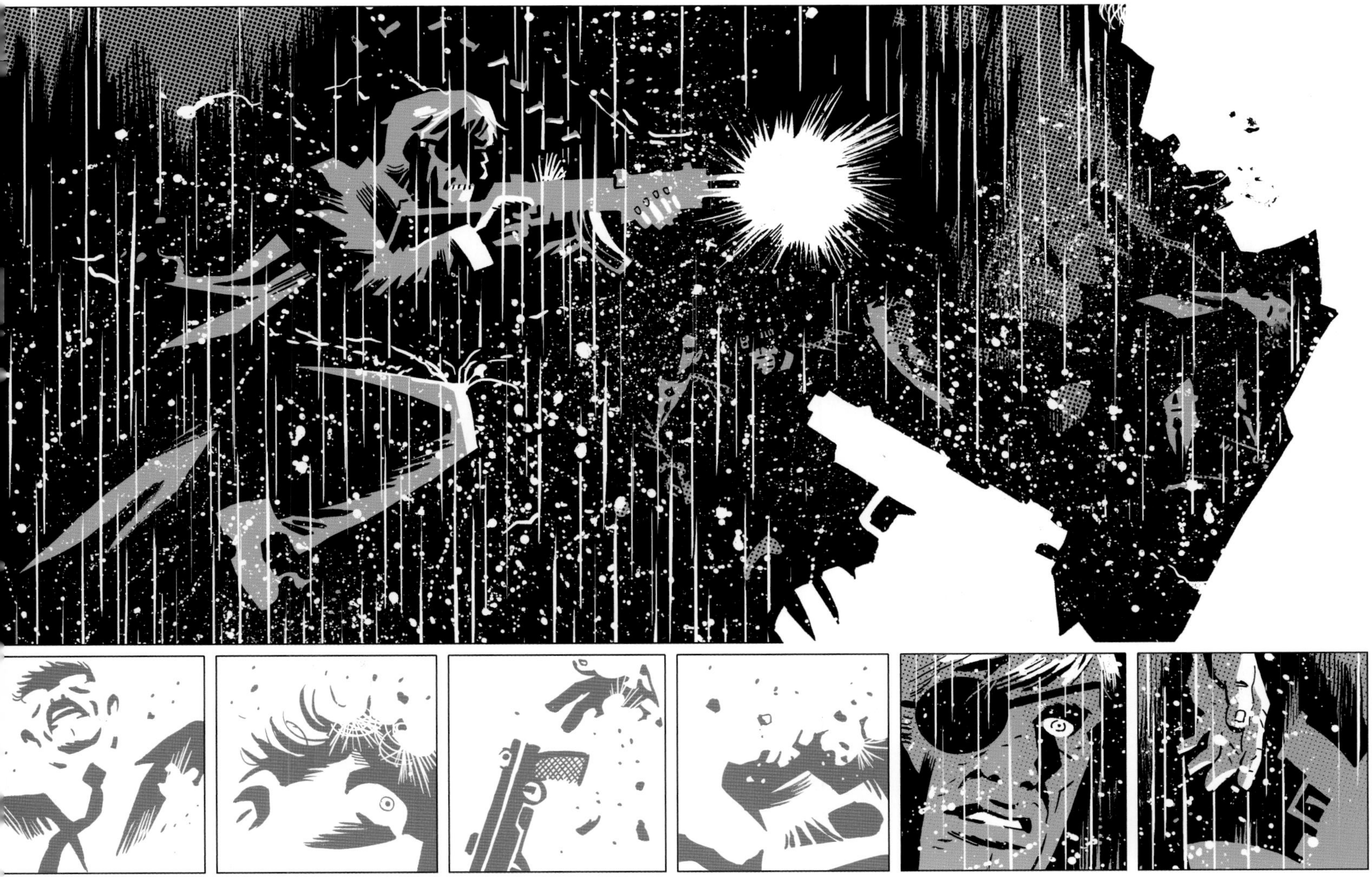

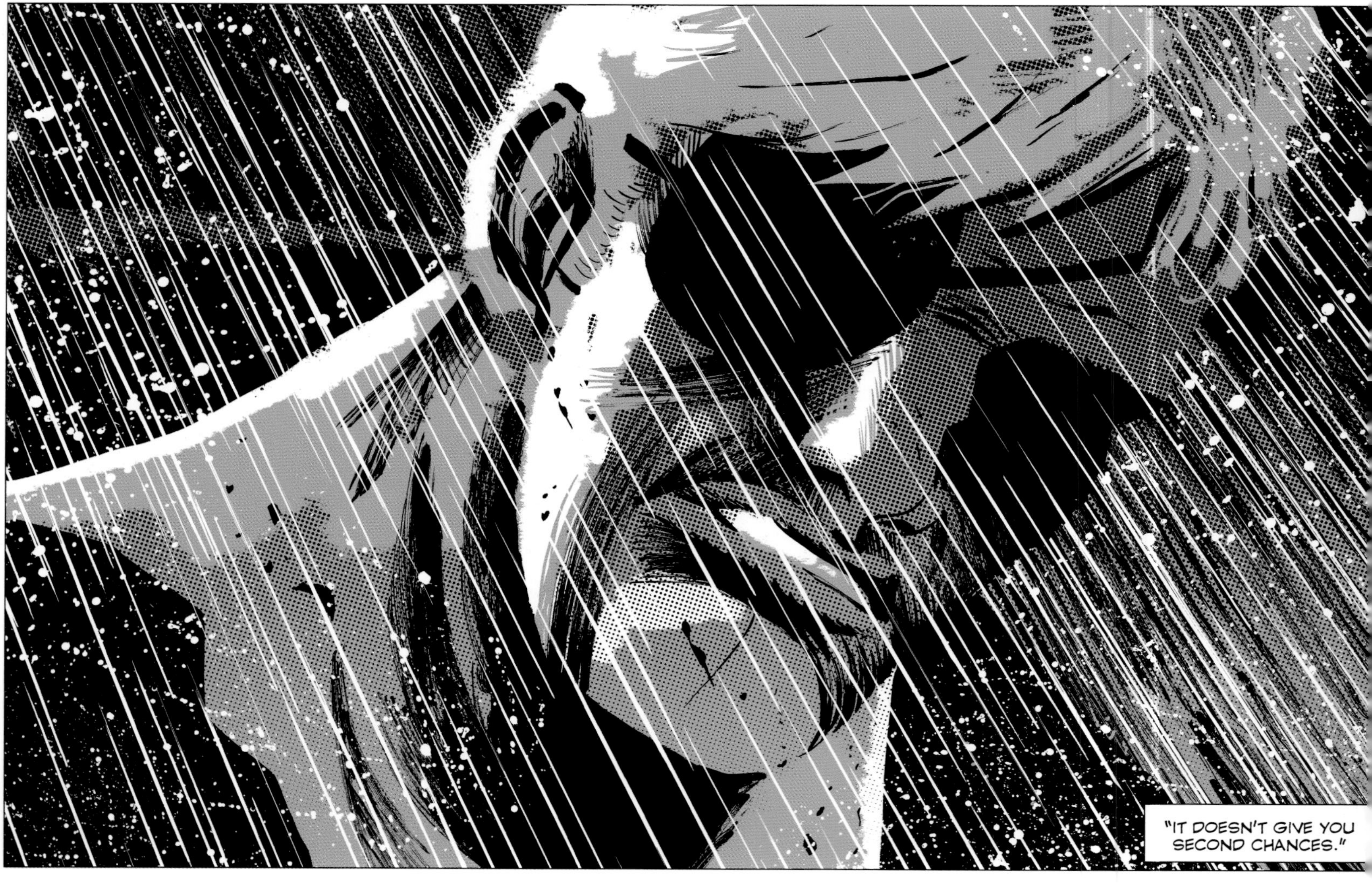
"IT DOESN'T GIVE YOU SECOND CHANCES."

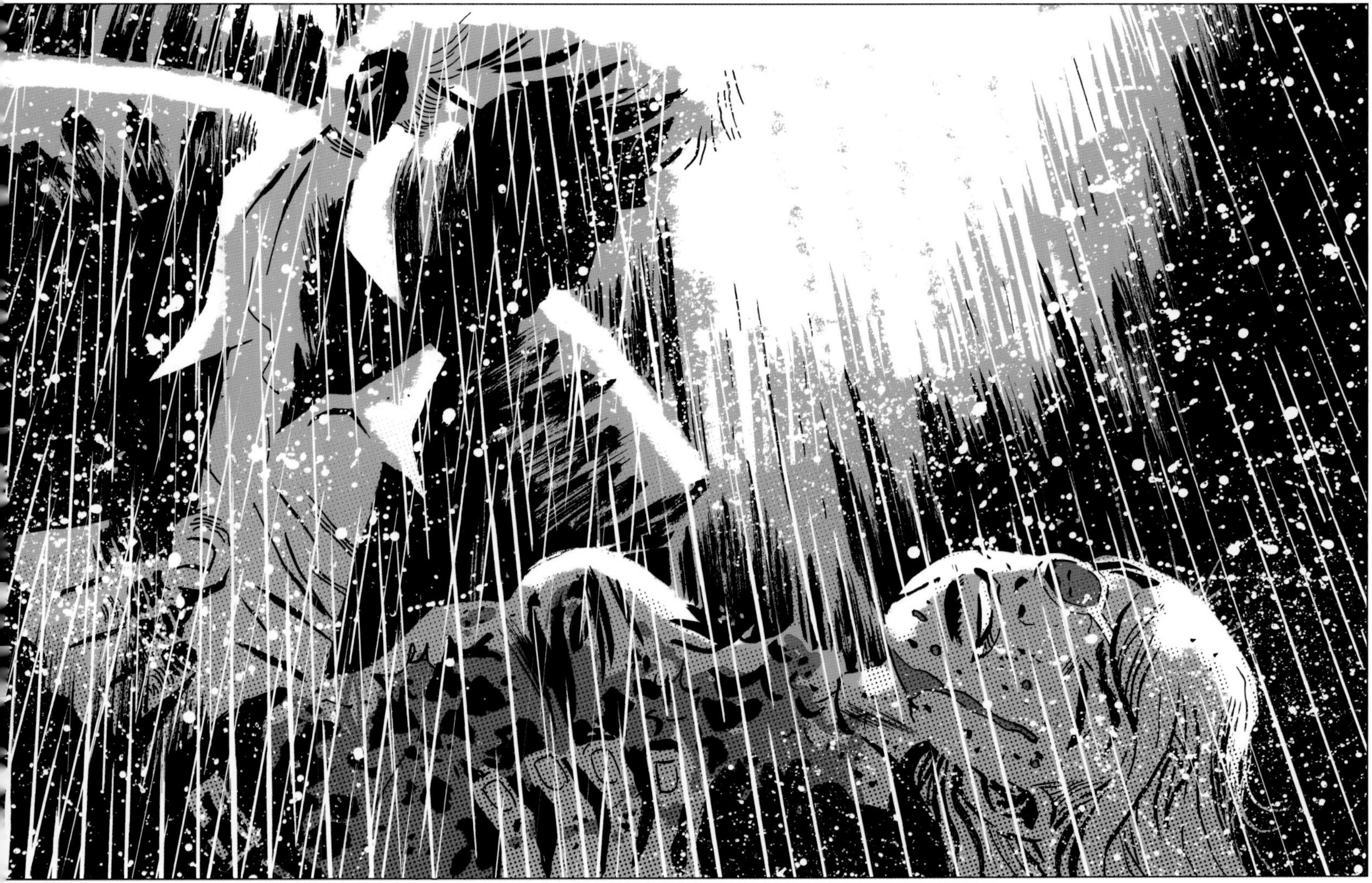

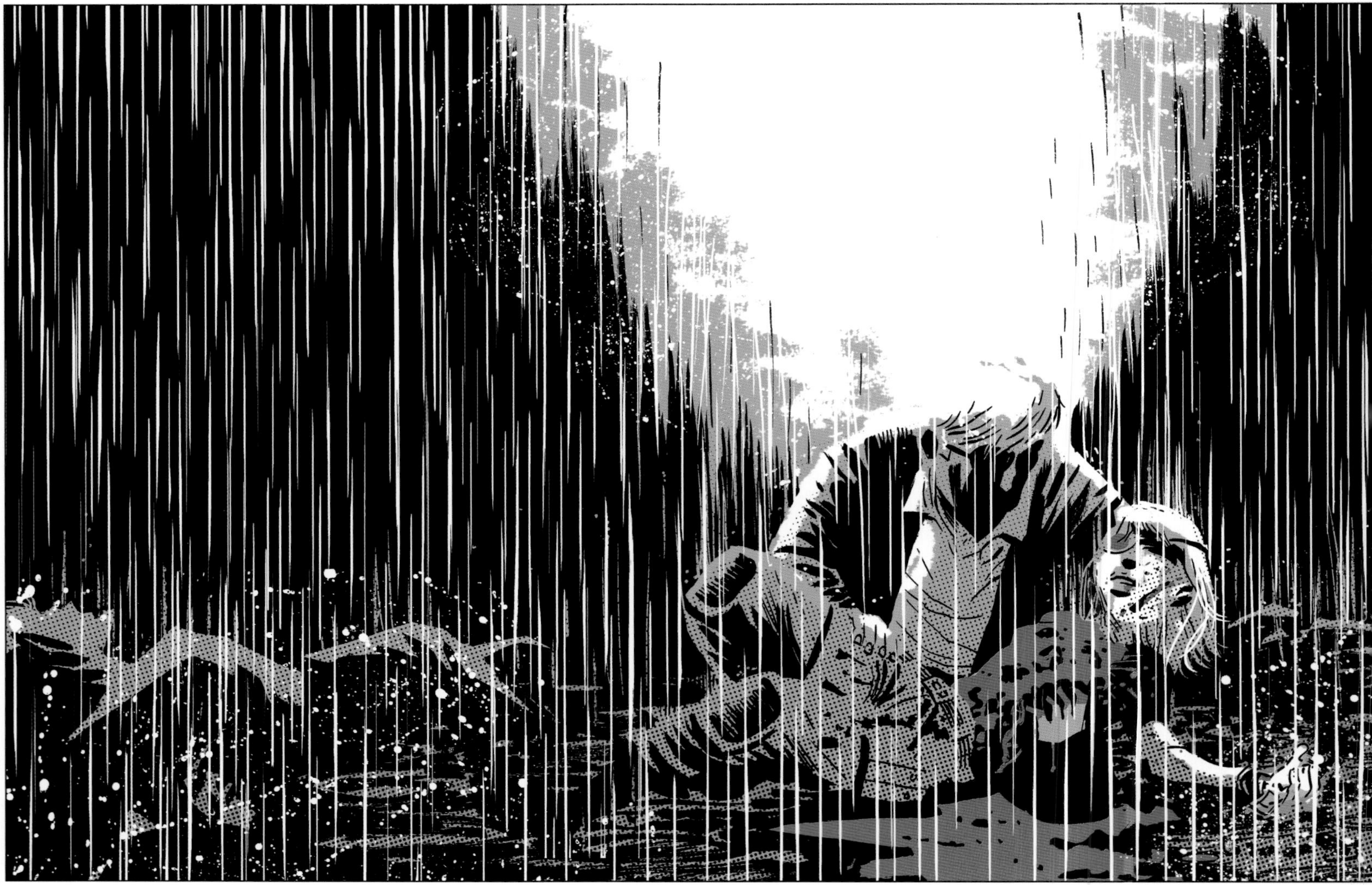

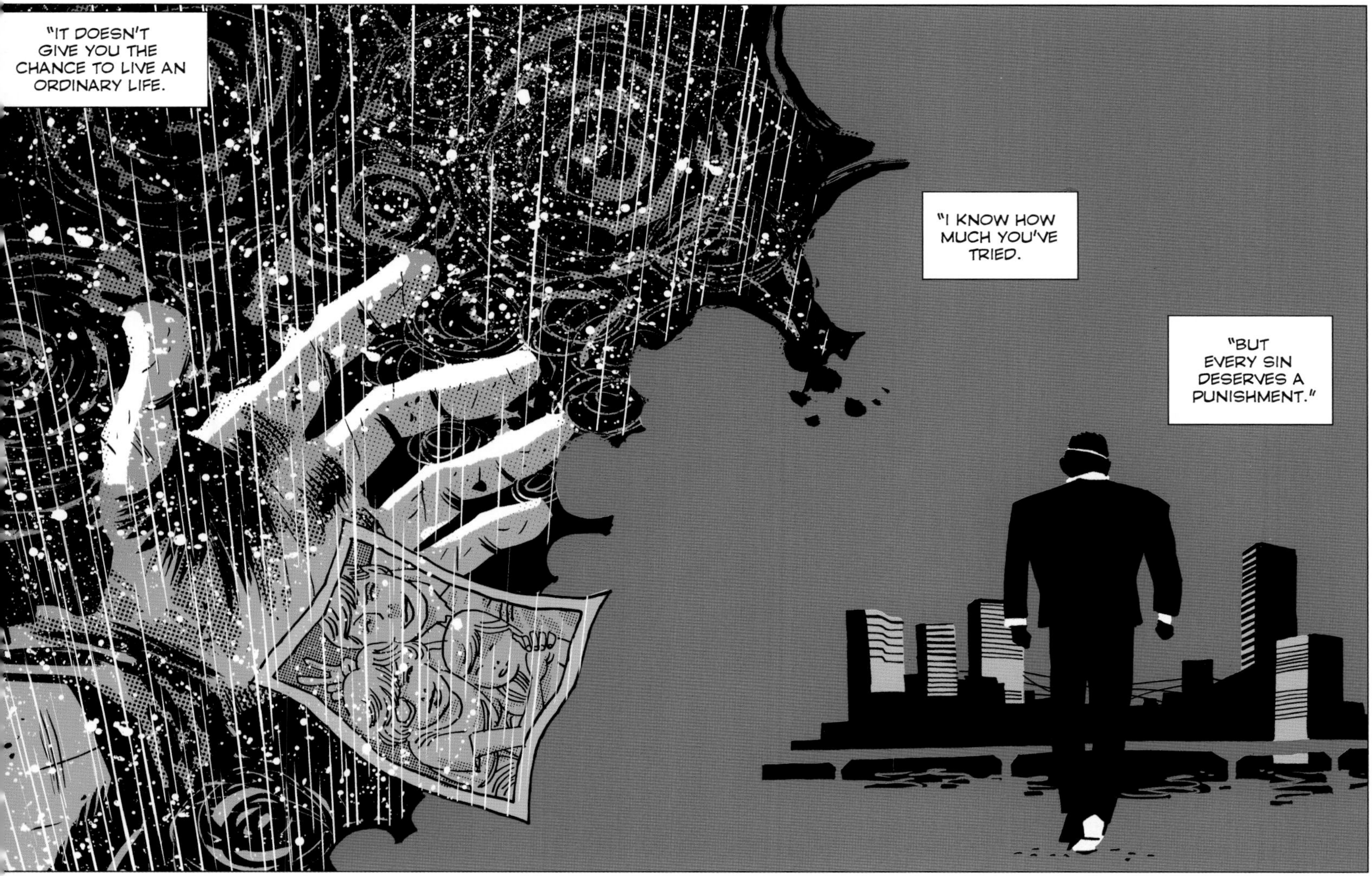
"IT DOESN'T GIVE YOU THE CHANCE TO LIVE AN ORDINARY LIFE.
"I KNOW HOW MUCH YOU'VE TRIED.
"BUT EVERY SIN DESERVES A PUNISHMENT."

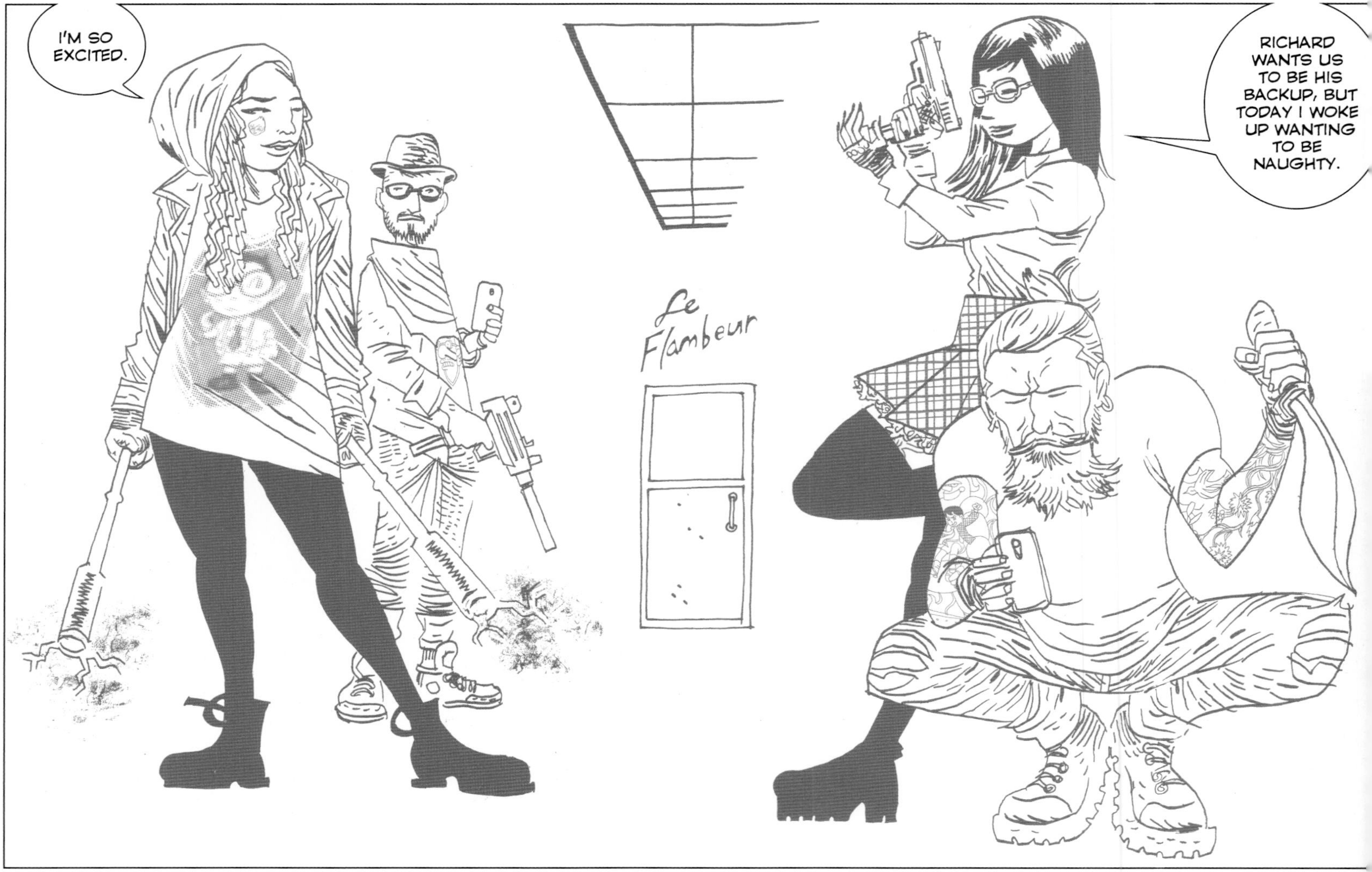
I'M SO EXCITED.
Le Flambeur
RICHARD WANTS US TO BE HIS BACKUP, BUT TODAY I WOKE UP WANTING TO BE NAUGHTY.

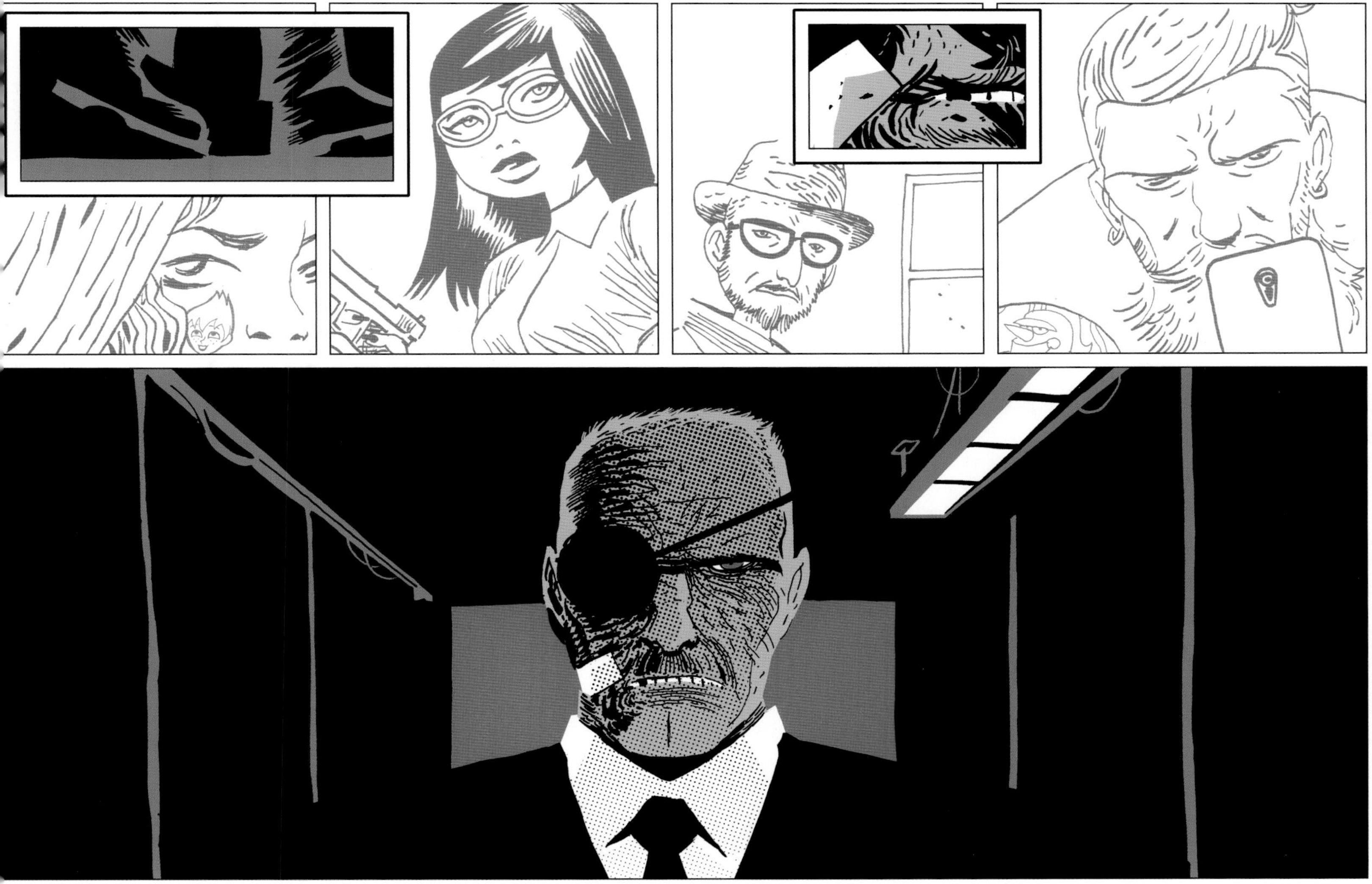

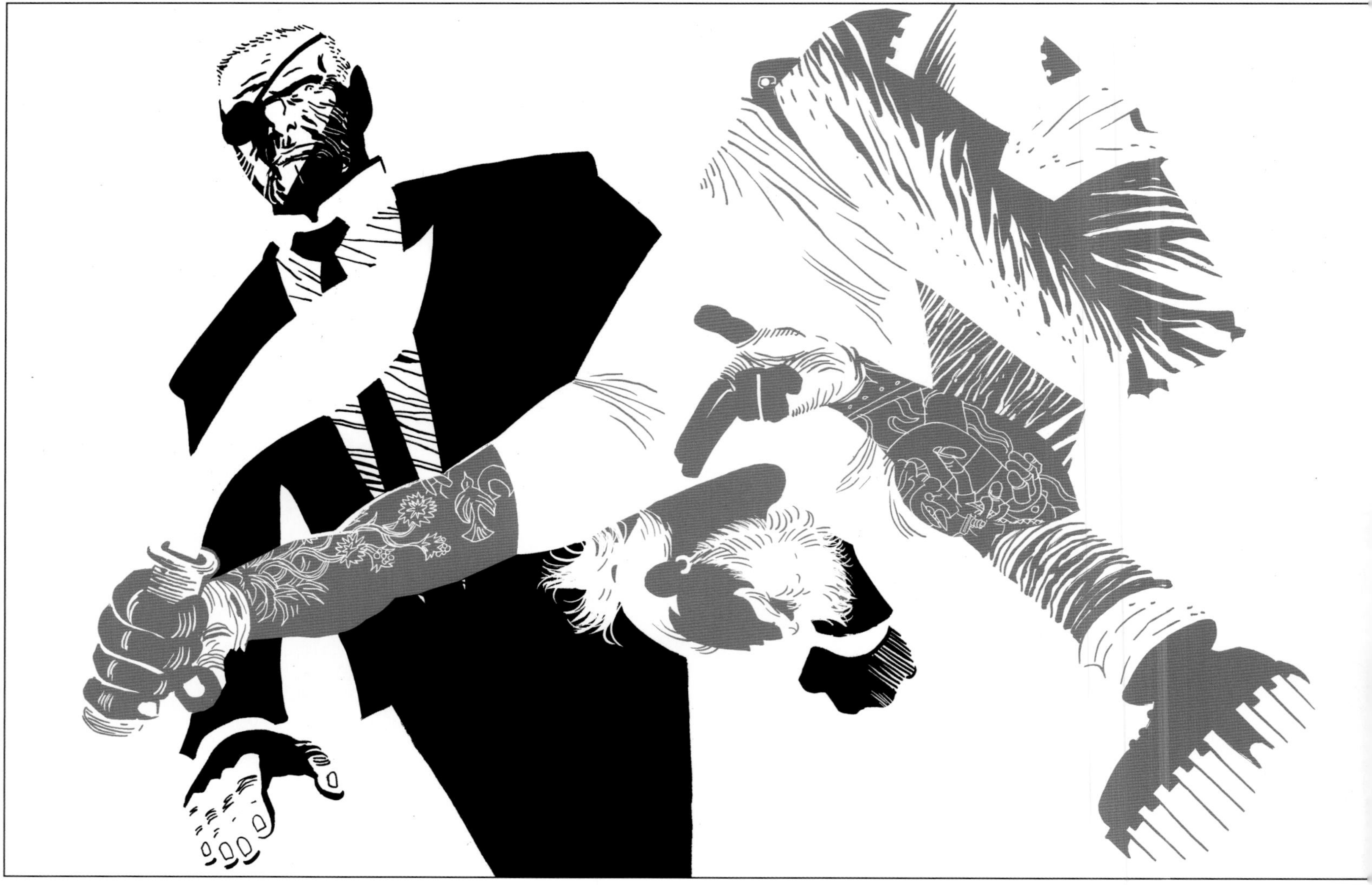

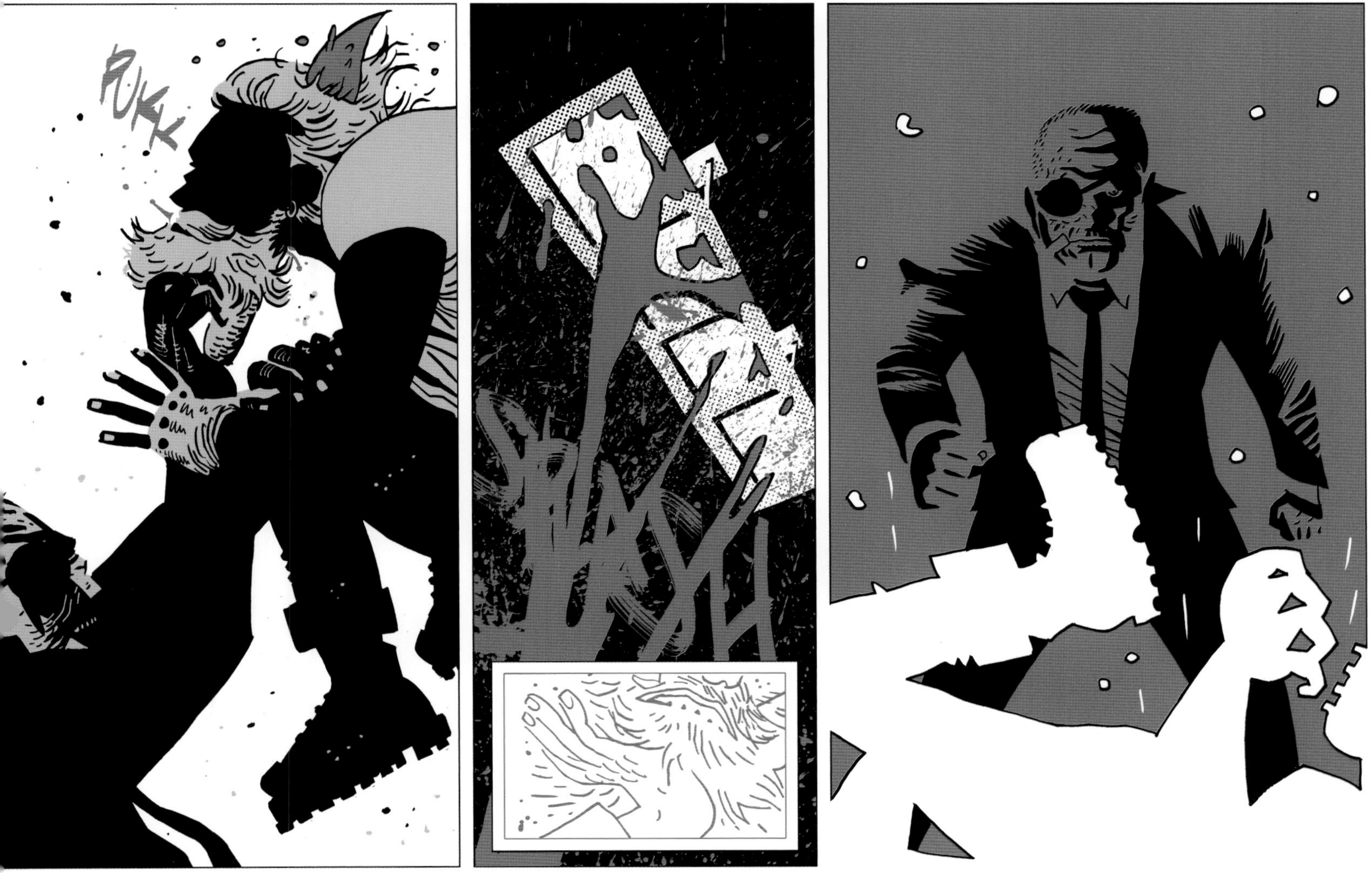
PUKK
SPLASH

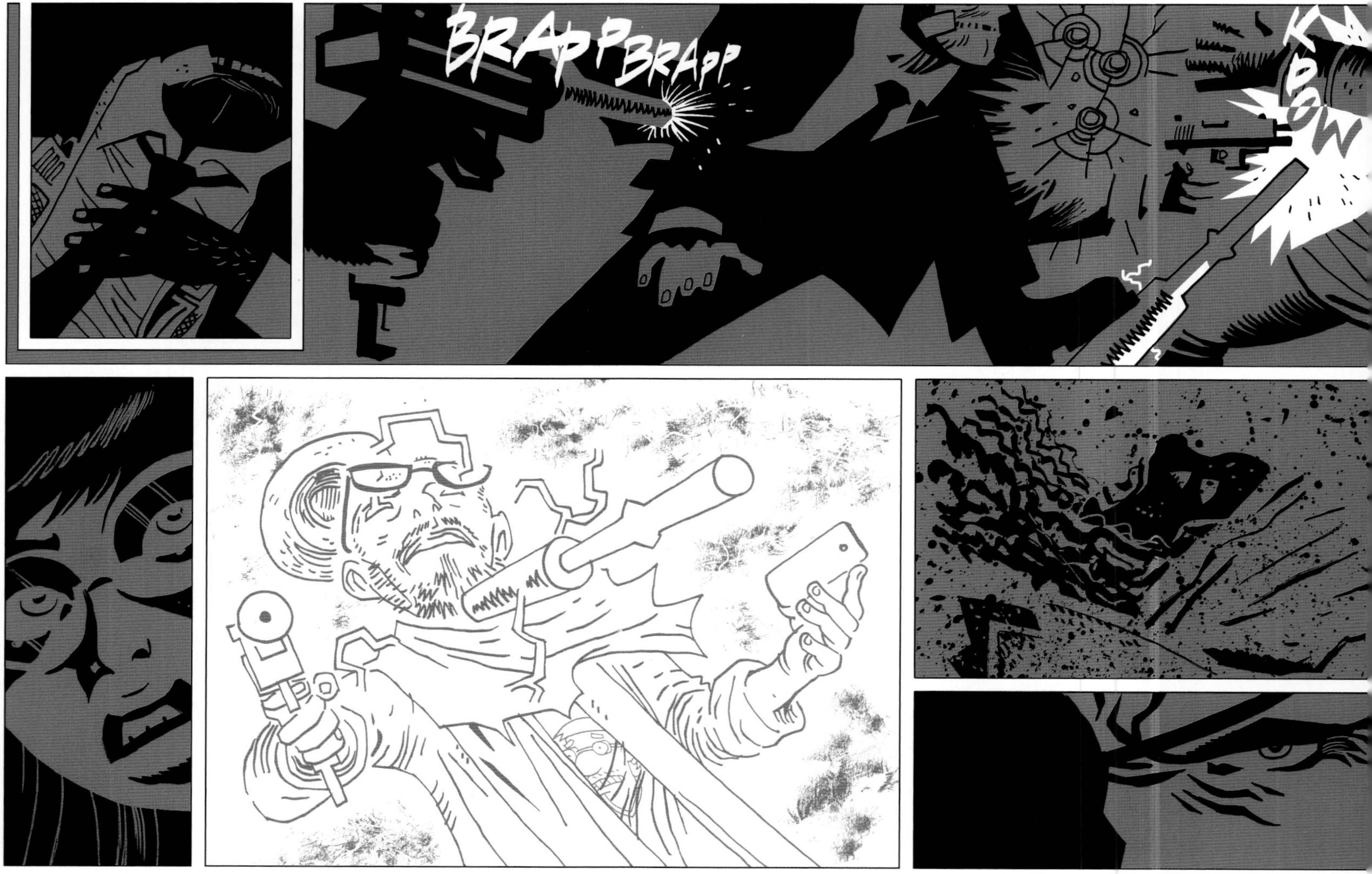
BRAPP BRAPP

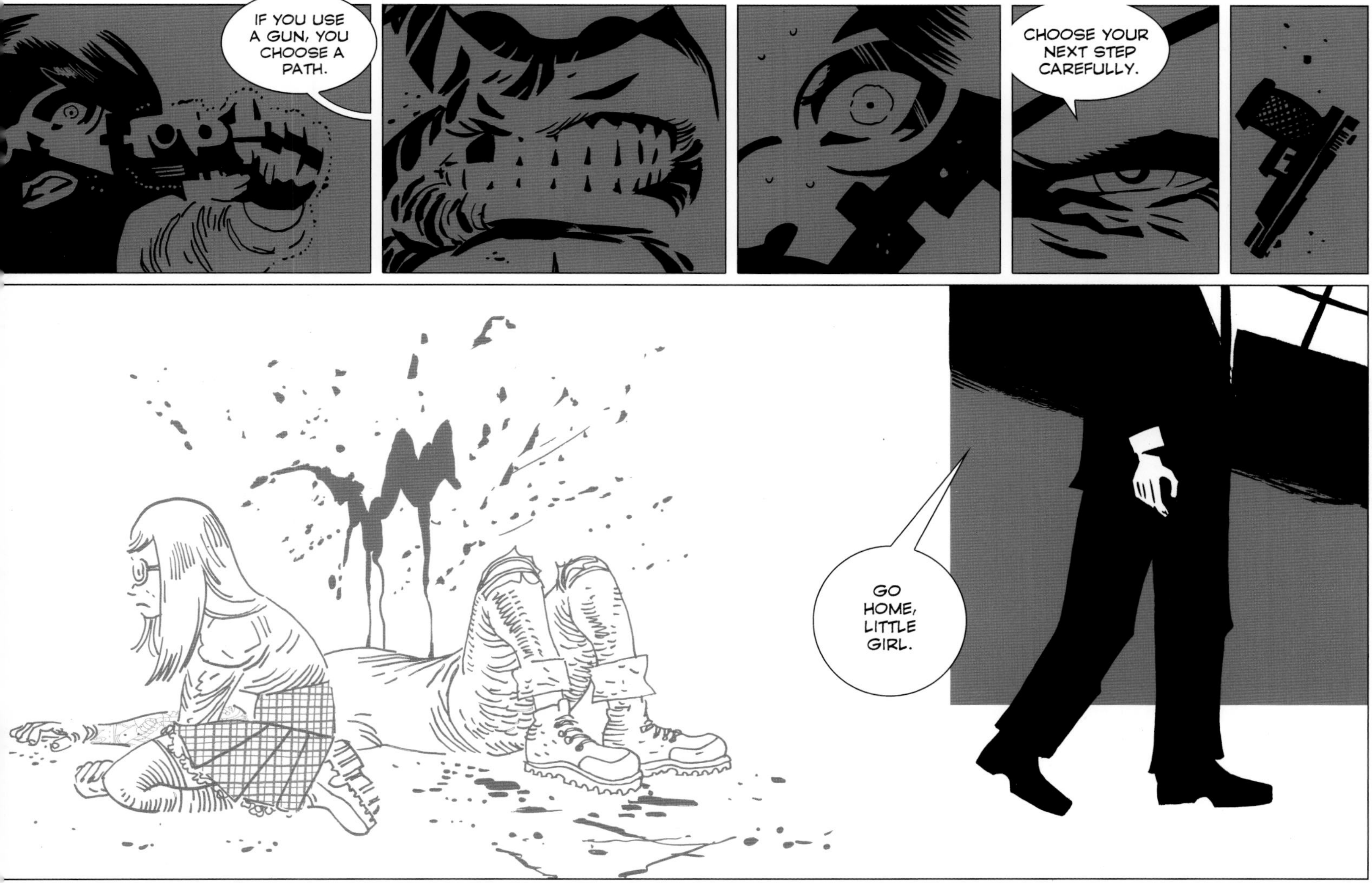
IF YOU USE A GUN, YOU CHOOSE A PATH.
CHOOSE YOUR NEXT STEP CAREFULLY.
GO HOME, LITTLE GIRL.

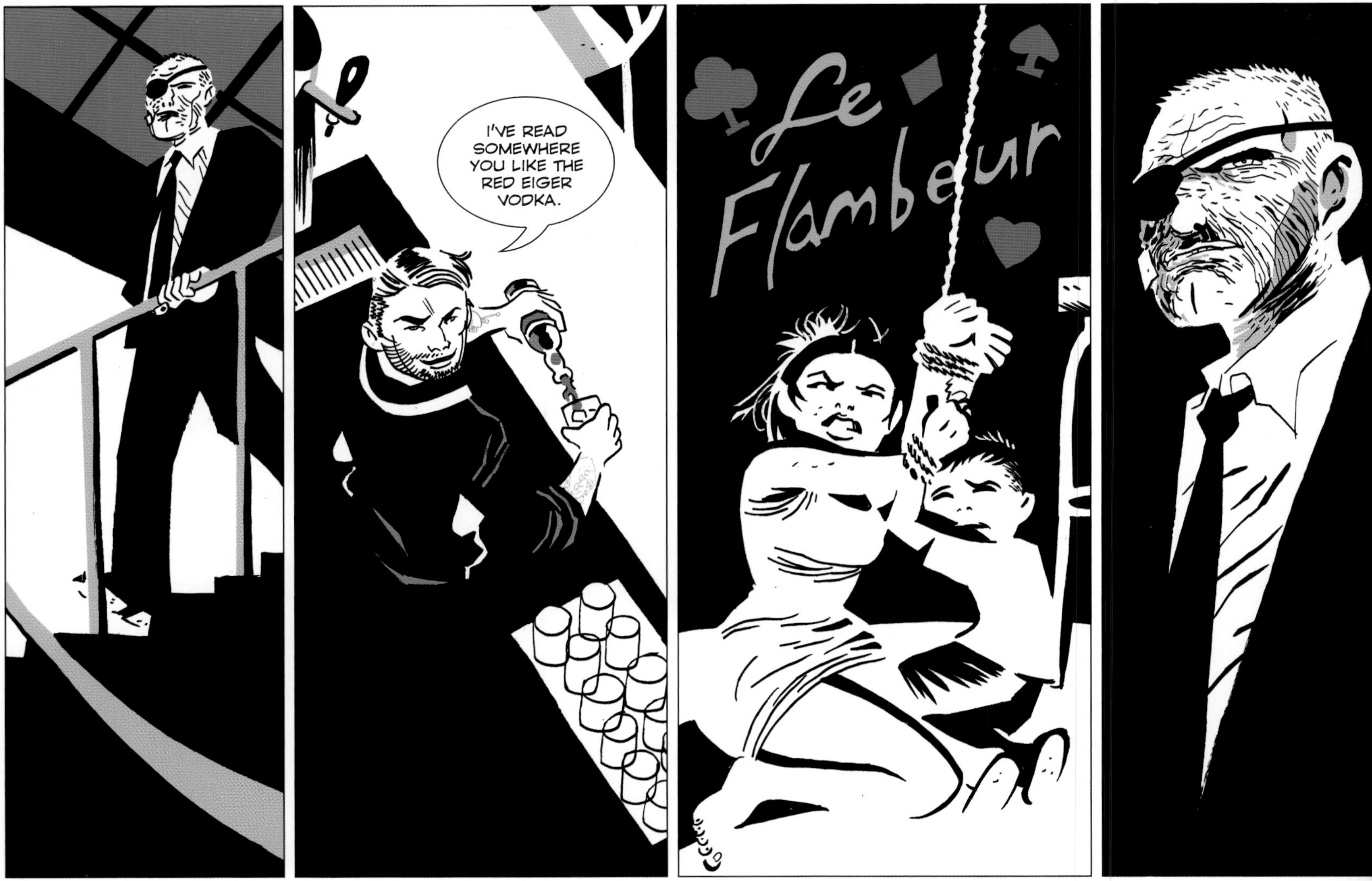
I'VE READ SOMEWHERE YOU LIKE THE RED EIGER VODKA.
Le Flambeur

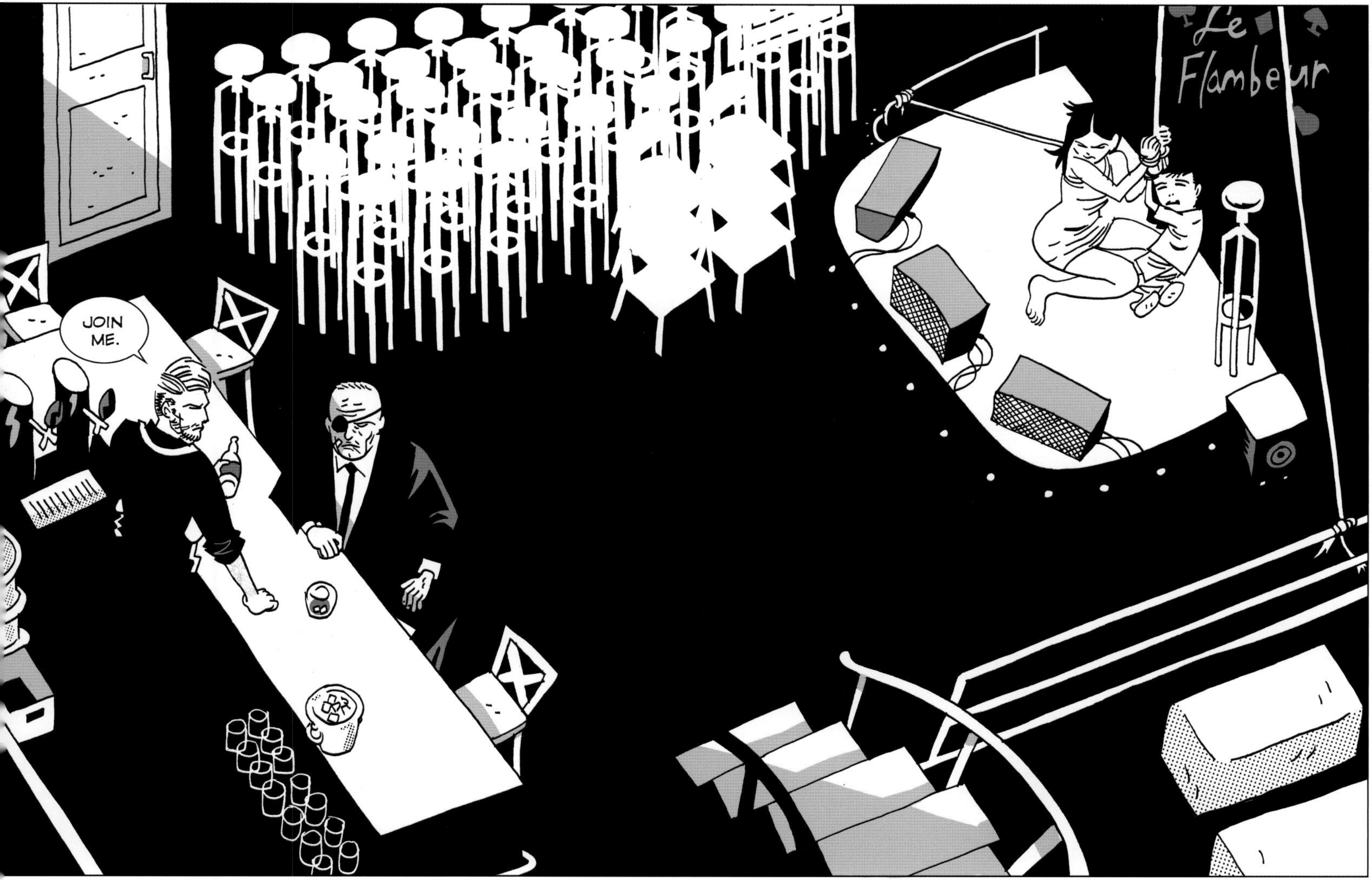
JOIN ME.
Le Flambeur

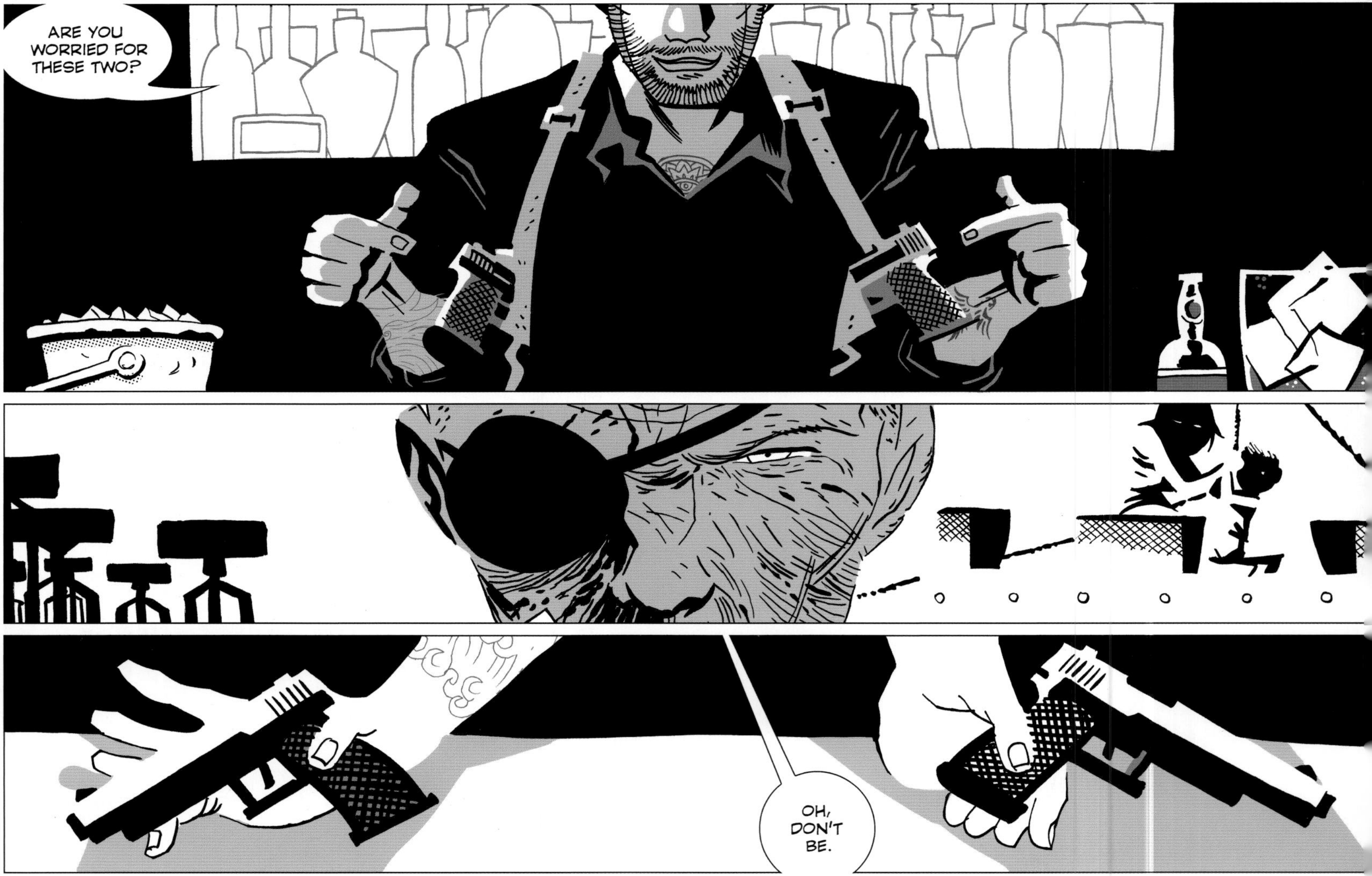
ARE YOU WORRIED FOR THESE TWO?
OH, DON'T BE.

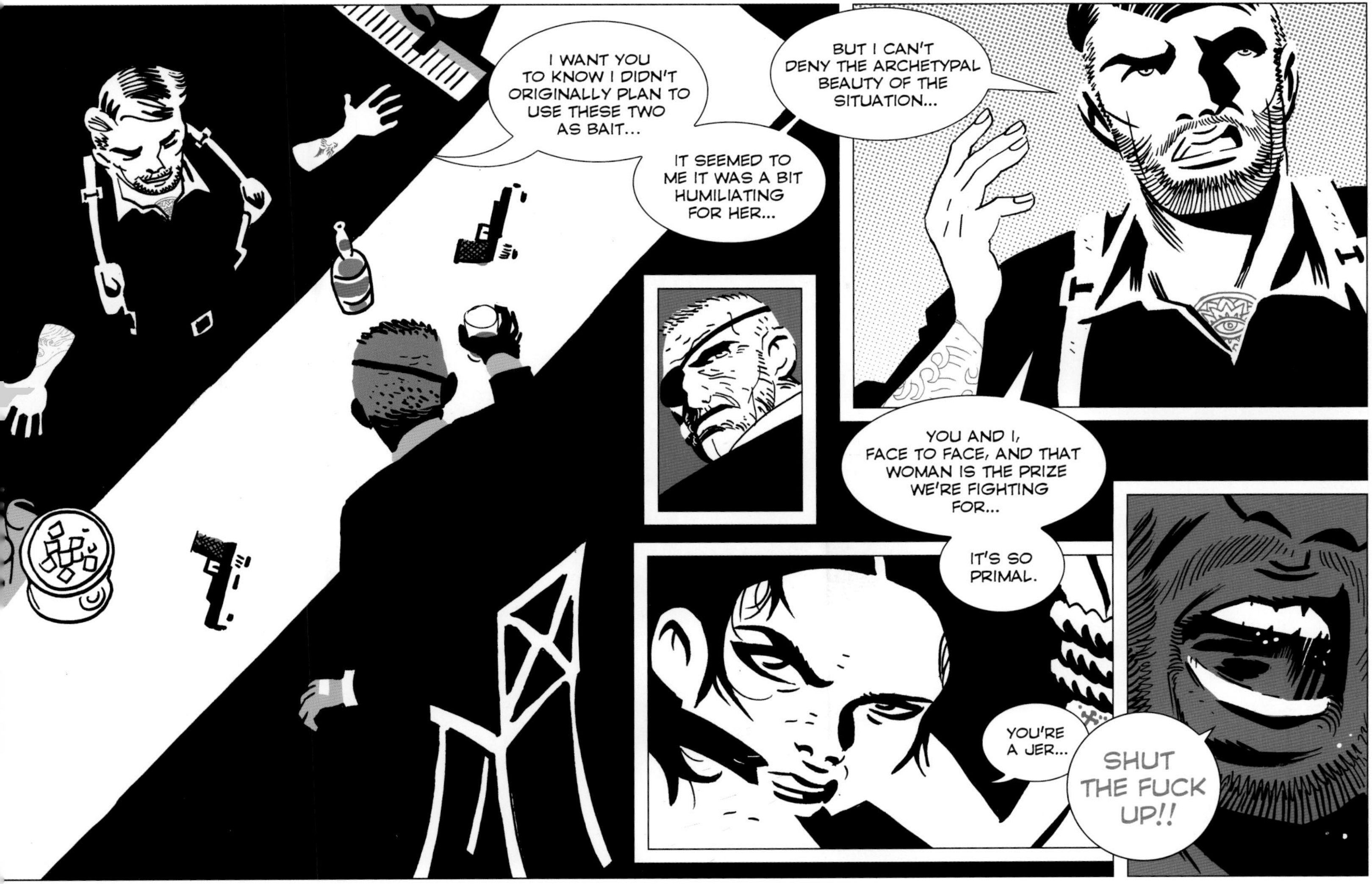
I WANT YOU TO KNOW I DIDN'T ORIGINALLY PLAN TO USE THESE TWO AS BAIT...
IT SEEMED TO ME IT WAS A BIT HUMILIATING FOR HER...
BUT I CAN'T DENY THE ARCHETYPAL BEAUTY OF THE SITUATION...
YOU AND I, FACE TO FACE, AND THAT WOMAN IS THE PRIZE WE'RE FIGHTING FOR...
IT'S SO PRIMAL.
YOU'RE A JER...
SHUT THE FUCK UP!!

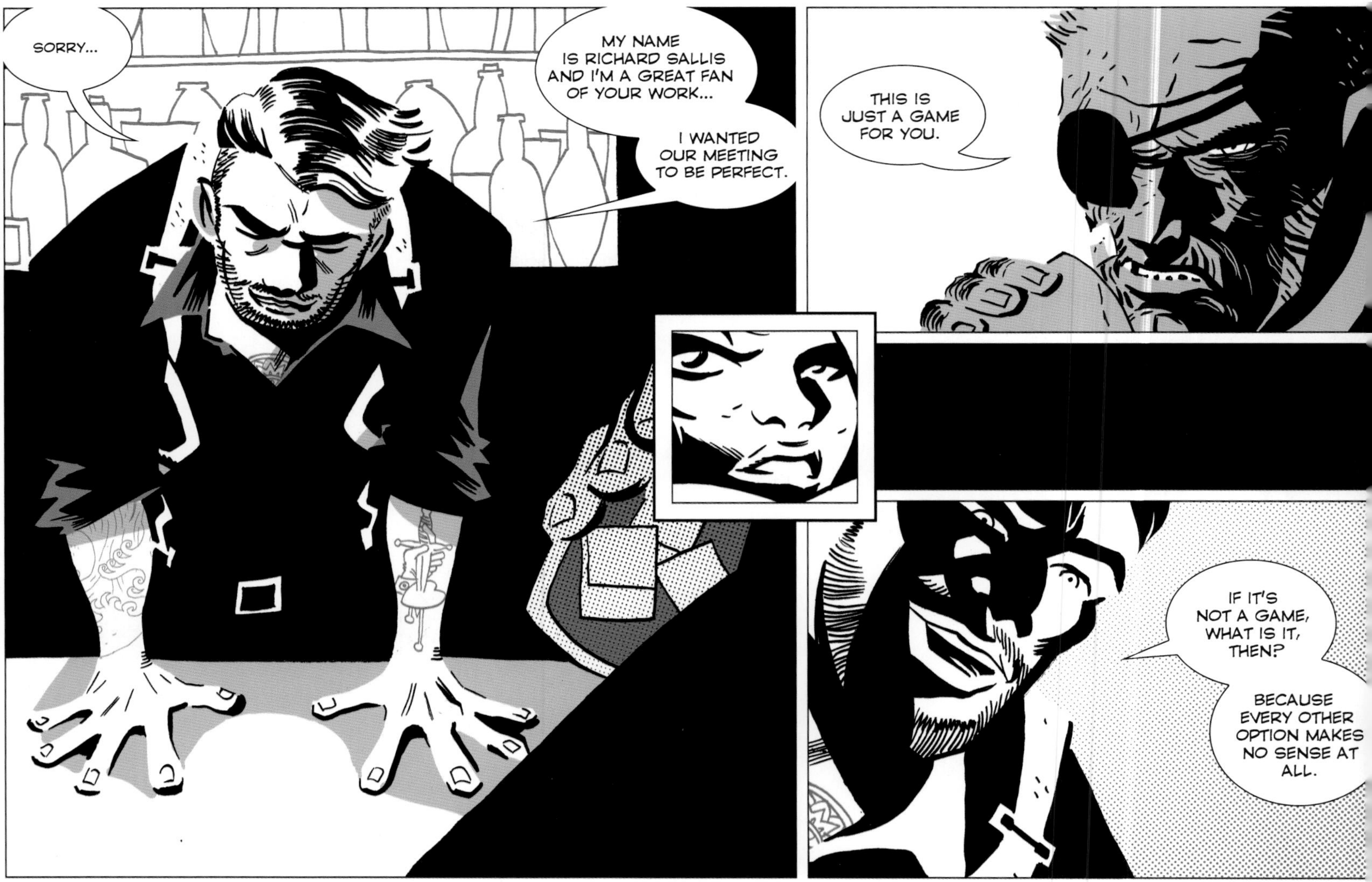
SORRY...
MY NAME IS RICHARD SALLIS AND I'M A GREAT FAN OF YOUR WORK...
I WANTED OUR MEETING TO BE PERFECT.
THIS IS JUST A GAME FOR YOU.
IF IT'S NOT A GAME, WHAT IS IT, THEN?
BECAUSE EVERY OTHER OPTION MAKES NO SENSE AT ALL.

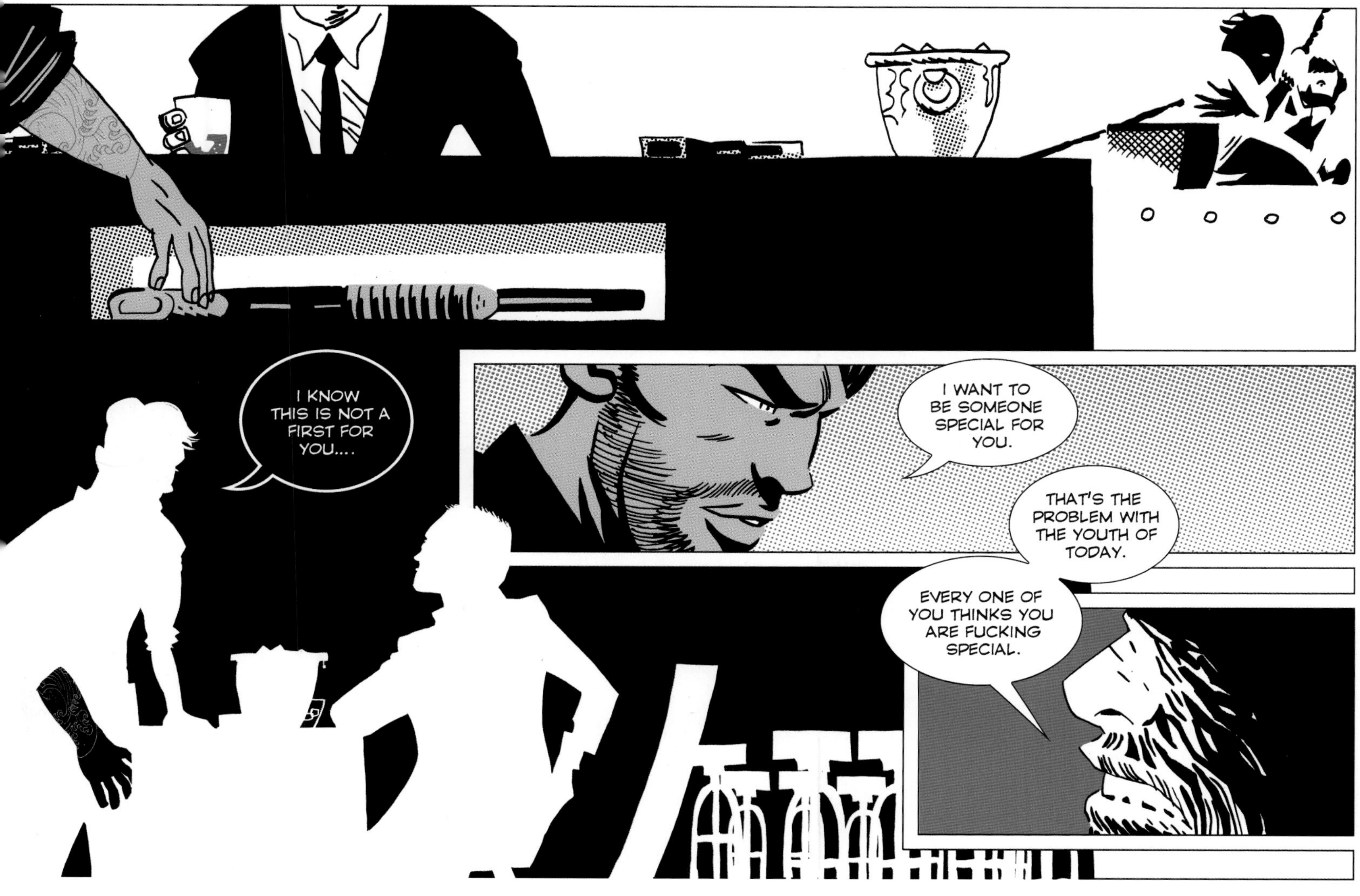
I KNOW THIS IS NOT A FIRST FOR YOU....
I WANT TO BE SOMEONE SPECIAL FOR YOU.
THAT'S THE PROBLEM WITH THE YOUTH OF TODAY.
EVERY ONE OF YOU THINKS YOU ARE FUCKING SPECIAL.

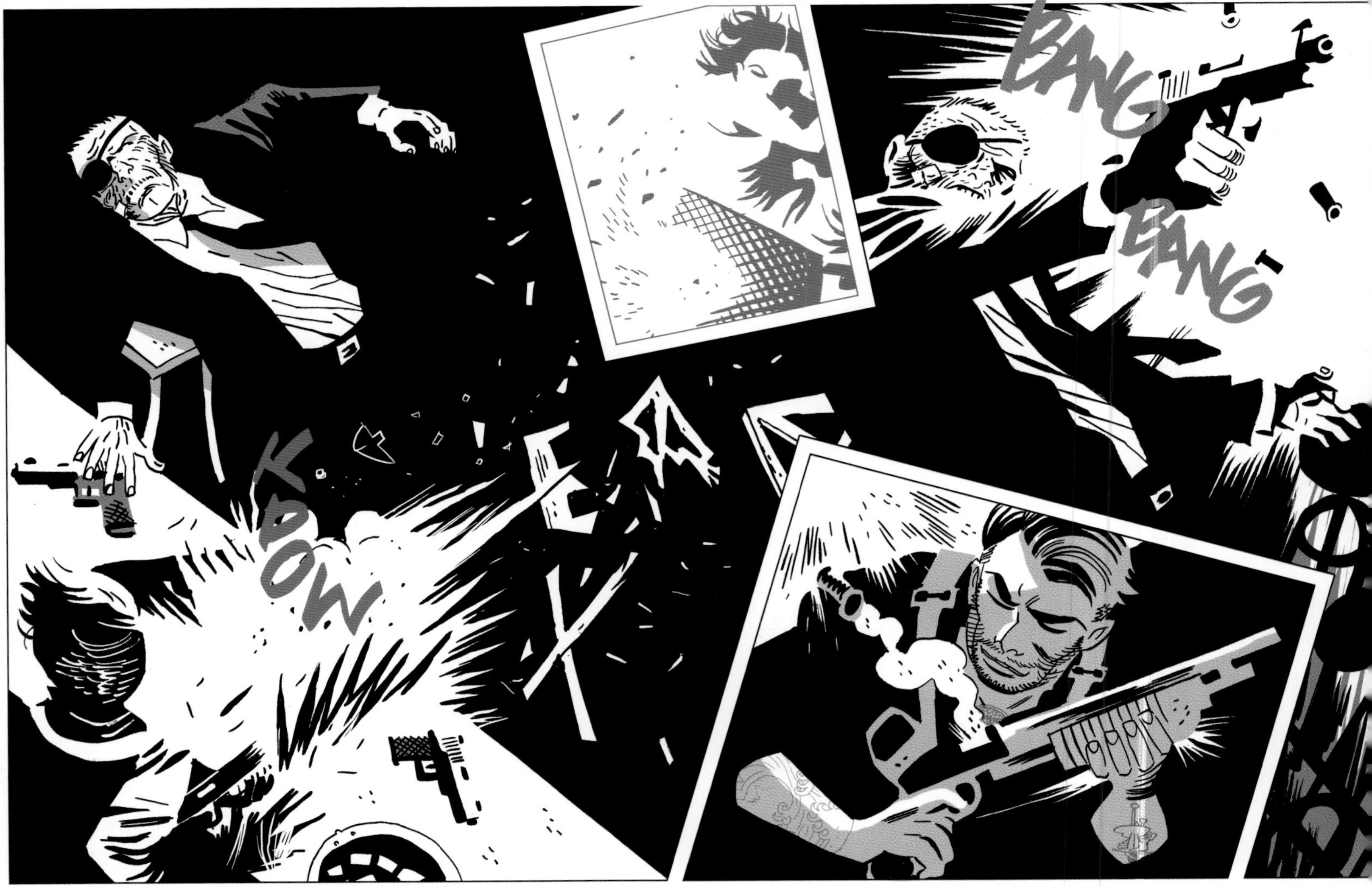
BANG
BANG
KBOOM

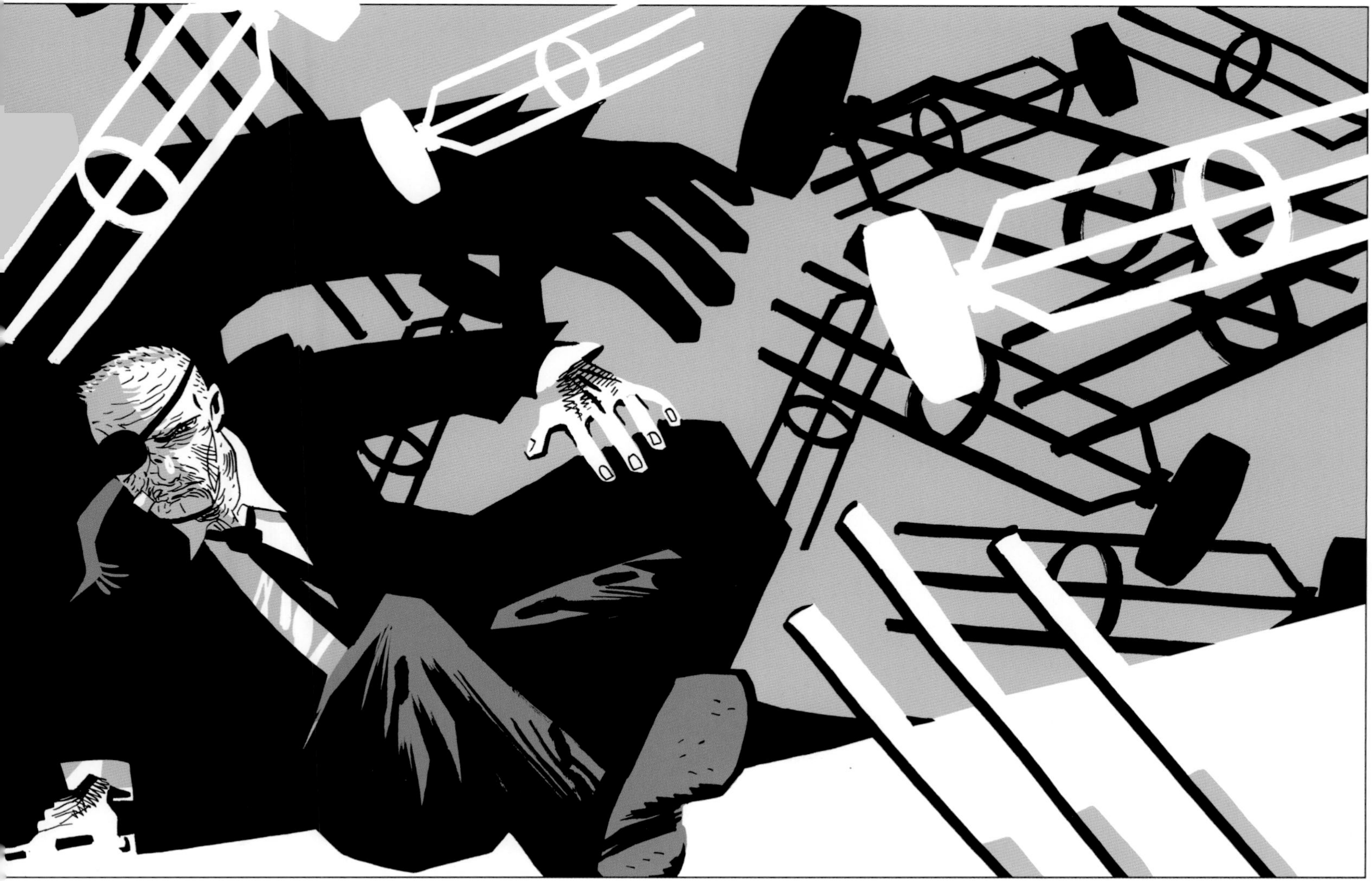

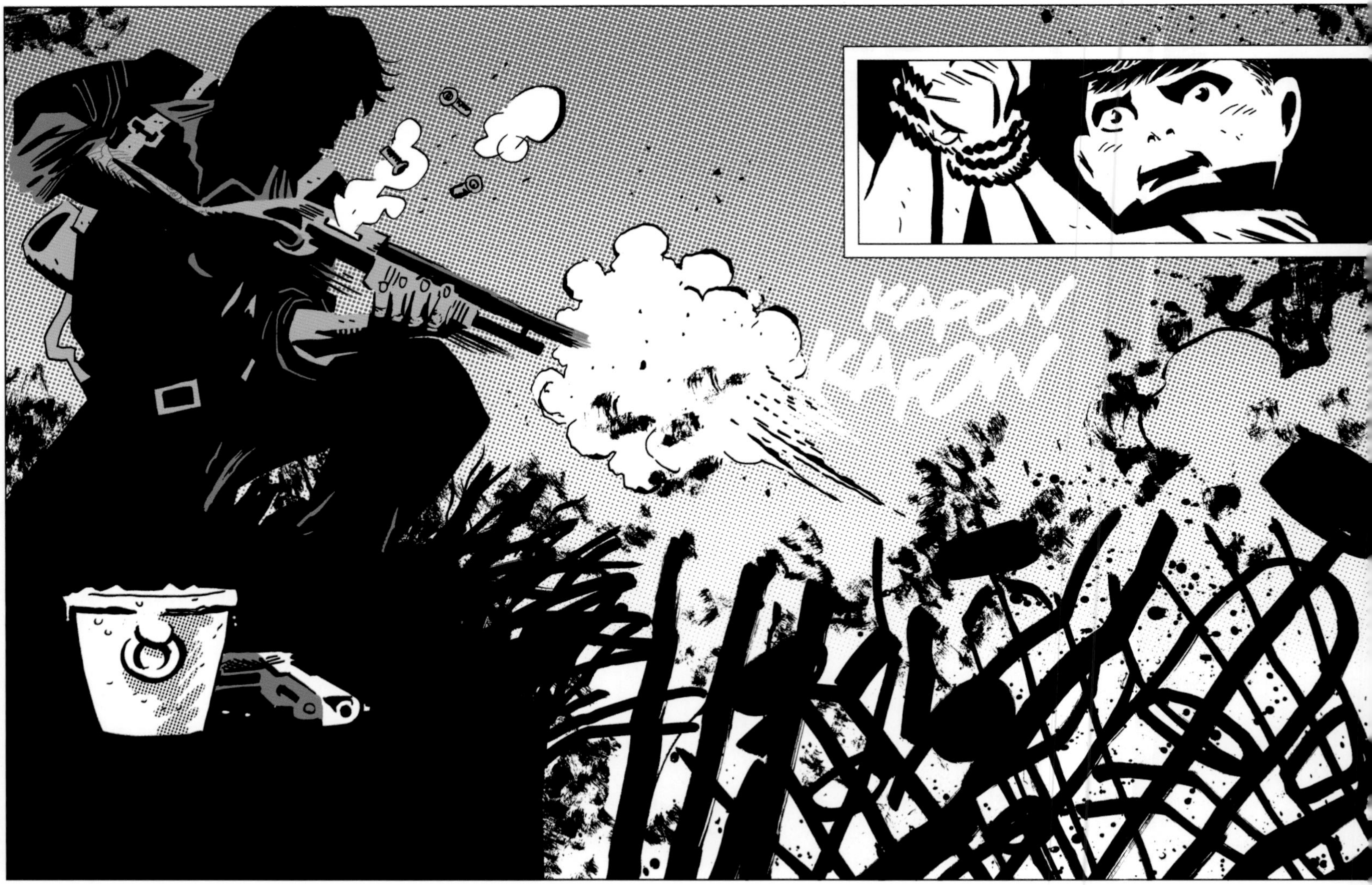
KAPOW
KAPOW

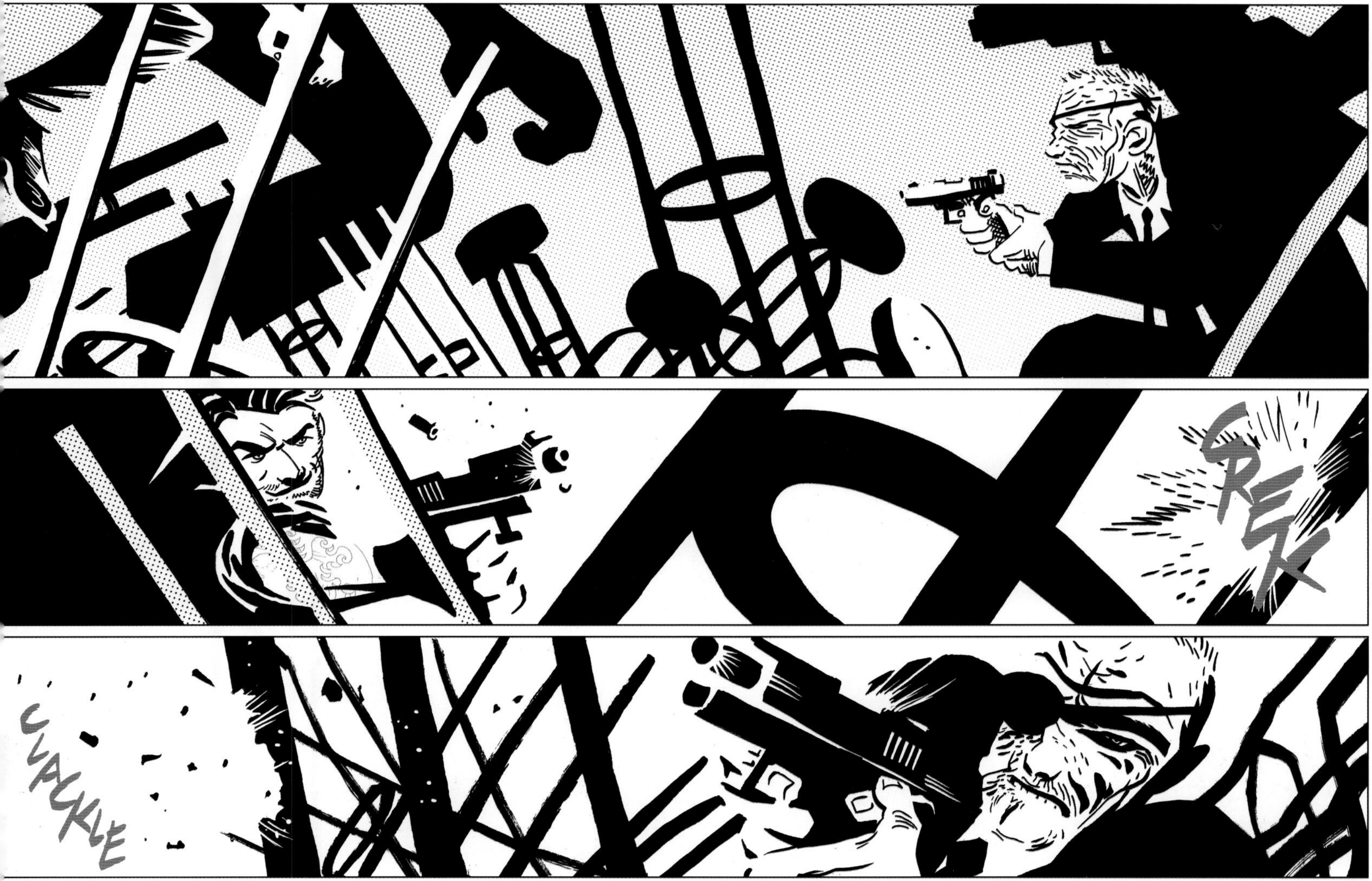
CREK
CLACKLE

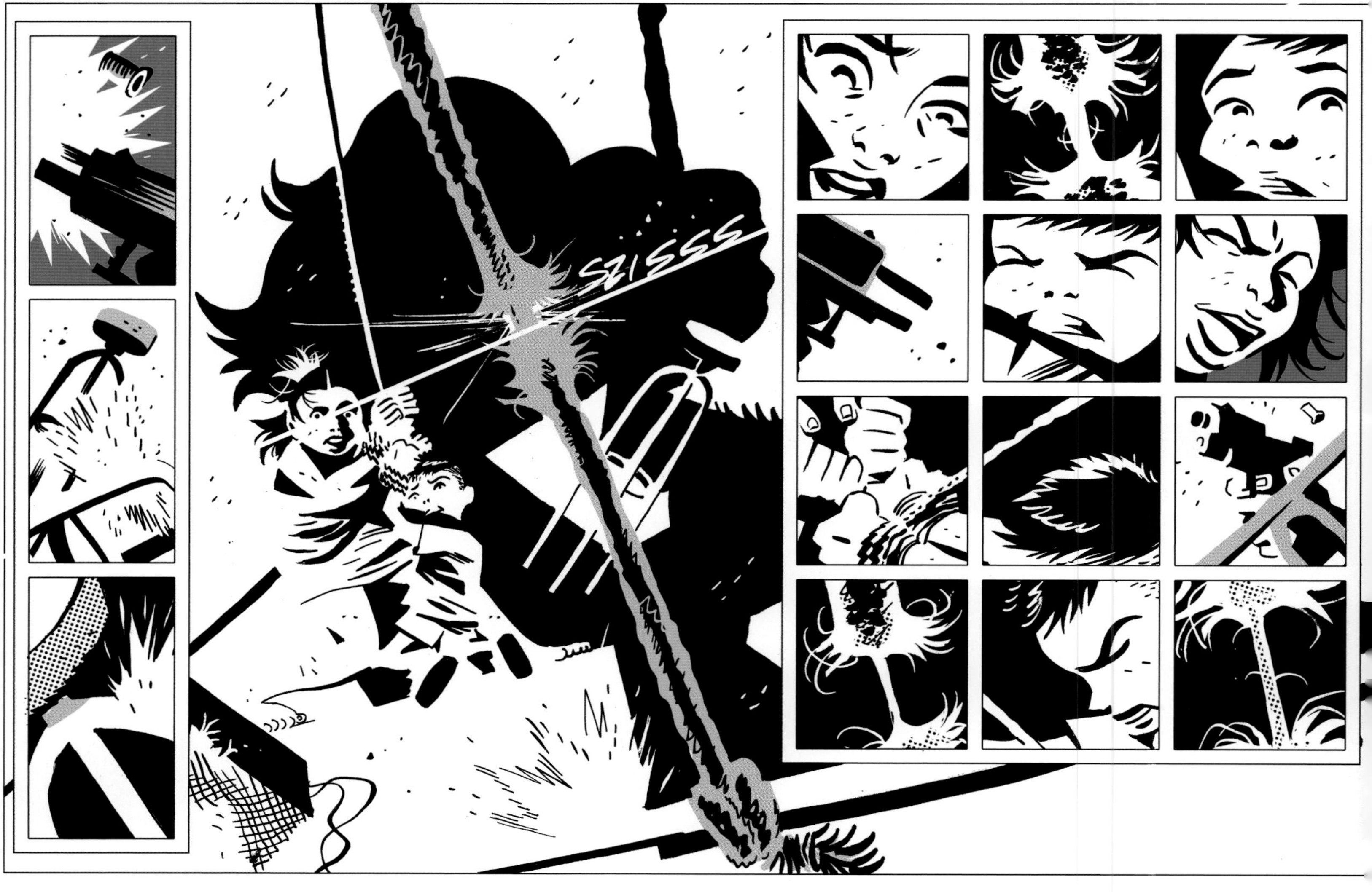
SZISSS

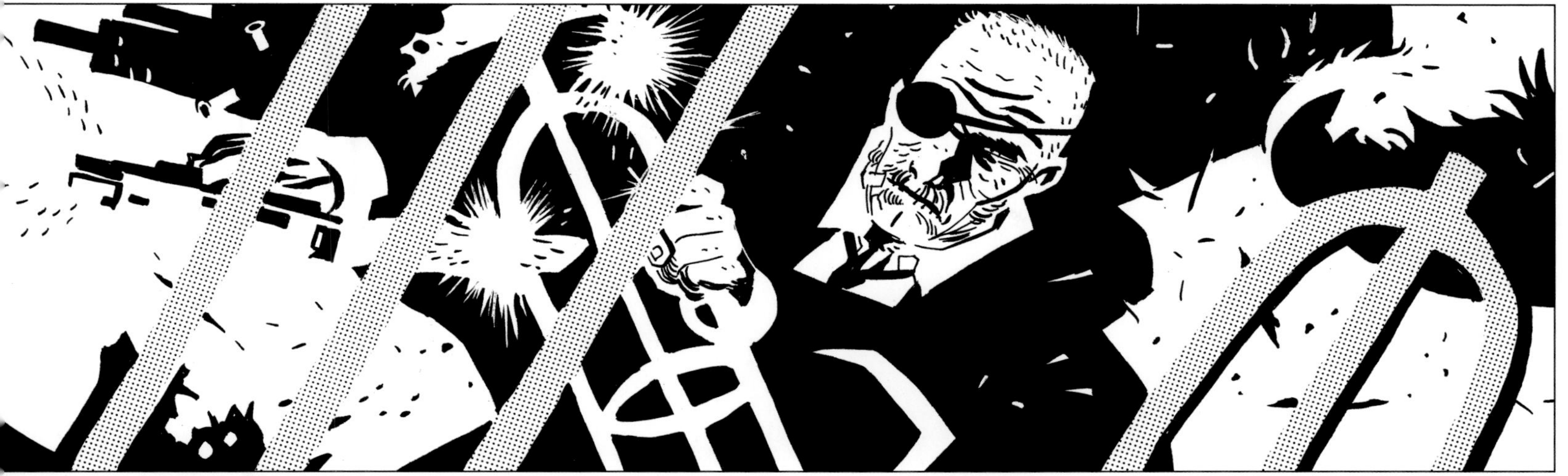

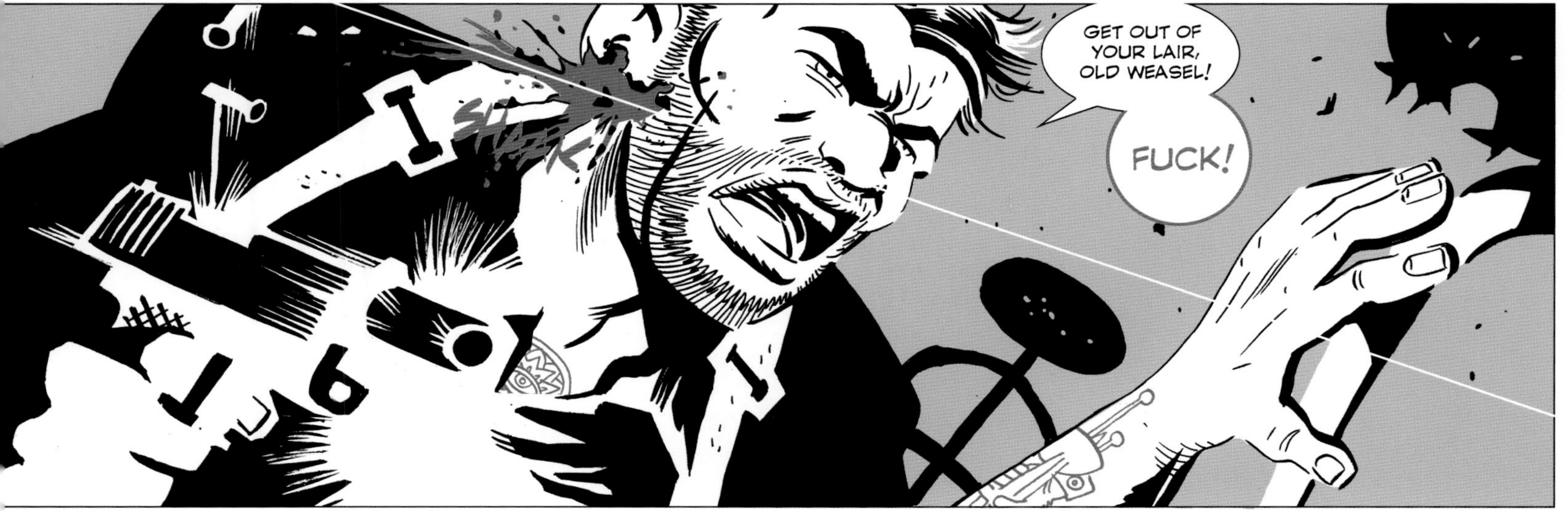
GET OUT OF YOUR LAIR, OLD WEASEL!
FUCK!

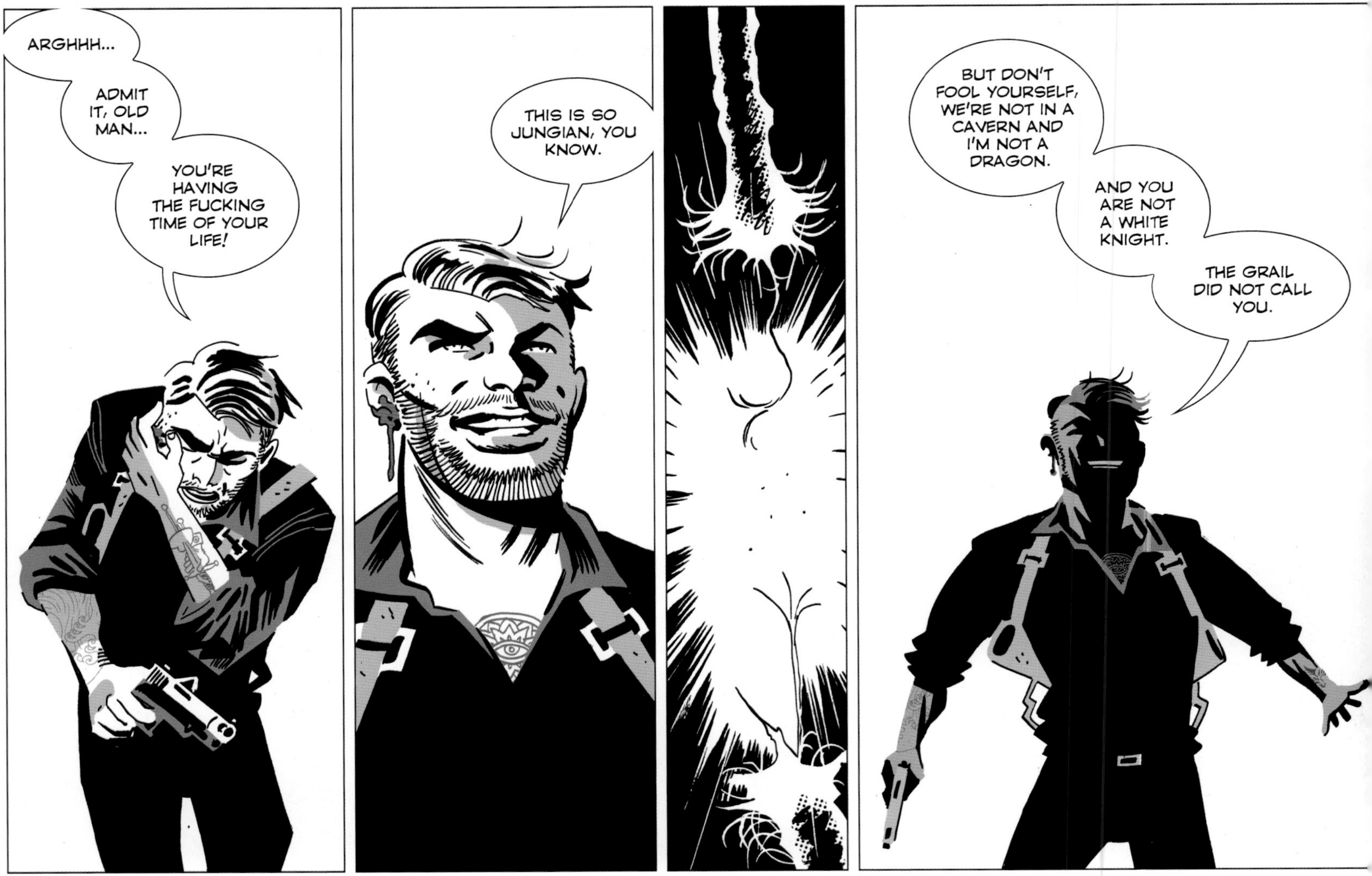
ARGHHH...
ADMIT IT, OLD MAN...
YOU'RE HAVING THE FUCKING TIME OF YOUR LIFE!
THIS IS SO JUNGIAN, YOU KNOW.
BUT DON'T FOOL YOURSELF, WE'RE NOT IN A CAVERN AND I'M NOT A DRAGON.
AND YOU ARE NOT A WHITE KNIGHT.
THE GRAIL DID NOT CALL YOU.

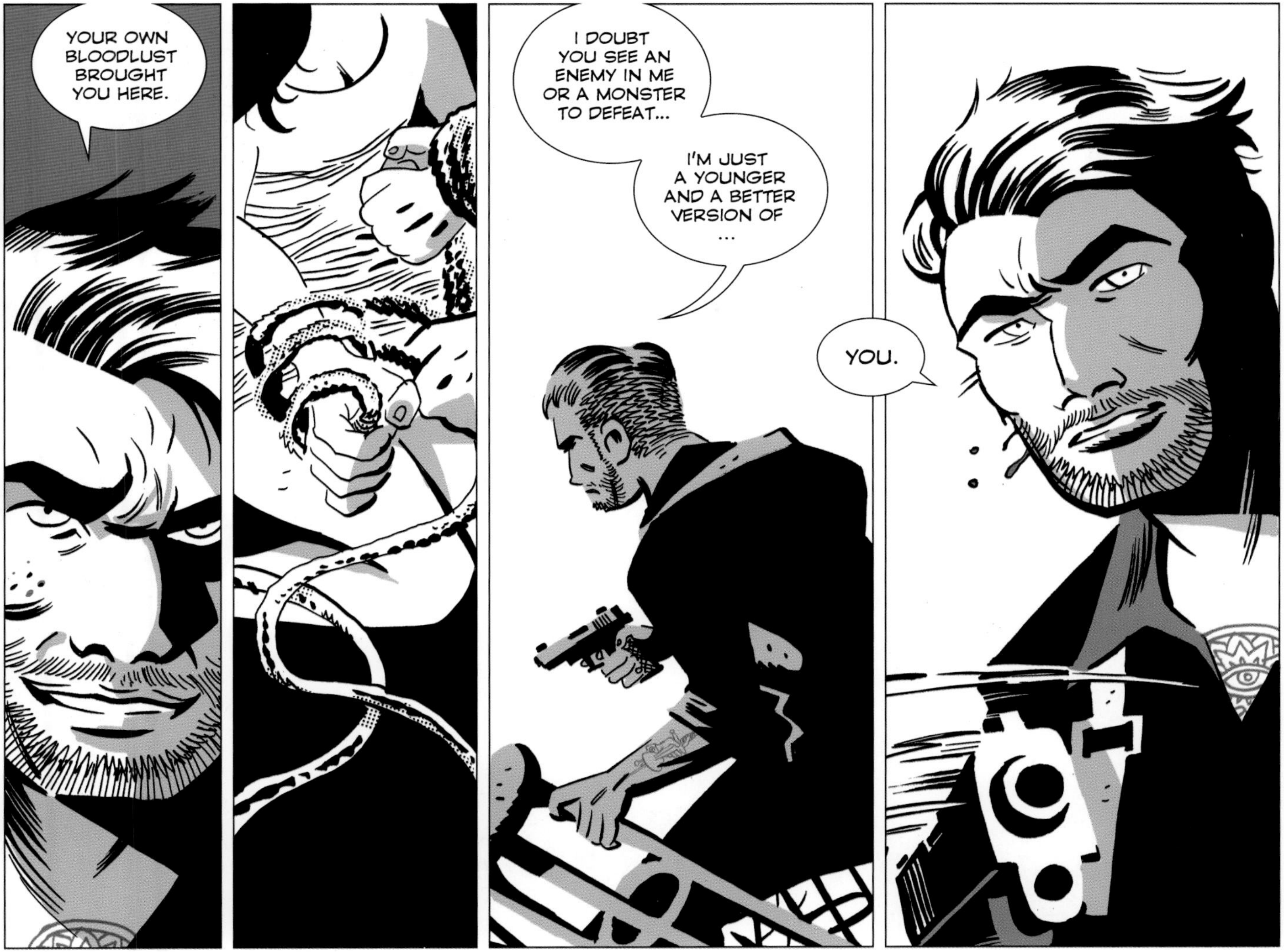
YOUR OWN BLOODLUST BROUGHT YOU HERE.
I DOUBT YOU SEE AN ENEMY IN ME OR A MONSTER TO DEFEAT...
I'M JUST A YOUNGER AND A BETTER VERSION OF ...
YOU.

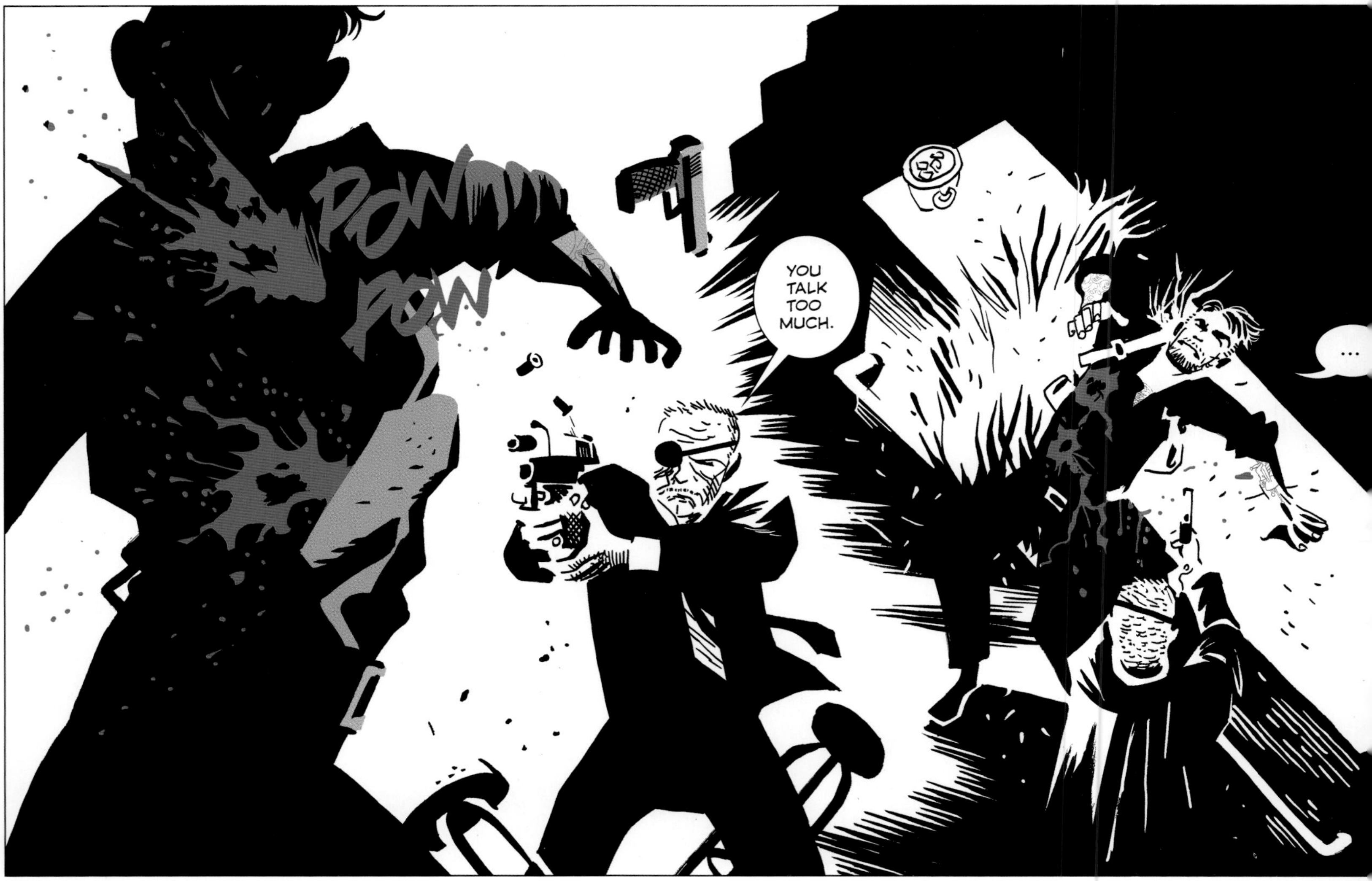
POW
POW
YOU TALK TOO MUCH.
...

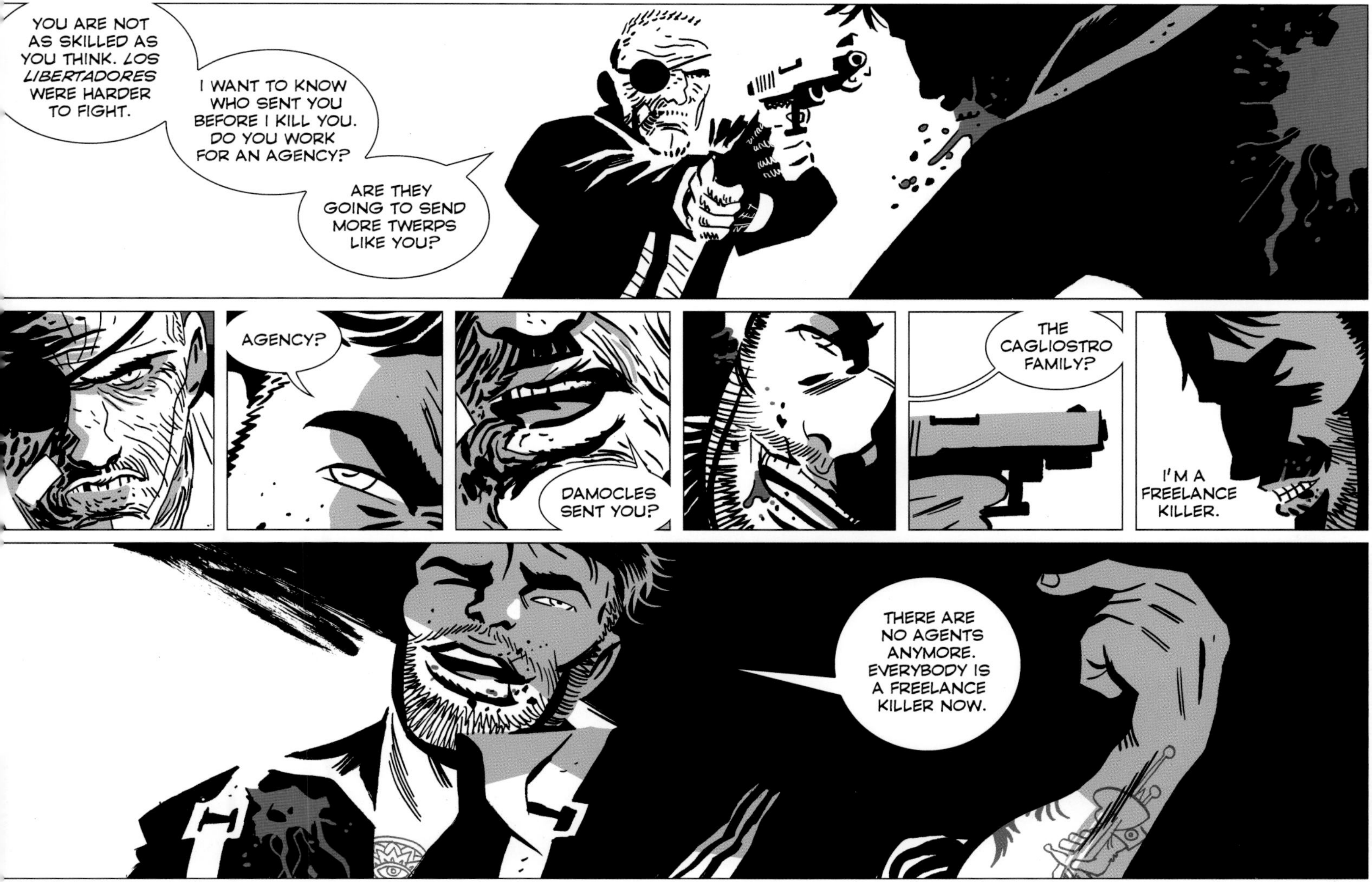
YOU ARE NOT AS SKILLED AS YOU THINK. *LOS LIBERTADORES* WERE HARDER TO FIGHT.
I WANT TO KNOW WHO SENT YOU BEFORE I KILL YOU. DO YOU WORK FOR AN AGENCY?
ARE THEY GOING TO SEND MORE TWERPS LIKE YOU?
AGENCY?
DAMOCLES SENT YOU?
THE CAGLIOSTRO FAMILY?
I'M A FREELANCE KILLER.
THERE ARE NO AGENTS ANYMORE. EVERYBODY IS A FREELANCE KILLER NOW.

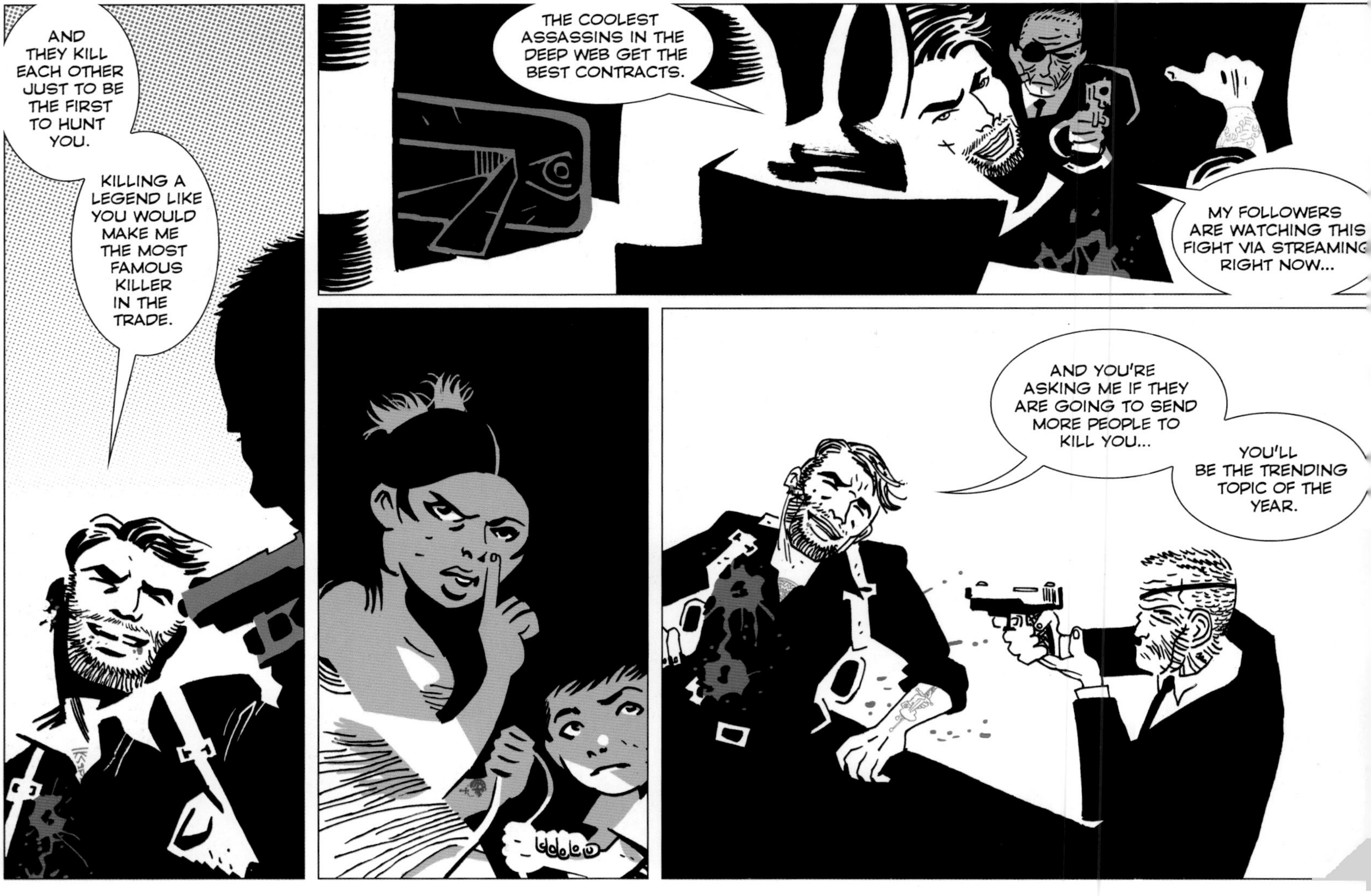
AND THEY KILL EACH OTHER JUST TO BE THE FIRST TO HUNT YOU.
KILLING A LEGEND LIKE YOU WOULD MAKE ME THE MOST FAMOUS KILLER IN THE TRADE.
THE COOLEST ASSASSINS IN THE DEEP WEB GET THE BEST CONTRACTS.
MY FOLLOWERS ARE WATCHING THIS FIGHT VIA STREAMING RIGHT NOW...
AND YOU'RE ASKING ME IF THEY ARE GOING TO SEND MORE PEOPLE TO KILL YOU...
YOU'LL BE THE TRENDING TOPIC OF THE YEAR.

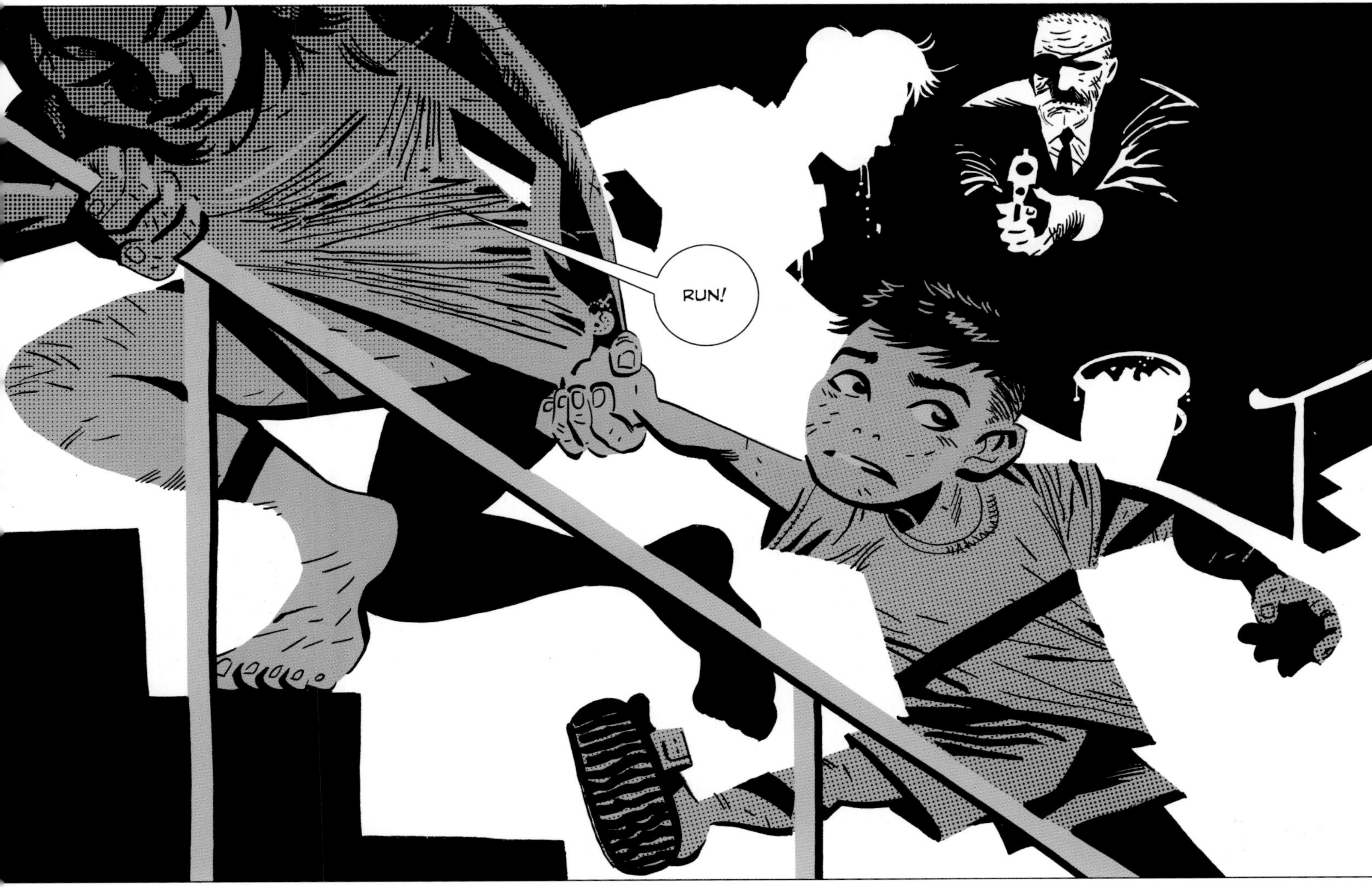
RUN!

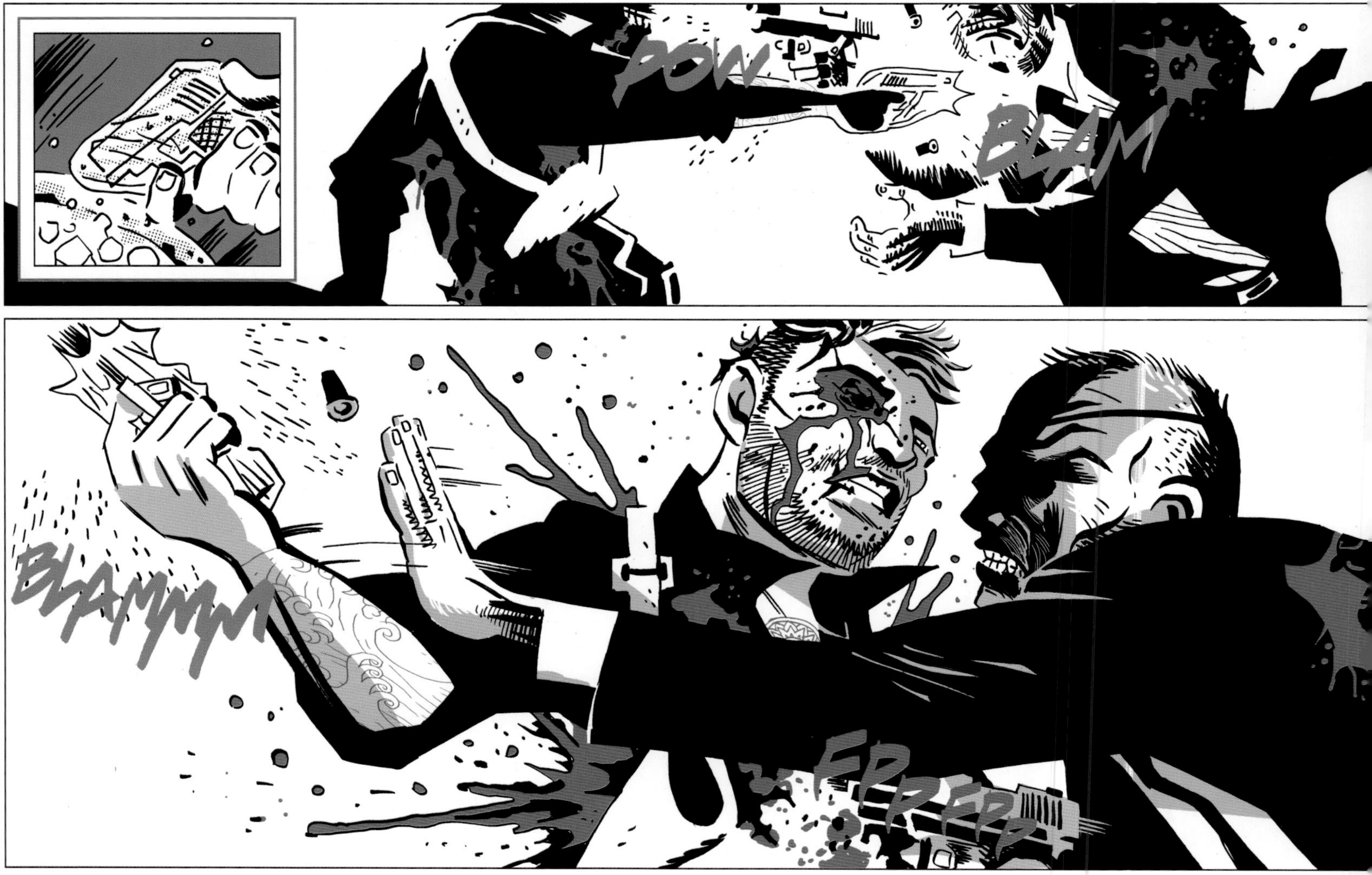
POW
BLAM
BLAMMM
FPP
FPP FPP

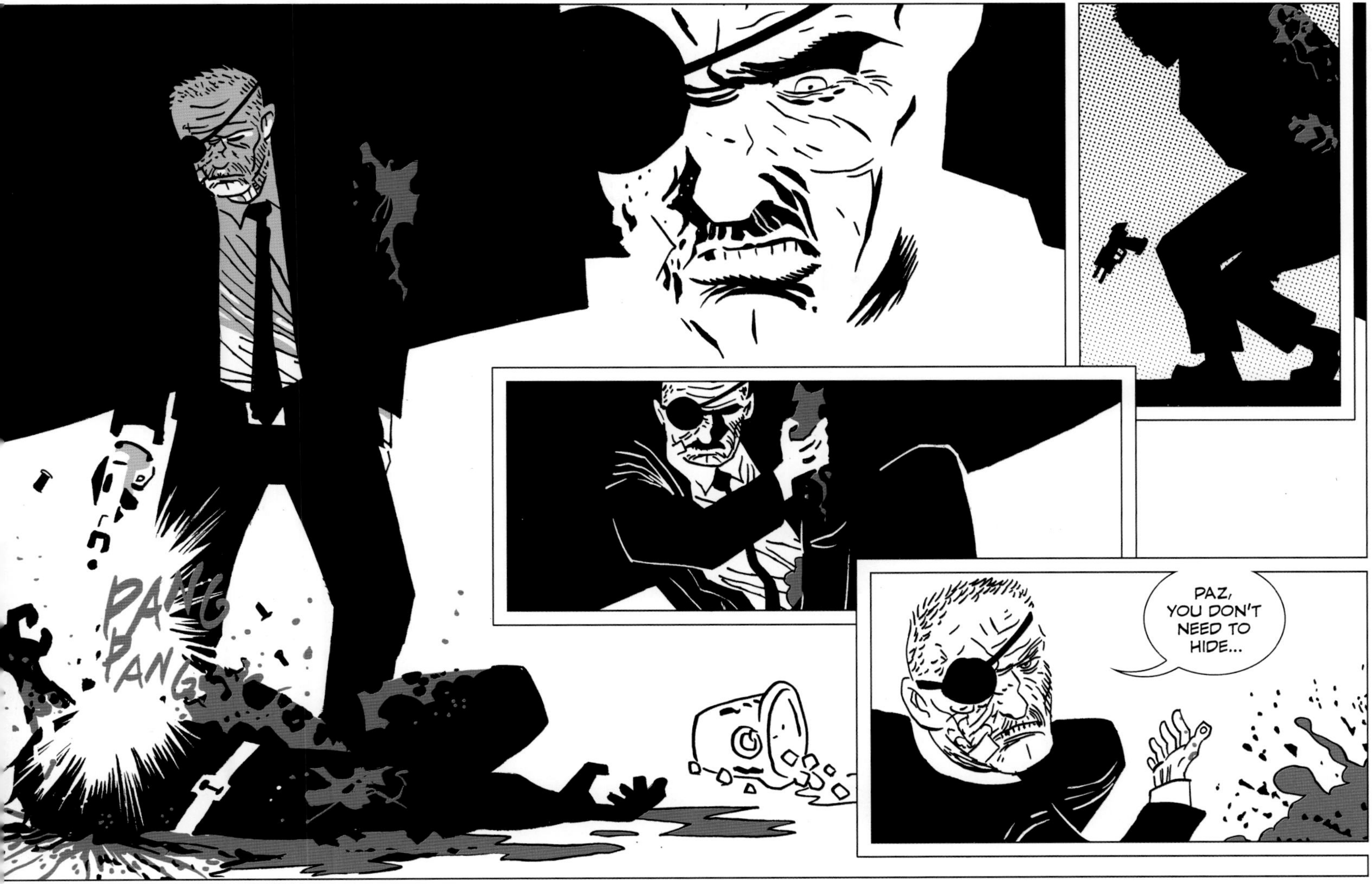
PANG
PANG
PAZ, YOU DON'T NEED TO HIDE...

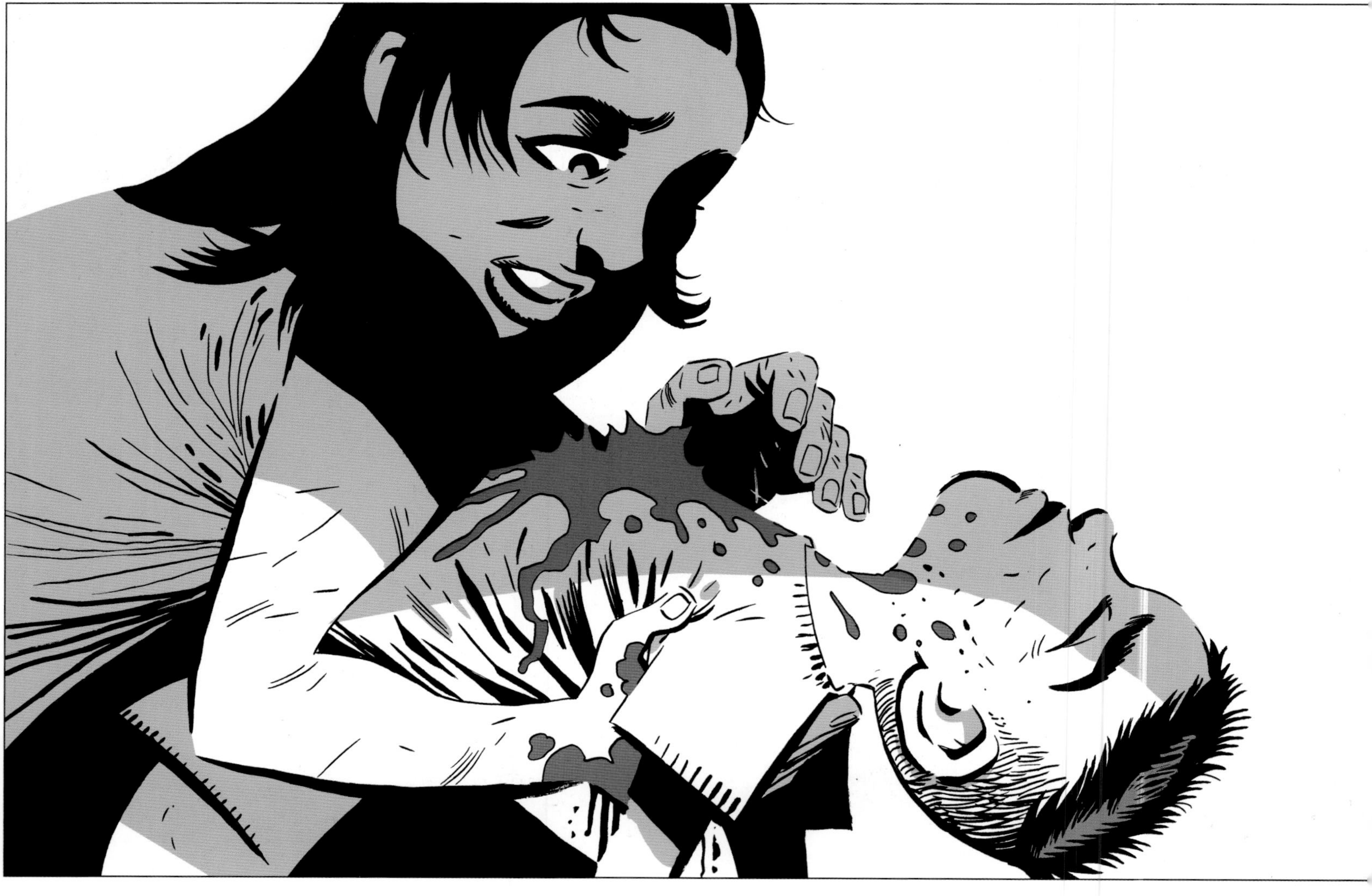

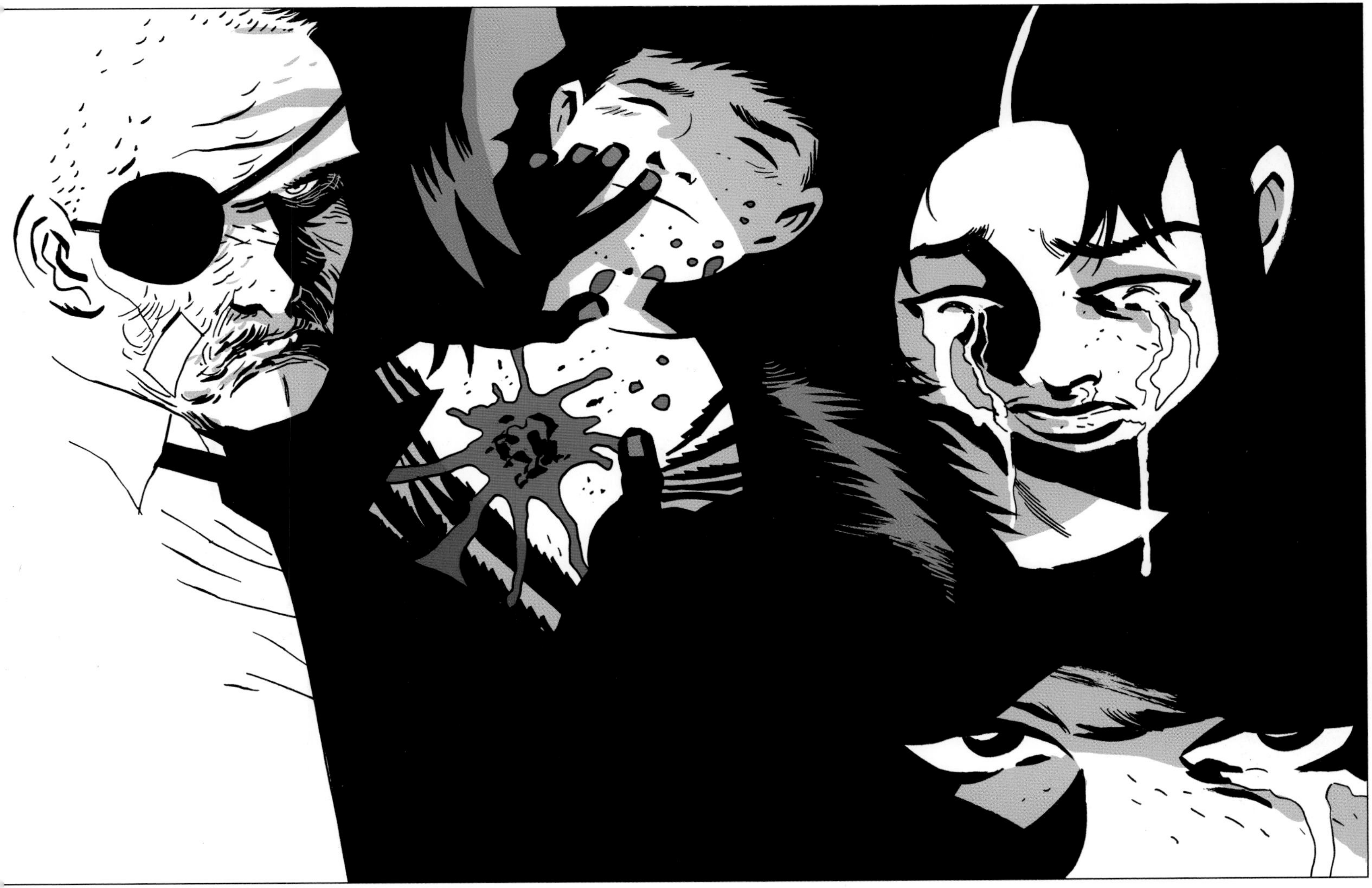

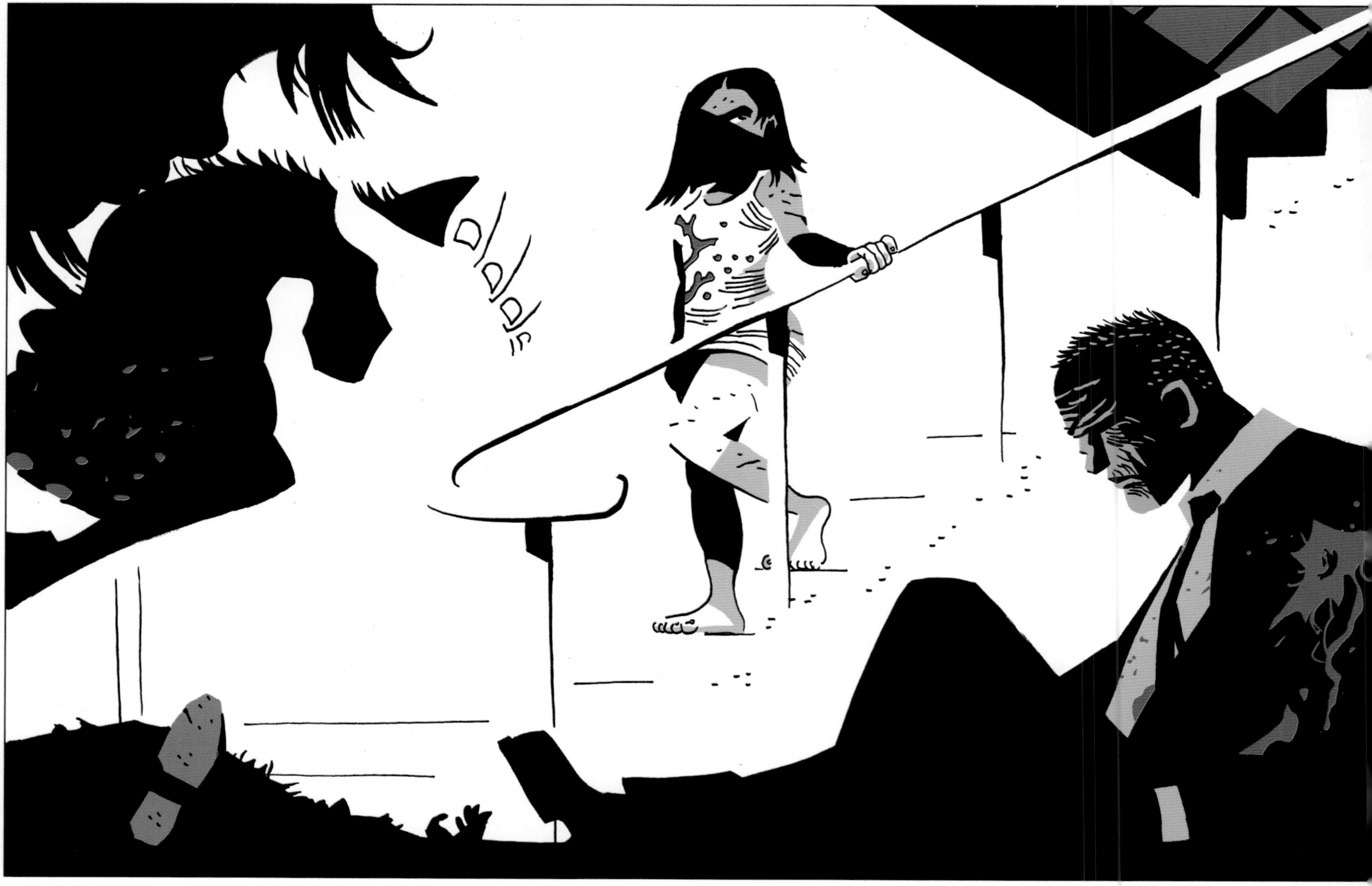

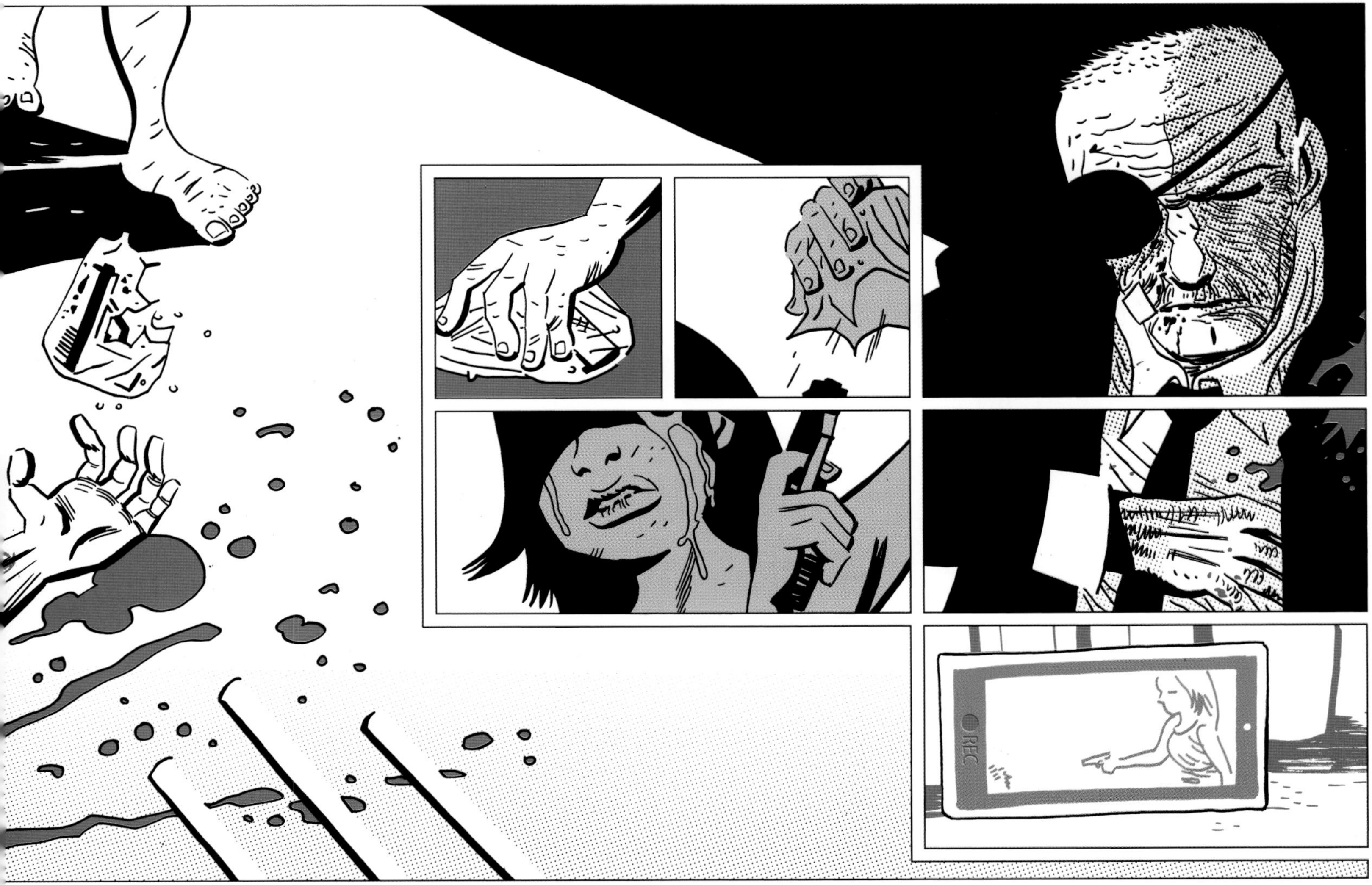
REC

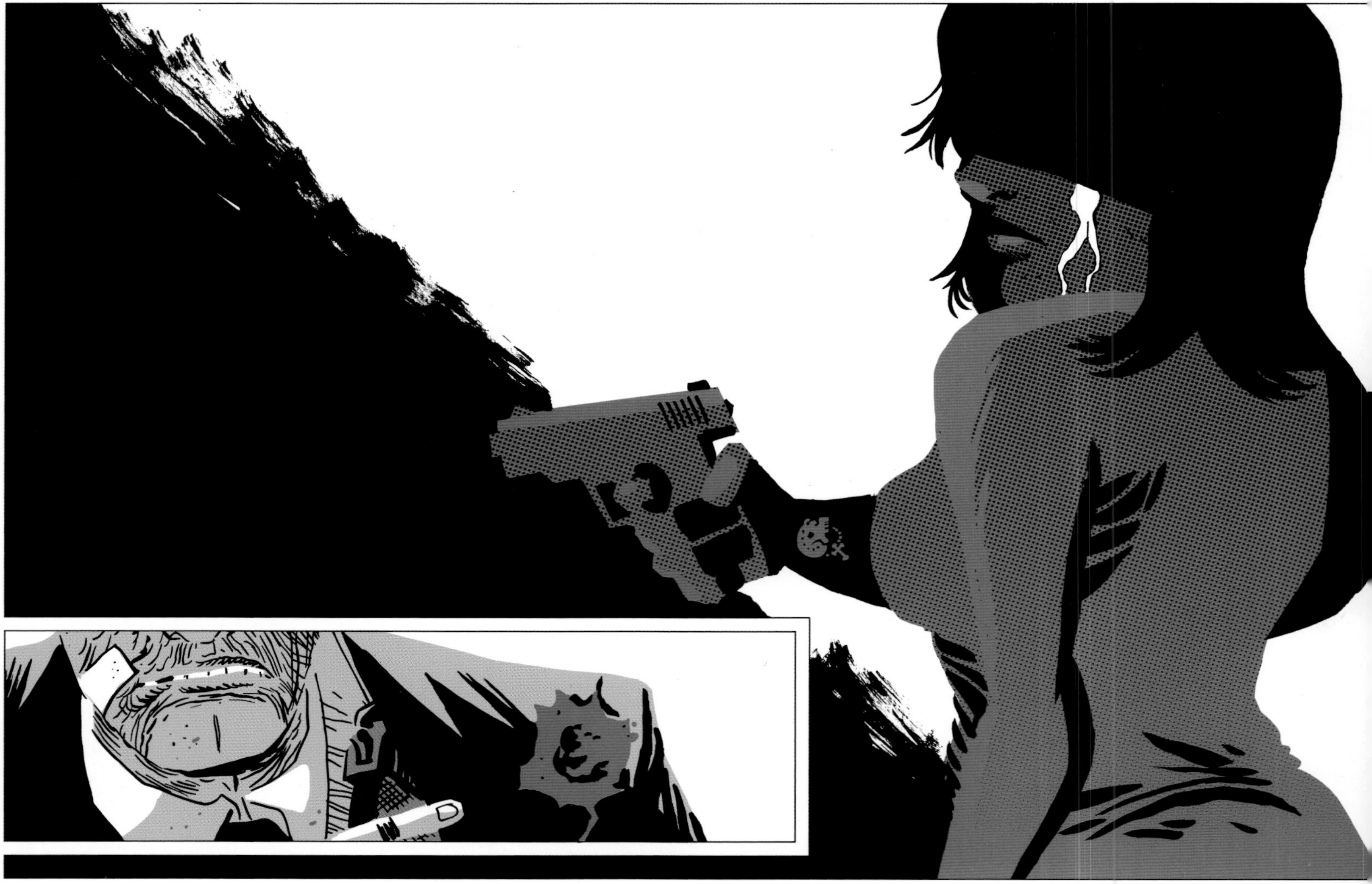

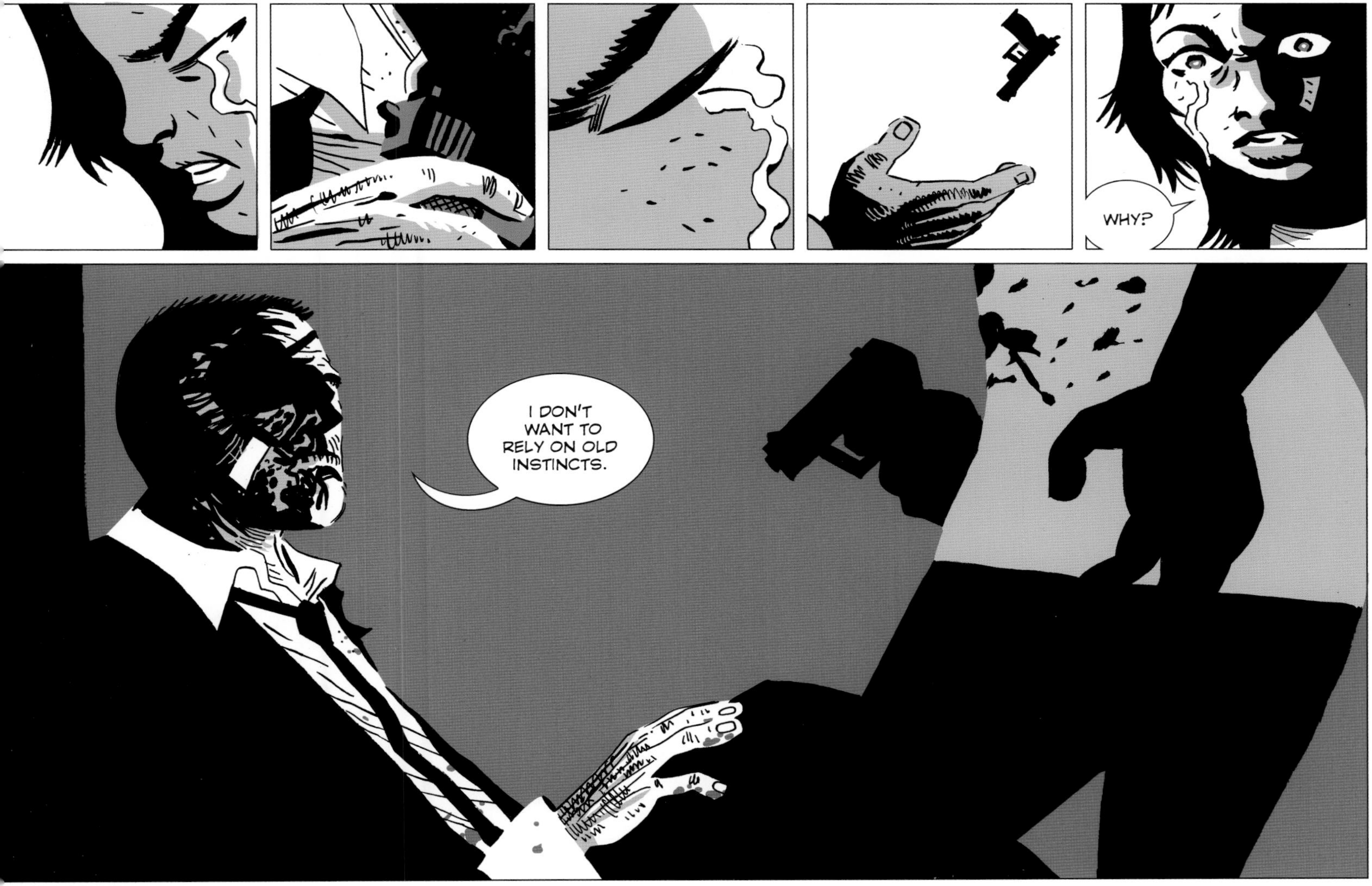
WHY?
I DON'T WANT TO RELY ON OLD INSTINCTS.

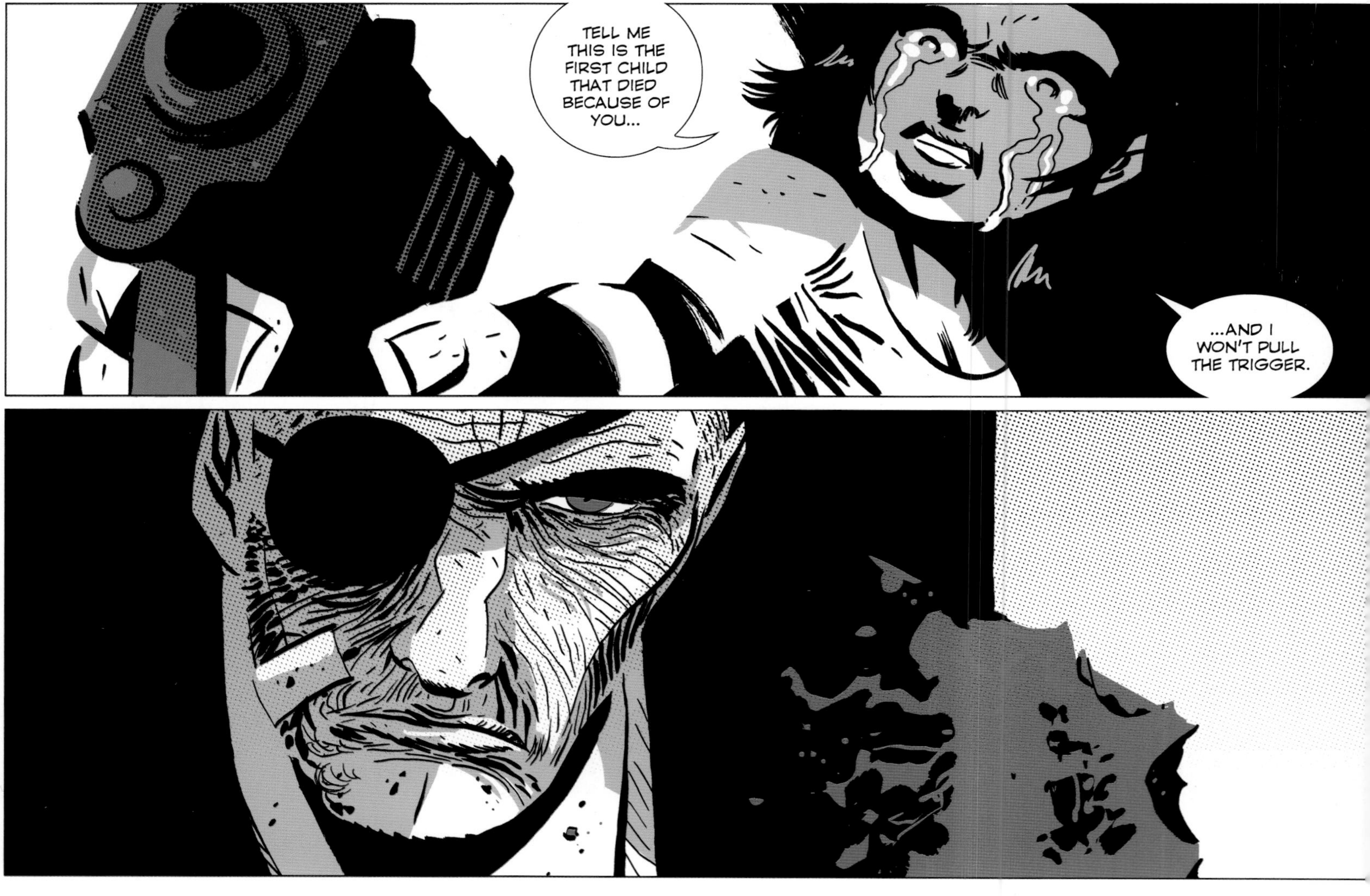
TELL ME THIS IS THE FIRST CHILD THAT DIED BECAUSE OF YOU...
...AND I WON'T PULL THE TRIGGER.

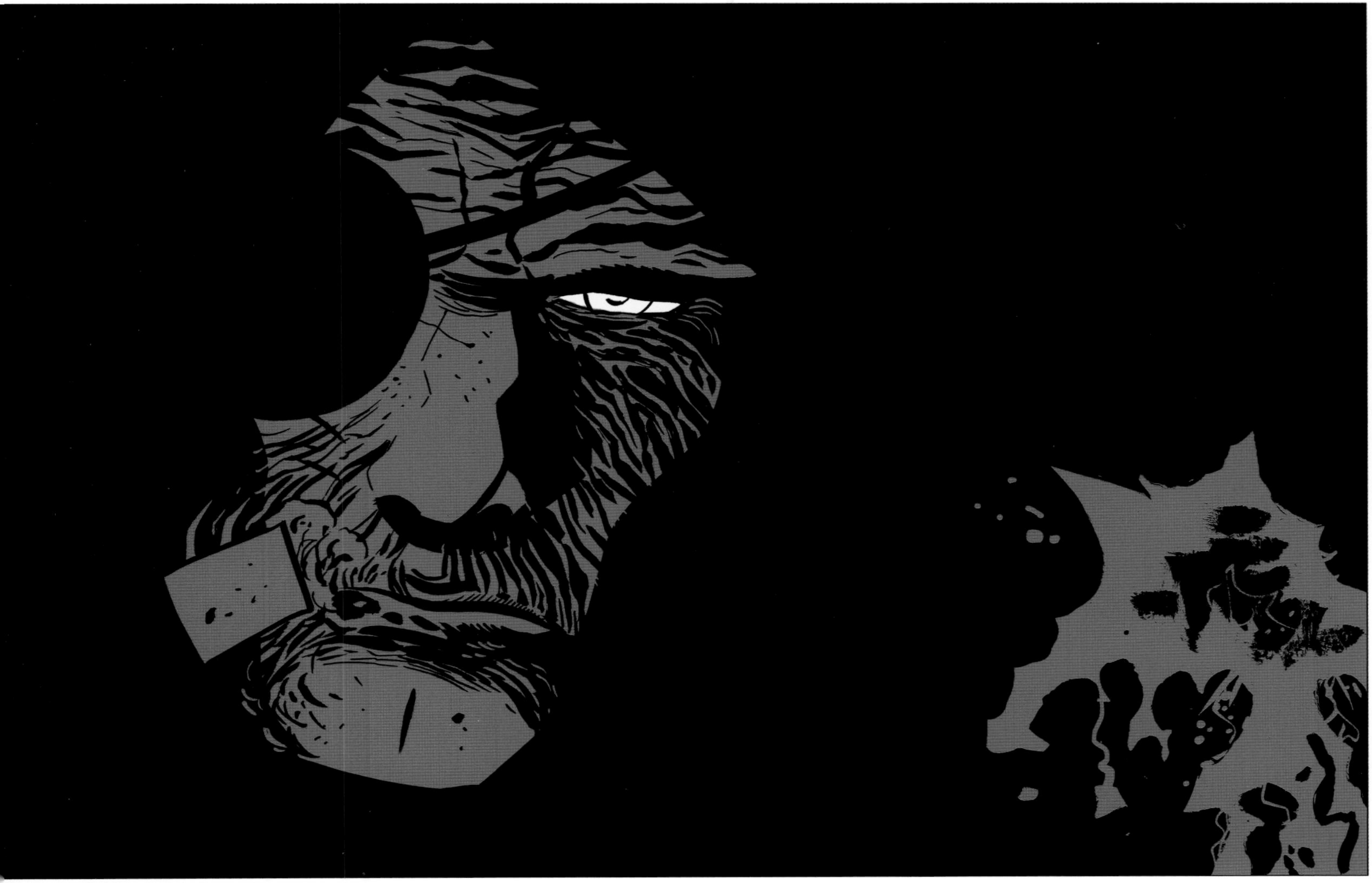

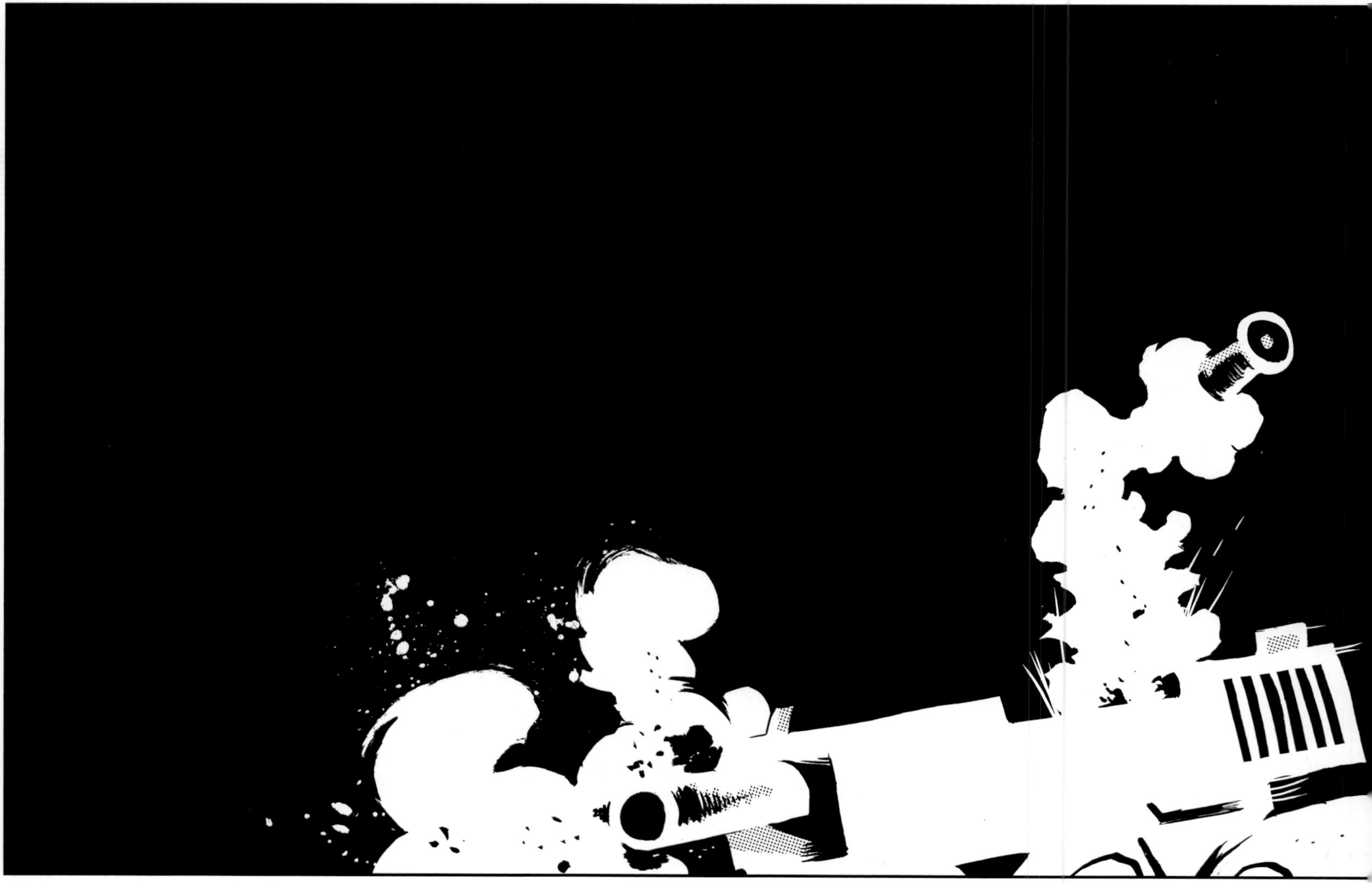

BONUS STORY
NEON

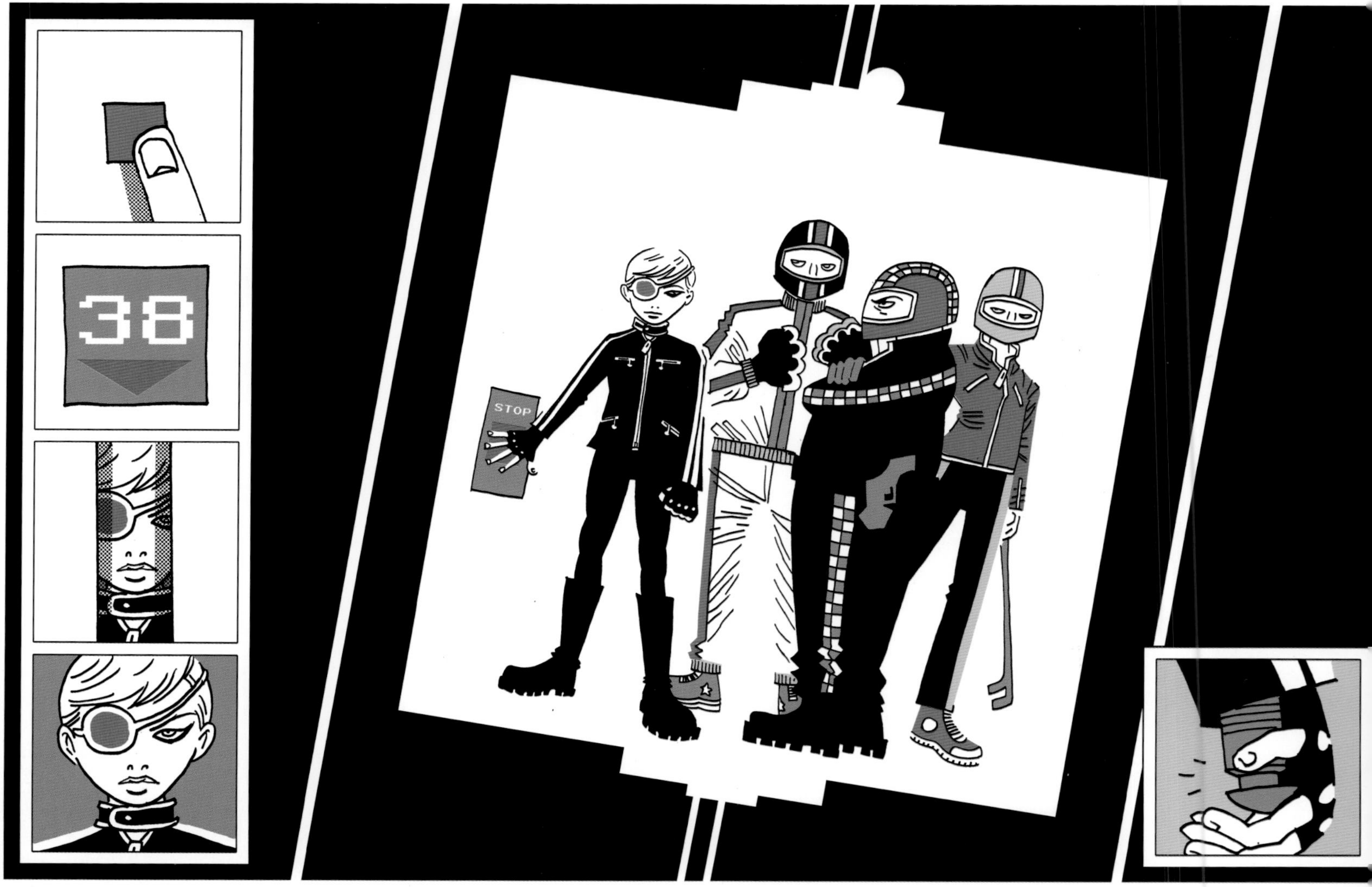
38
STOP

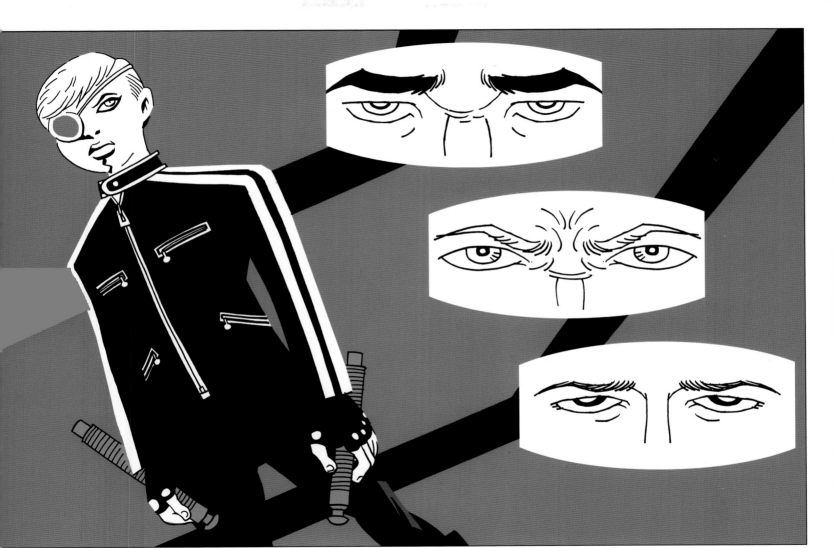

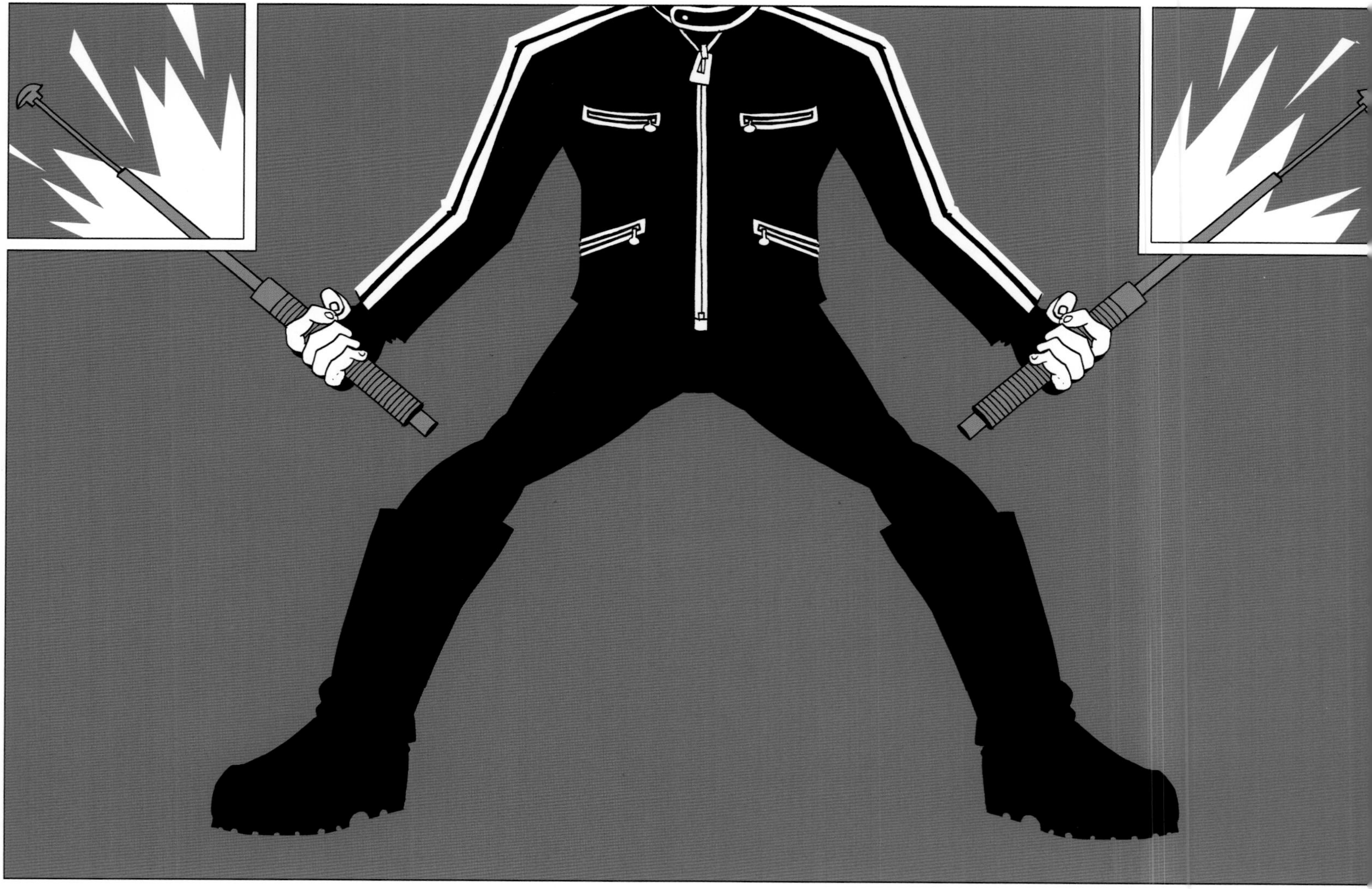

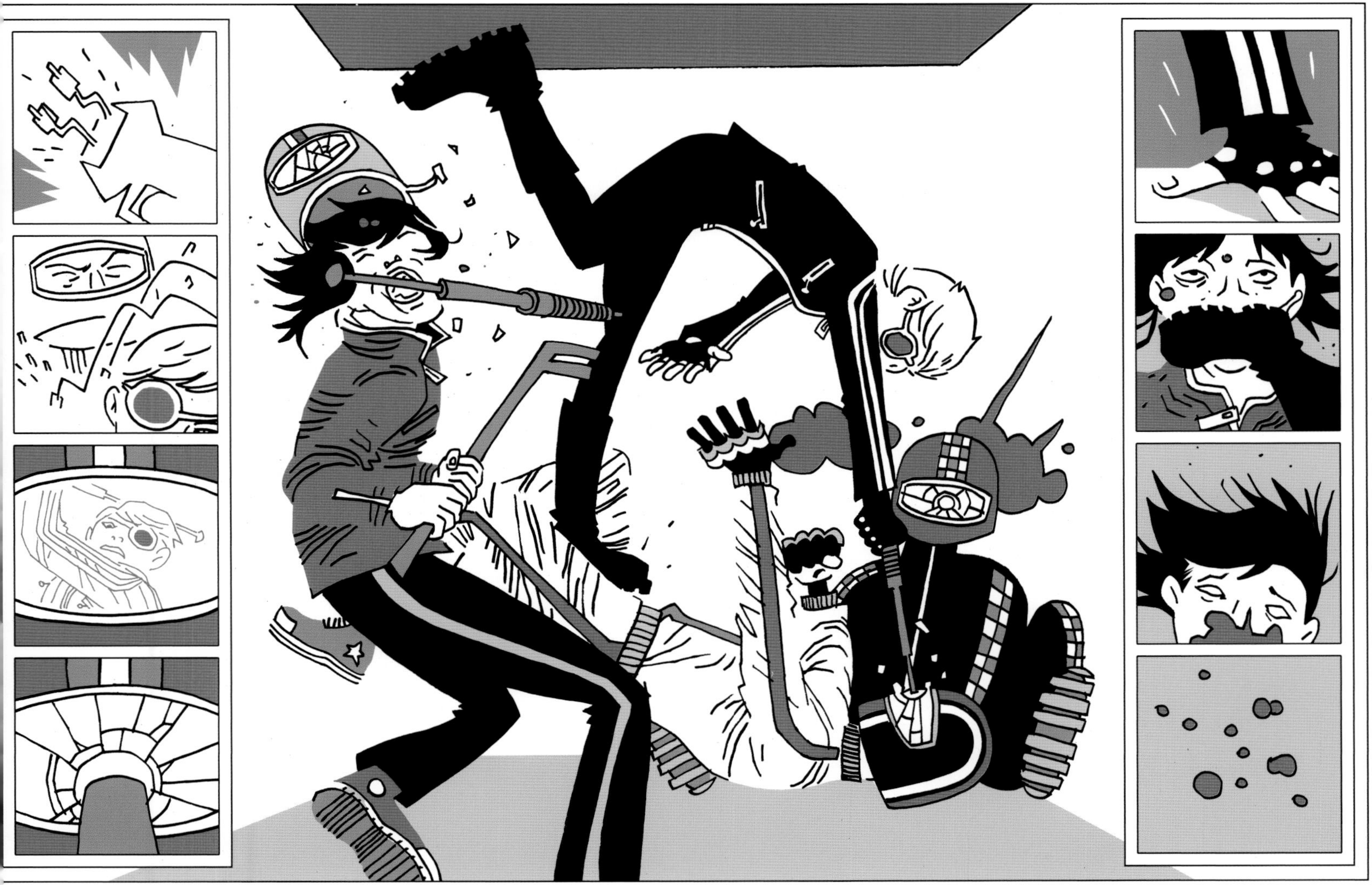

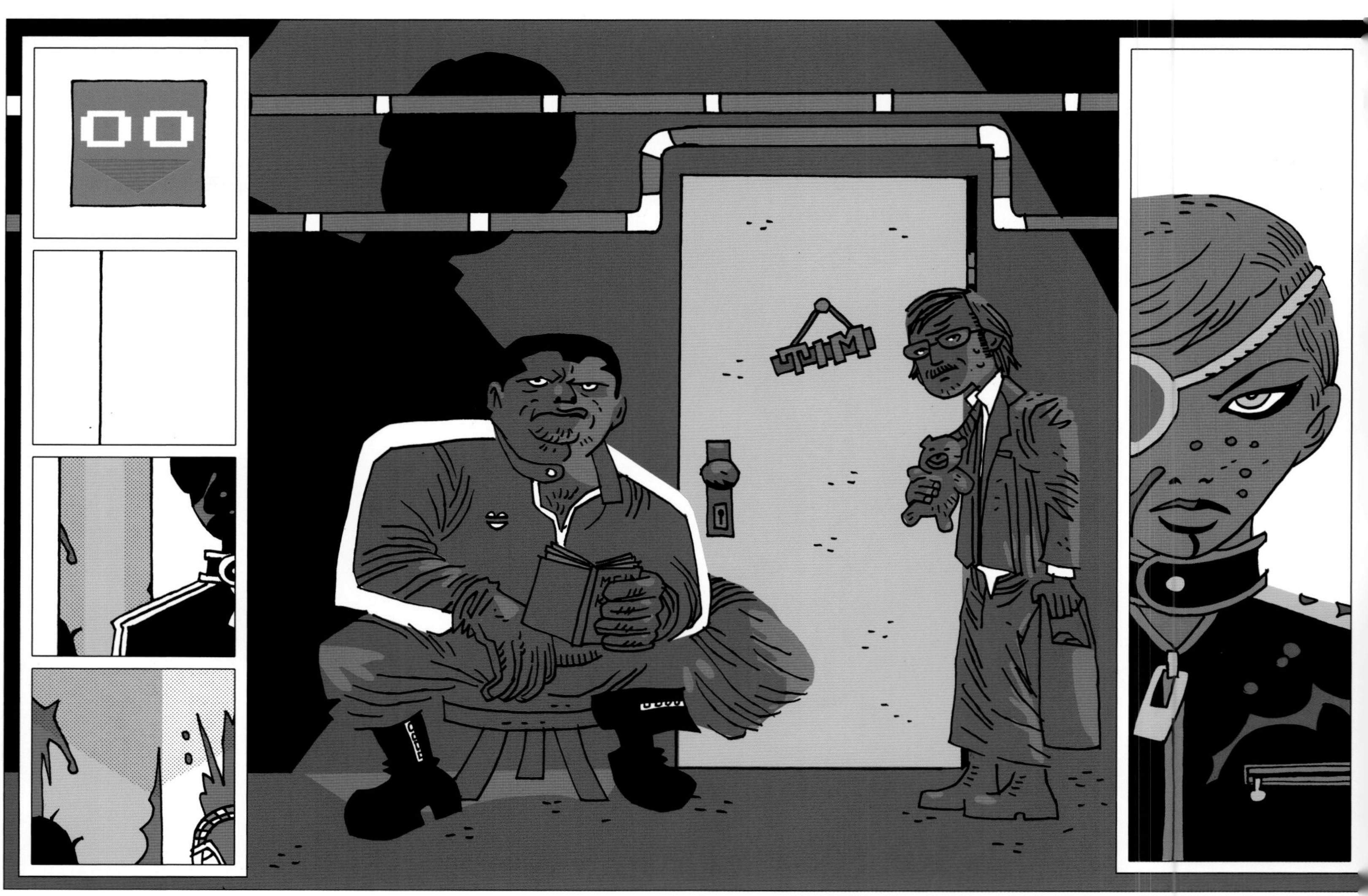
TIM

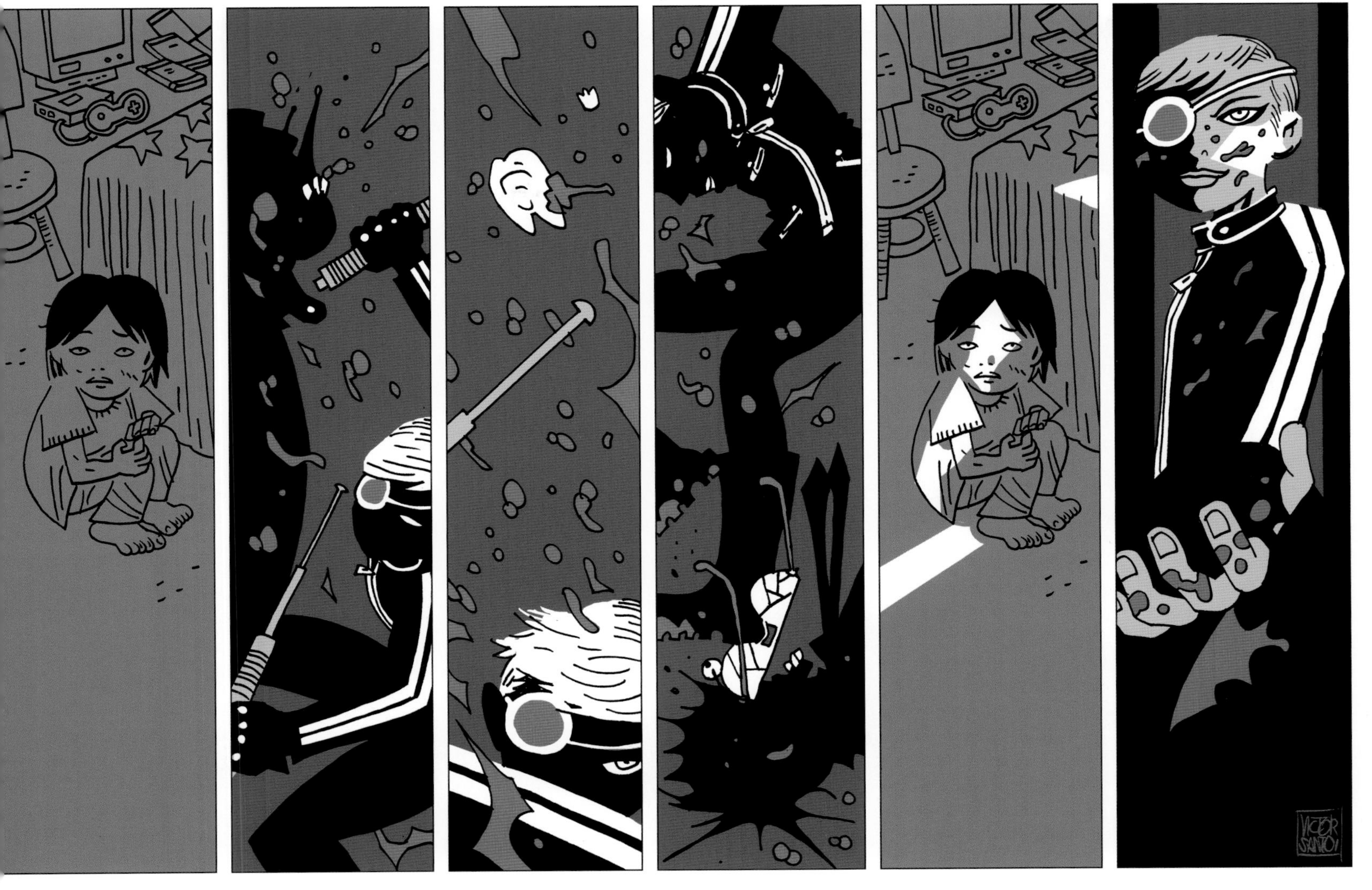
VICTOR SANTOS

THE KAISER FALLS SKETCHBOOK
ADDITIONAL ILLUSTRATIONS AND SKETCHES
BY VICTOR SANTOS

Victor Santos's sketches for each of his *Polar* covers are an incredible insight into the themes of his books. In each rough concept the Black Kaiser looks grizzled and worn, but still ready for a fight.

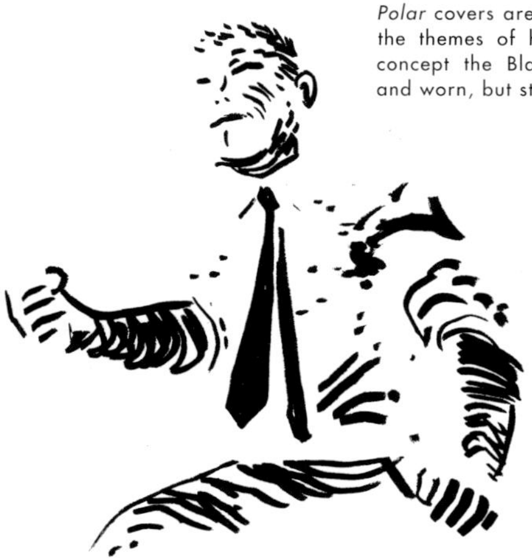

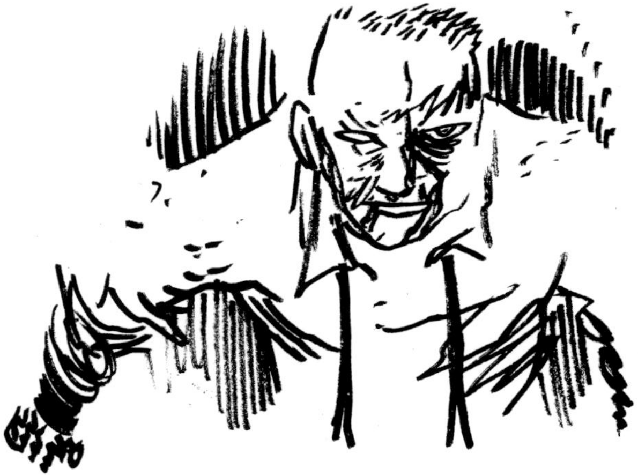

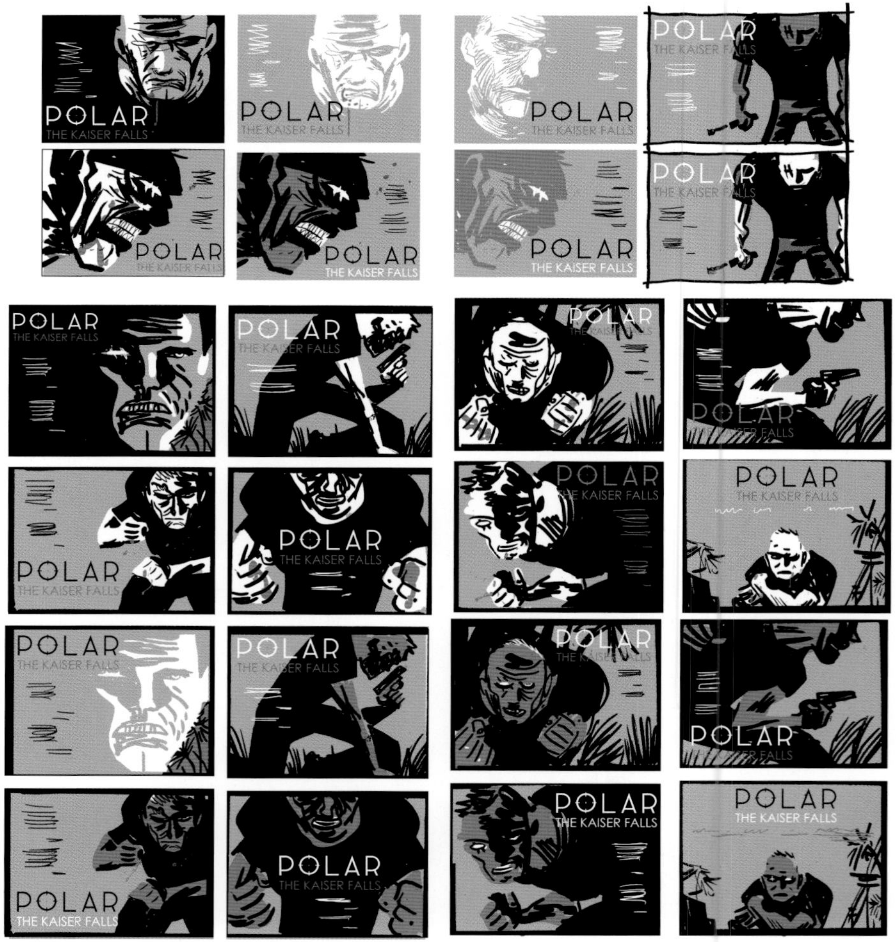
POLAR
THE KAISER FALLS

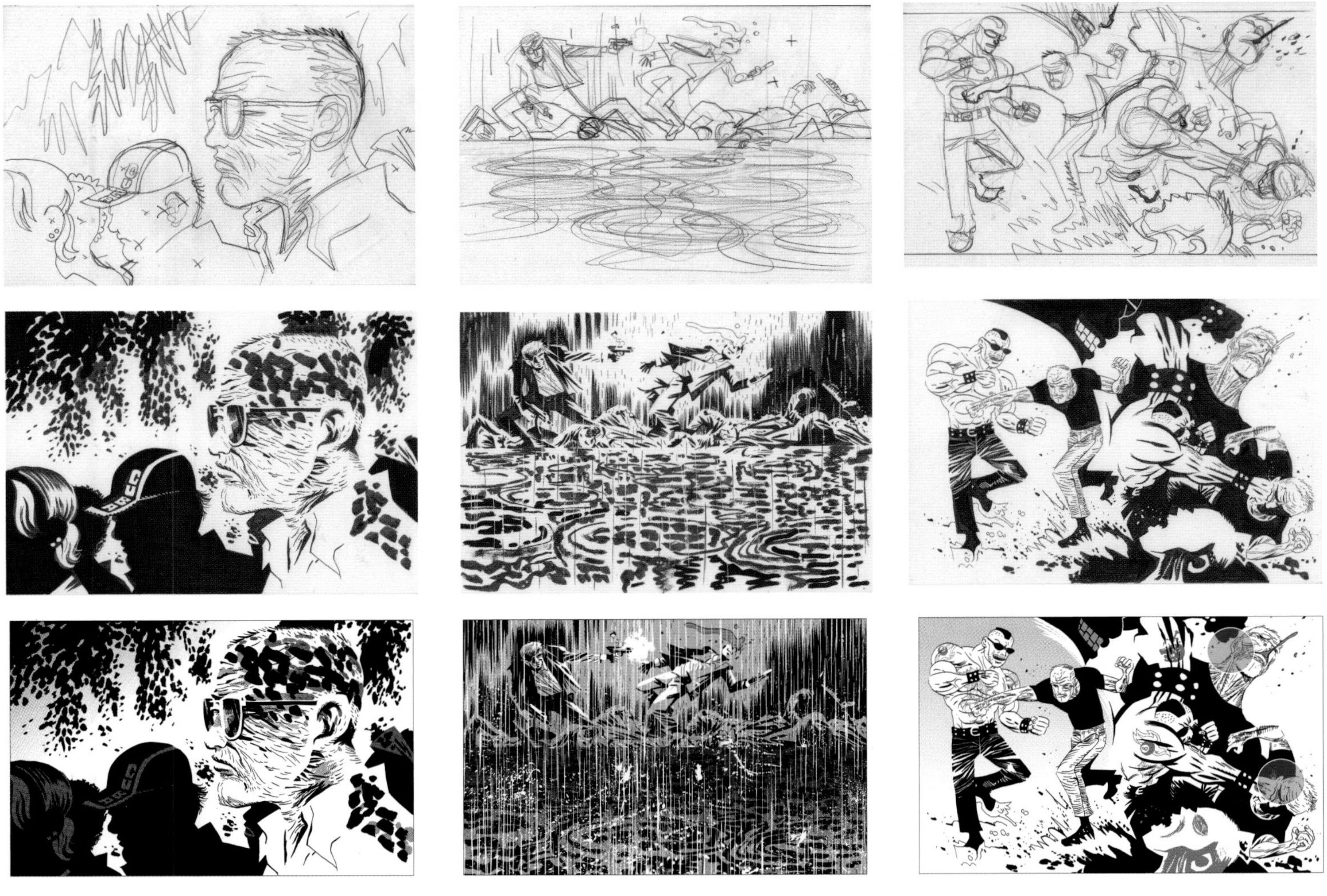

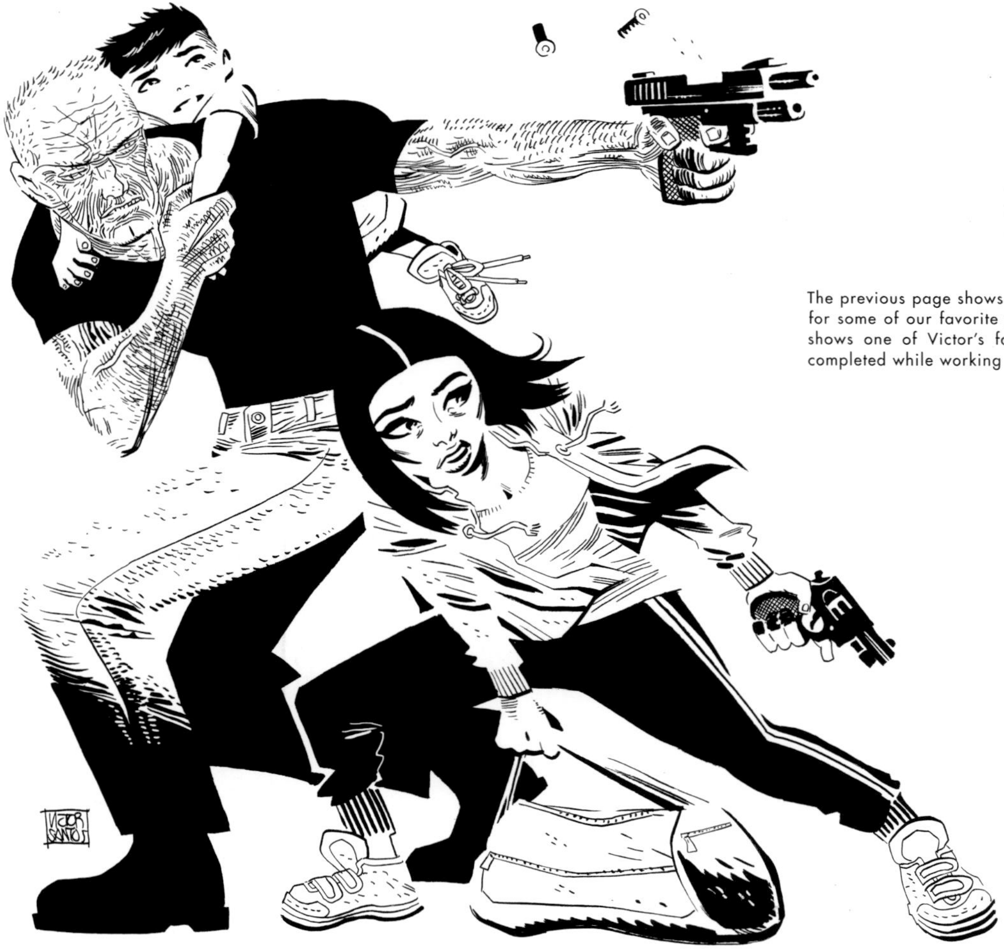
VICTOR SANTOS

The previous page shows the process work for some of our favorite pages. This page shows one of Victor's favorite pieces he completed while working on this book.

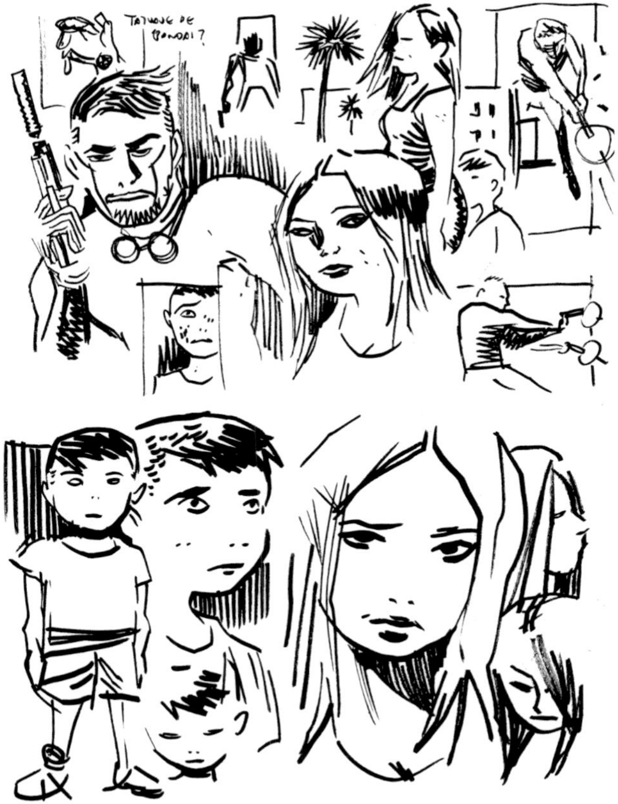
TATUAGE DE BONDI ?

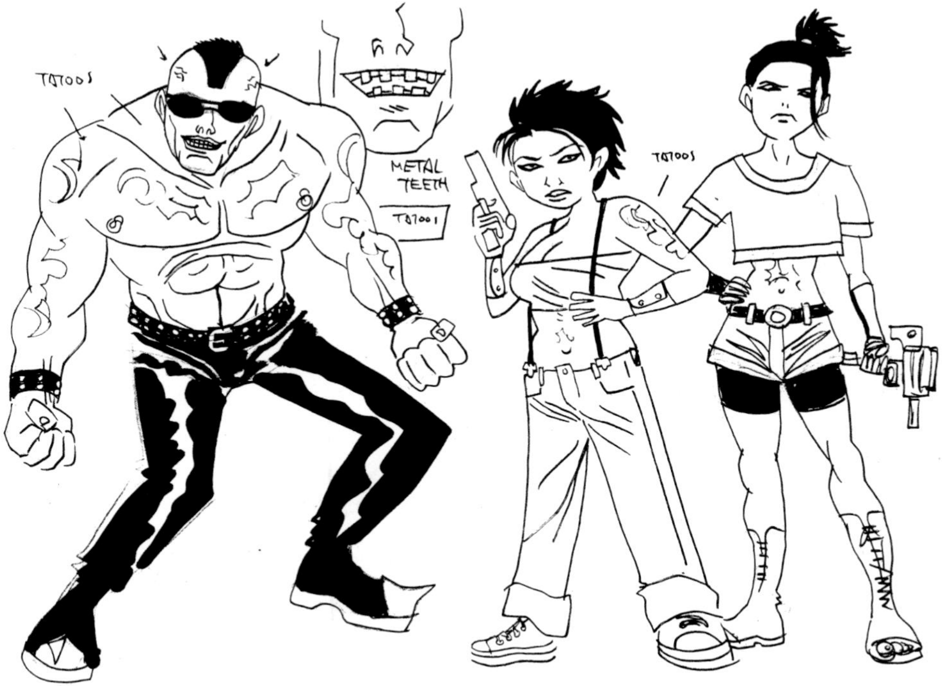
TATOOS
METAL TEETH
TATOOS

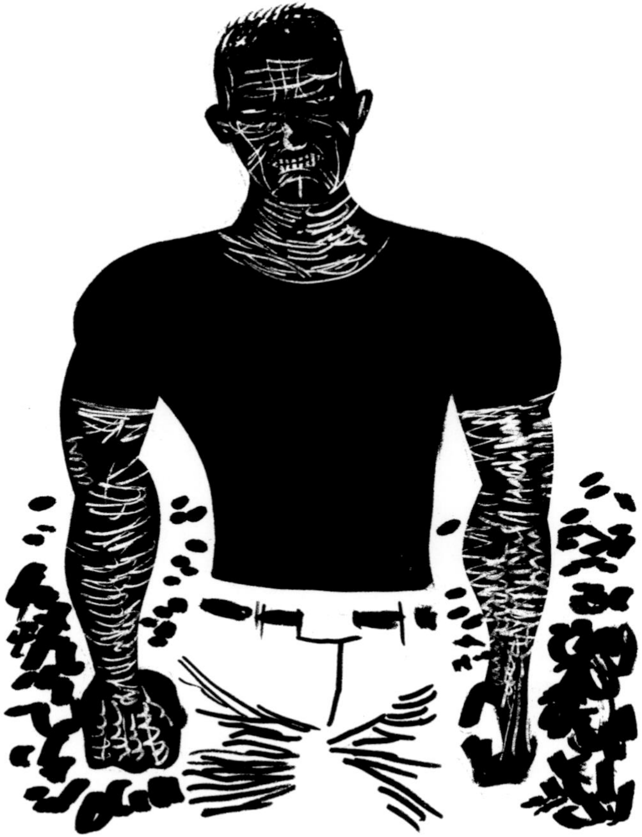

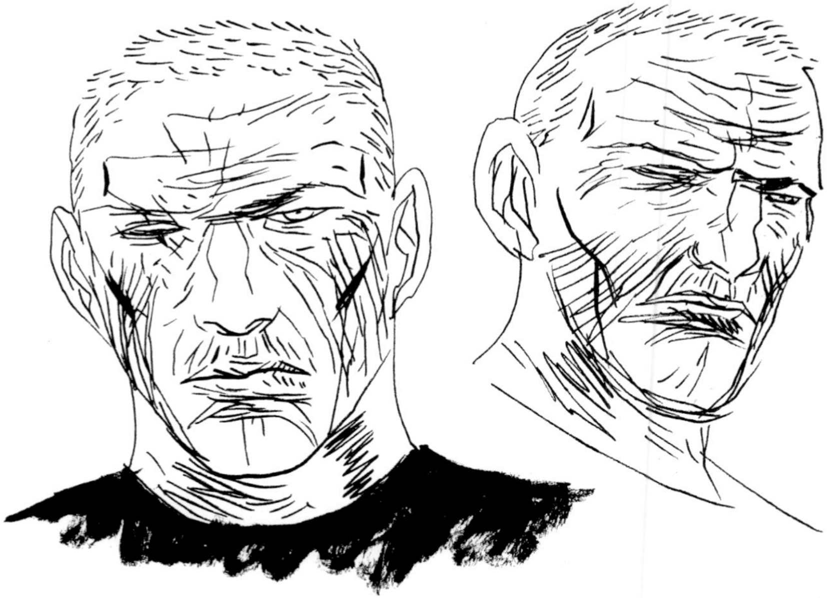

The Black Kaiser has seen better days, but Victor's sketches here show a wizened and formidable killer.

ABOUT THE AUTHOR

Born in Valencia in 1977, Victor Santos began his career writting and drawing a variety of comics published in Spain and France, including *Los reyes elfos* (*The Elf Kings*), *Pulp Heroes*, *Young Ronins* and *Infinity: Outrage*.

Santos has illustrated numerous comics in the United States, including the fantasy epic *The Mice Templar*, written by Bryan J. L. Glass and Michael Avon Oeming, James Patterson's *New York Times* best-selling *Witch & Wizard* series, written by Dara Naraghi, and DC Comics' *Filthy Rich* with Brian Azzarello.

His latest works are the Image comics series *Violent Love*, written by Frank Barbiere, the graphic novel *Bad Girls*, written by Alex de Campi for Simon & Schuster, and his solo project *Rashomon*, a noir story placed in feudal Japan, revisiting Ryūnosuke Akutagawa's classic novel.

His most personal work, the noir/spy graphic novel series *Polar*, has been adapted as a major motion picture by Constantin Films and Netflix, with star Mads Mikkelsen as the main character, Black Kaiser.

Santos has won six awards at the Barcelona international comic convention for his work and three at the Madrid comics convention. In 2014 he was nominated for the prestigious Harvey Award for his work in *Polar: Came from the Cold*. The original art of the *Polar* graphic novels had a succeful exhibition in the Glénat Gallery in Paris in 2016.

He lives in Bilbao, Spain.

@POLARCOMIC   VICTORSANTOSCOMICS.COM   POLARCOMIC.COM

UNCOVER THE LEGEND OF THE BLACK KAISER!

NOW A **NETFLIX** ORIGINAL FILM

"A visual tour de force. With *Polar*, Victor Santos takes his seat at the table of the great graphic storytellers. A book to read again and again."
—Brian Azzarello *100 Bullets, Wonder Woman*

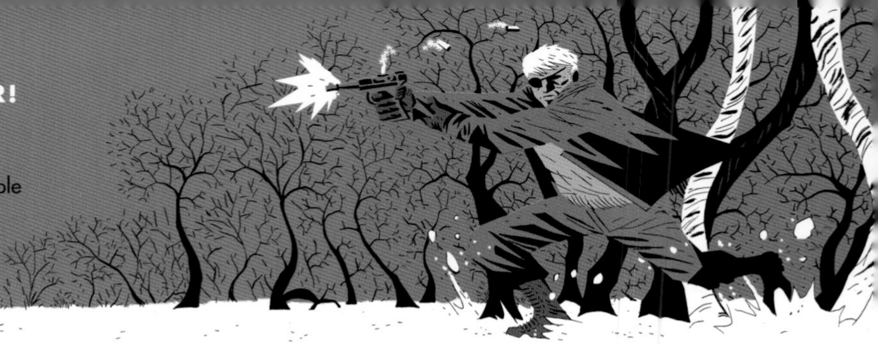

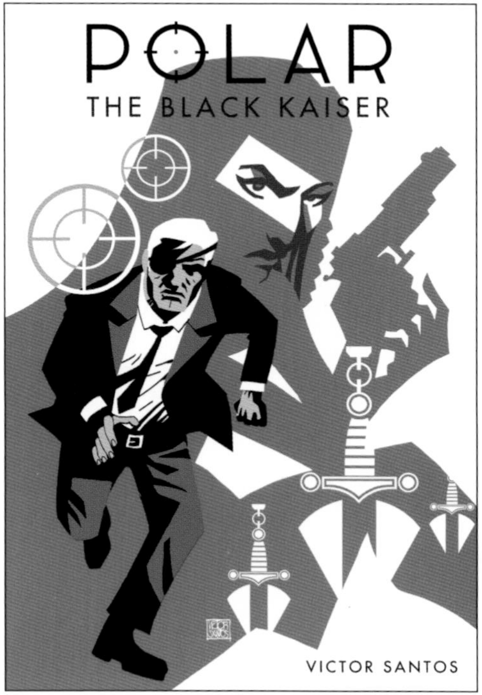
POLAR
THE BLACK KAISER
VICTOR SANTOS

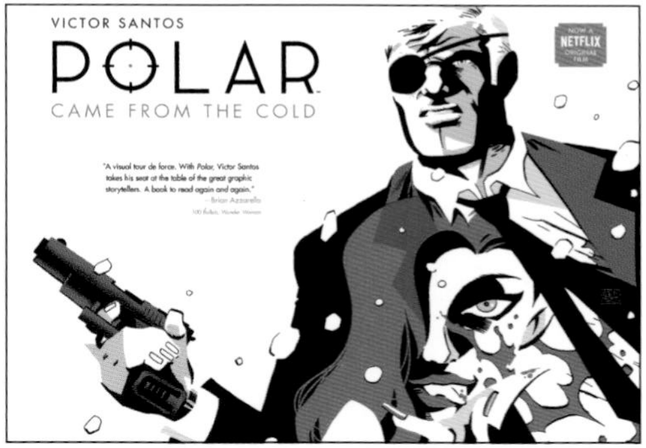
VICTOR SANTOS
POLAR
CAME FROM THE COLD
NOW A NETFLIX ORIGINAL FILM

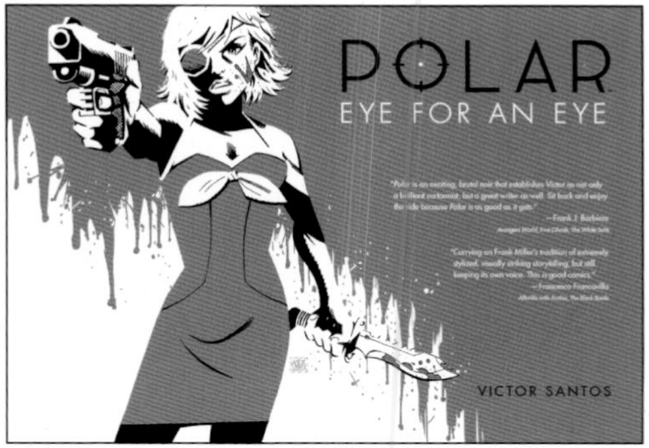
POLAR
EYE FOR AN EYE
VICTOR SANTOS

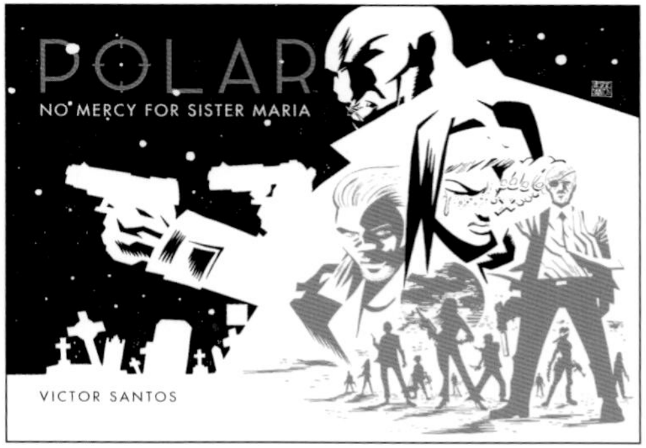
POLAR
NO MERCY FOR SISTER MARIA
VICTOR SANTOS

Polar Volume 0: The Black Kaiser
ISBN 978-1-50671-251-2
$17.99

Polar Volume 1: Came from the Cold 2nd Edition
ISBN 978-1-50671-118-8
$19.99

Polar Volume 2: Eye for an Eye
ISBN 978-1-61655-616-7
$17.99

Polar Volume 3: No Mercy for Sister Maria
ISBN 978-1-50670-053-3
$17.99

AVAILABLE AT YOUR LOCAL COMICS SHOP OR BOOKSTORE! TO FIND A COMICS SHOP IN YOUR AREA, VISIT COMICSHOPLOCATOR.COM.
For more information or to order direct: On the web: DarkHorse.com • Email: mailorder@darkhorse.com • Phone: 1-800-862-0052 Mon.–Fri. 9p.m to 5p.m Pacific Time.

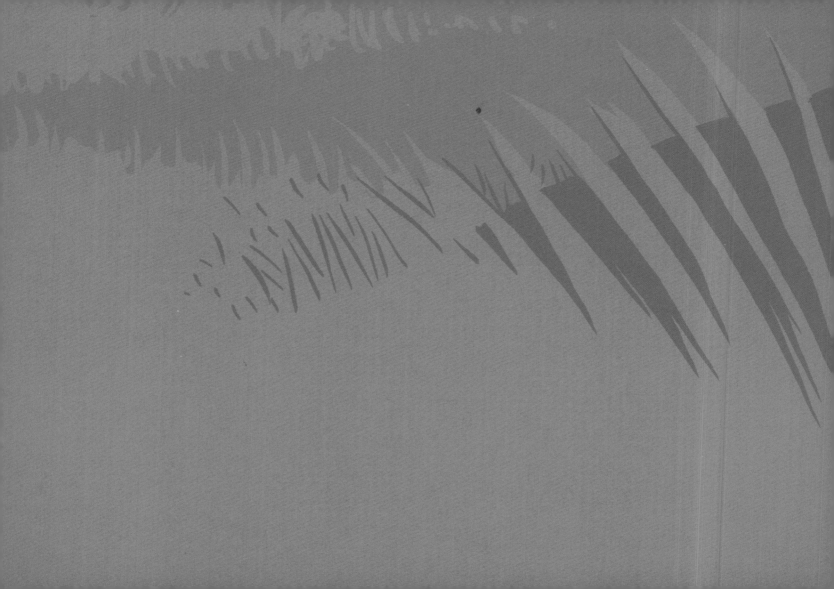